Andrew Leigh

RANDOM HOUSE
BUSINESS BOOKS

For all the MLA community

First published in 1999 by
Random House Business Books
Random House, 20 Vauxhall Bridge Road,
London SW1V 2SA

Random House Australia (Pty) Limited
20 Alfred Street, Milsons Point, Sydney
New South Wales 2061, Australia

Random House New Zealand Limited
18 Poland Road, Glenfield, Auckland 10,
New Zealand

Random House (Pty) Limited
Endulini, 5A Jubilee Road, Parktown 2193,
South Africa

The Random House Group Limited Reg. No. 954009

Papers used by Random House are natural, recyclable
products made from wood grown in sustainable forests. The
manufacturing processes conform to the environmental
regulations of the country of origin

ISBN 0 7126 8405 0

Designed by Roger Walker

Typeset in Concorde and Officina Sans
by MATS, Southend-on-Sea, Essex

Printed and bound in Great Britain by
Biddles Limited, Guildford and King's Lynn

Companies, institutions and other organisations wishing to
make bulk purchases of any business books published by
Random House should contact their local bookstore or
Random House direct:
Special Sales Director
Random House, 20 Vauxhall Bridge Road,
London SW1V 2SA
Tel 0171 840 8470   Fax 0171 828 6681

www.randomhouse.co.uk
businessbooks@randomhouse.co.uk

Contents

ACKNOWLEDGEMENTS

I'd like to offer special thanks to:

Maynard Leigh Associates consultants Gay Barnes, Chris Ettridge, Nigel Hughes and Tessa Morton for their contributions made between busy schedules of running courses.

My business partner Michael Maynard for his invaluable support, encouragement and creative suggestions. Anyone who reads a draft book by the pool on holiday has to be someone really special.

Jim Greenfield of the United Nations Food and Agricultural Organisation for sharing his thirty years experience of talking to non-English-speaking audiences around the world.

Mel Holford of MLA for her unique contribution.

The following generously and unselfishly shared their know-how and experience of large-scale presentations:

Robert Pye, Director of Sales, Ernst and Young
Frank Lee, Head of Energy and Utilities Director, Sema Group
Peter Jackson, Head of Bids and Proposals, Computer Sciences
    Corporation
Peter Hill, Business Development Manager, Rolls-Royce plc
Richard Godfrey, International Accounts Director, UDV
Ray Barratt, Industrial Business Unit Manager, SAP
David Hughes Solomon, Technical Director, SAP
Alex Gethin, Senior Manager, Marketing, KPMG
Brian Pollock, Diector, Management Consulting Services,
    PriceWaterhouse Coopers

Thanks also to Simon Wilson of Random House who helped clarify the focus for the book.

Quotations came from a wide variety of resources but the most redoubtable war horses were:

Quotations by Women, Rosalie Maggio, Beacon Press, 1996
The International Thesaurus of Quotations, compiled by Eugene
    Ehrlich and Marshall De Bruhl, Harper Perennial, 1996
Bloomsbury Thematic Dictionary of Quotations, 1990

Finally, special thanks go to Gillian for not smashing the computer and for providing her usual loving encouragement and support.

Preparation

I s your business presentation really necessary? Sounds a curious way to start preparing, doesn't it? Yet those on the receiving end are the ones who count. They don't always want or need a formal presentation.

Take Igor Andronov, for example. As a top Lloyds TSB executive he frequently sits through high-powered presentations to his company. Often these performances are about contracts worth millions. So what passes through his mind?

'I get really annoyed if people are going through the motions of a presentation when it's unnecessary. People often give me a document and then they present it. Many bids could simply be outlined on a couple of pages.' To prove the point he fishes in a filing cabinet, extracting a high-value bid which, despite its significance, indeed fits on just two sides of paper.

'Generally I think our proposals are too large,' admits one director of complex bids for a major IT concern. 'I think it's easier to write and present a hundred-page document than a fifty-page document – because with a shorter one you've got to think more about what you're saying.'

Peter Hill, Business Development Manager in the civil aerospace, defence and energy company Rolls-Royce plc, regularly steers high-level investments, through to completion. Such schemes undergo a gamut of internal appraisal, whether financial, technical or commercial. While many of his presentations remain formal, 'we are increasingly moving towards informal ones. The company is trying to shift towards a more open, flatter structure with less hierarchy and the informal-presentation approach seems to be more accepted and appropriate.'

Rather than forcing the audience to sit through an explanation of your written material why not just ask if they've read it?

briefing
devising
luck
Murphy's Law
prepare
rules

1

Making it Outstanding

Top 10 Tips!

★ Decide your key message
★ Invest in thorough preparation
★ Find your passion and use it
★ Explain what's in it for the listener
★ Be willing to take it slowly
★ Stay fully present the whole time
★ Stand up, balanced on both feet or sit forward in your chair
★ Use your personality, allowing your gestures to grow from your natural enthusiasm
★ Move around without falling over or tripping up
★ Speak clearly and loudly enough to be fully heard

None of these actions are beyond you. We'll be covering all of them and more.

To be what we are,
and to become what we are capable of becoming,
is the only end of life.

BARUCH SPINOZA

Learning the lessons

improve
know-how
reviewing

Even if you never become involved in complex, large-scale bids and presentations, these still provide many valuable lessons. For example, those regularly making such presentations realise that preparation often begins long before there is even a definite opportunity to make a formal presentation.

Major business presentations are normally part of a broader sales and marketing effort which in many cases is a highly attenuated procedure, lasting weeks, months and sometimes even years.

Chart 1, for example, shows the main stages of obtaining a large contract leading up to the formal presentation.

These various stages usually blend seamlessly into each other with the time for each varying considerably. Clarity about the process and knowing how to control it explains why some of the

CHART 1: THE LARGE CONTRACT PROCESS

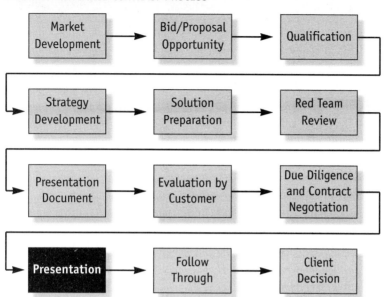

most successful contractors and sales teams make such an impact with their presentations.

Large-scale complex bids are normally highly secret affairs, involving scores of people working intensively in teams for months on end. Sometimes these teams are spread across the world, never meeting physically to present their work.

To gain control over the process, complex bids are usually steered by experienced project managers whose job is to ensure the whole protracted journey is completed on time in the least costly way.

In many companies there are professional 'bid support teams'. These specialist groups take on the tough assignment of helping those who must make presentations. Their job is often a thankless task. If a bidding team loses, the support group may be blamed, while if it wins you can guess where all the credit goes.

'Our role is that we're coaches to bid teams in the proposal process,' explains Brian Polk of PriceWaterhouseCoopers' (PWC) bid support unit. 'We build capability within the business, to manage it better next time, not to manage it *for* those doing the bids. We're dedicated to helping and coaching them through the process of winning work. By virtue of being involved in a lot of these things you start to understand and be able to give guidance on the strategies that will win in particular markets. You develop a sense of "what is a professional process? How is it managed?

What kind of team do you need to structure. What are the important interventions that we need to make in the process that will help them win?'"

'It's the Audience, Stupid'

audience
size
children
conference
expectations
foreign audiences
listen
tuning in

Campaigning for election against George Bush, President Clinton's team displayed a prominent notice in their headquarters saying 'It's the Economy, Stupid.' This reminded everyone to stay focused on the fundamental issue without becoming distracted.

You too may need to find ways to keep reminding yourself about the prime importance of the audience. Lose sight of this and your presentation will almost certainly be off target. Focus on two essential audience goals:

★ Detailed knowledge about those involved

★ Build a relationship with the potential audience

Master presenters go to extraordinary lengths to pursue both these aims. Their sheer persistence explains why, in competitive situations, they frequently succeed, despite facing competitors who may have more or better resources.

Knowing the audience enables you to create a presentation with confidence. If you allow enough time really to listen, the audience will 'tell' you what it wants to hear. Though it's a vital first step, knowing who will be there is not enough.

Clarifying purpose

ACTION

Whether a complex bid, a sole trader's pitch to a single buyer, a conference speech, a team briefing or a meeting with employees, most business presentations usually imply: action.

Even presentations arguing for *inaction* are really seeking a decision and are therefore implicitly about action. Talking at a

conference for example, may seem mainly about imparting information, or building a profile. Yet you probably want some kind of result, such as hoping the audience will some day think of you or your company and therefore make contact.

Likewise, at an interview for a new job, the presentation succeeds if you're hired. Or if you want a pay rise your presentation wins only if you're offered it or learn how you could eventually obtain it.

Presentations resulting in no action are soon forgotten. In business terms they're a failure. So in devising a presentation it's important to be clear what result you want. Since your presentation concerns action, how do you devise one that is convincing and persuasive? The best place to start is with your audience.

Making sense of purpose

Every business presentation has a

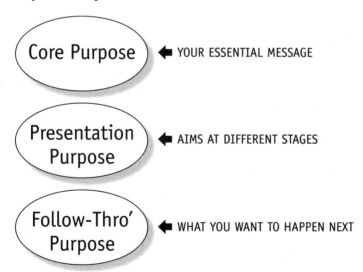

Core Purpose ⬅ YOUR ESSENTIAL MESSAGE

Presentation Purpose ⬅ AIMS AT DIFFERENT STAGES

Follow-Thro' Purpose ⬅ WHAT YOU WANT TO HAPPEN NEXT

CORE PURPOSE

Confusion over core purpose explains why so many business presentations fail to hit the mark. Typically there are too many aims, leaving both presenter and audience confused. You can nearly always reduce the core purpose of your presentation to

★ a single, headline statement

Wherever possible, express this core purpose in terms of action:

Headlines

A single action-focused headline can sum up most business presentations.

For example:

★ 'You need a culture shift, choose us and you'll achieve it.'

★ 'You want more from IT investment, get it by outsourcing to us'

★ 'After meeting me you'll know you've found your top-flight account manager'

★ 'Talking at this conference will lead to some people calling us about our work'

★ 'Our new document handling system will inspire you to agree a free company survey'

★ 'We'll show how to make major energy savings so you'll hire us to deliver them'

> *The purpose of life is to believe,*
> *to hope and to strive.*
>
> INDIRA GANDHI

headline ⊂ The core purpose may emerge at the start of the bid and proposal
logo process, or evolve as you dig down and understand your audience better. Write it on a large card or flip chart and put it on display during the entire preparation period.

Reducing an entire presentation message to a single headline, word, or even logo may involve a series of steps, gradually whittling down the many messages to perhaps just two or three. Finally one overall message may emerge from the work. It's more art than science.

Where the stakes are high it may be worth asking a professional design house to create memorable copy and a brand logo.

PURPOSE DURING THE PRESENTATION

You will also have different intentions at various stages throughout the presentation itself. For example, at some point you may want to

★ Make people laugh
★ Challenge current thinking
★ Sow seeds of doubt
★ Make people anxious
★ Gain agreement
★ Offer new insight
★ Stimulate involvement
★ Provoke questions

goals
objective
opinion
why

If you view the presentation as mainly about giving information you'll risk losing sight of these different kinds of intentions. They make a presentation richer and more interesting to watch.

As you plan your performance, if at any stage you realise that you are unsure about why you are including something ask:

★ Why am I telling them this now?
★ What effect am I trying to achieve at this moment?

Think of taking your audience on a journey. At different stages you want to achieve different things and this intention can guide you in shaping your presentation material.

For example, if at some stage the purpose is to wake people up you could do anything from shout, bang the table, play some rousing music, or get them working in small groups. Or, if at a particular point you want to make people challenge you, the answer might be to make a particularly provocative point. If you are trying to get them thinking you might allow lots of silence, put up an insightful quotation, run a quiz, do an interactive exercise and so on.

Knowing what you want to achieve at different moments means careful planning ahead and rehearsing.

FOLLOW-THROUGH PURPOSE

Once you end the presentation what do you want to happen next? Audiences need clear guidance about what is expected of them. For example, if you want a decision to go ahead with an investment, it's important to say that clearly at the end of the presentation.

Likewise, if you want to be chosen as a favoured supplier, having given your presentation, then say so, making it clear what you want to happen next. Because most business presentations are so grounded in action it is usually fairly easy to state the next steps required.

Even if you are merely presenting and explaining a report you still need to indicate what you think should be the next steps. The required action may come down to asking people to go away and think about what you've said – but with a view to what? Get clear what you are asking of your audience. Sometimes it pays to become even more specific and clarify what you want different members of the audience to do. For example, you might ask that as part of the follow-through action you want to meet with certain individuals, invite others to a special seminar and request certain people to send you information.

The folklore of sales presentations is 'always ask for the order'. This is often highly inappropriate and premature during complex bid situations. It may be far better to offer suggestions about further action, such as having a follow-up meeting. Or you might invite some of the audience to meet one of your satisfied customers to see your products or services at work.

★ Get clear on the follow-through action

Influencing strategies

In formal business pitches, by the time the audience sits in a room with you people should already know you, have shared their thoughts and wishes and be aware of what makes you different. To reach this situation requires an

★ Influencing strategy

Only rarely, such as in government tendering, will you be prevented from making advance personal contact with your audience. The top professionals regard exclusion from meeting and getting to know the audience as a sure sign that their presentation is unlikely to succeed.

Set out to discover

★ What makes your audience tick
★ What people want most from the presentation
★ How best you can serve them

To influence people to take action requires both knowledge of them and a relationship with them. Researching your audience is therefore a sign of strength, not weakness. Indeed, your audience may be impressed by how much effort you make to discover their needs. The most successful Master presenters go to incredible lengths to unearth facts and feelings about their audience.

Based on a brief phone call, it's easy to assume that you already know what people want from your presentation For example, you may *think* that your purpose is to 'sell' the benefits of using your company. Yet the audience may already know these and instead desire something entirely different – for instance to assess you and your team as people.

You may *think* you need to explain how your service works. The reality may be that the audience has checked this out previously and instead expects to experience in the room what makes you or your company special.

You may *think* that you must describe in depth the deal you are offering. Yet the audience may prefer to focus entirely on the credit terms, or how you'll handle production delays.

Even those who ought to know better sometimes allow their audience to suffer unnecessarily by offering what *isn't* wanted. For instance, when Maynard Leigh Associates tried to hire a specialist public relations company we invited half a dozen experienced practitioners to visit and make a case for obtaining our business.

Almost without exception they forced us to sit through computer-based slide shows on a small laptop screen, the contents of which were mainly bullet points and words. Yet what we were trying to assess was the presenters' ability to build relationships and convey our messages in powerful ways that gained interest and excitement.

★ *Clarifying influence*

A widely used method in complex sales presentations is one developed by Miller Heiman, which defines the audience into buyer influences:

★ **Economic buyer** – asks: 'What does this do for my bottom line?' This person's major concern is relating the cost to the final performance and can also override other buyers and veto decisions.

★ **User buyer** – asks: 'What does it do for me?' The role is to make judgements about the impact of the product or service on the job to be done.

★ **Technical buyer** – asks: 'Does it meet the requirements?' These people often throw rocks in the way and help to screen out proposals on technical grounds. There may be a whole team of people with this apparently negative role.

★ **Coaching buyer** – asks: 'Can I be associated with it?' These people have to be located and then developed. Once identified they can guide you in the proposal process, even assessing your intended presentation. Ideally the coach wants your solution and will help you get it.

Who is important?

Taking trouble to unravel the different sorts of buyer influences allows you to focus your presentation on the right people and target your message. 'Throughout the preparation phase we will have identified who are the important people within a buying process,' explains Brian Polk of PWC.

PWC uses a version of the Miller Heiman approach to clarify the nature of the audience and is evolving its own approach to decide who are the really important people to get to with a presentation.

'Where we've had really embarrassing meetings in the past is where we haven't done the homework to understand the different client communities that are represented in the meeting. And we haven't lined up the right people on our side to talk to those people during the session.

In large-scale proposals all four types of audience may need satisfying. Each sort of buyer influence may be a group of people, rather than a single person, and because of their different interests they may require their own separate business presentation.

So, for example, considerable time may be spent satisfying the technical buyer. When a committee plays this role it's often led by an important executive who must reassure top management that the proposal will meet technical requirements.

The coaching buyer is also a crucial person, guiding the preparation work and even perhaps helping to create the final presentation in partnership with you.

At Computer Sciences Corporation (CSC), for instance, presentation managers talk of finding a 'coach' who may sit in on a dress rehearsal of the presentation to guide them further in refining their message.

Dig down

The power of the audience to tell you exactly what it needs can hardly be exaggerated. When our company decided to pitch for a major project from one of the UK's leading pharmaceutical companies we prepared a package of key messages and graphics. However, we first sent the material through to the internal coach to comment on.

Back came the reply: 'It's what we'd expect of any company pitching for our business. We're wanting something more from you.' What was the 'more' the client needed? In this case it was a business presentation that told them

★ 'What it would be like working with you'
★ 'How you will add value and help us achieve our corporate ambitions'

So we relegated the formal side of the presentation to just ten minutes out of the allocated two hours. Instead, we devised something entirely new and interactive to convey our real message that it was fun working with us and that we knew how to guide them in a major culture change programme.

Understanding your audience

★ Research those to whom you will be talking to clarify
   * roles
   * formal and informal influence
   * opinions on the area in which you are presenting
   * attitudes towards your presentation – in favour, open, opposed, ambivalent
   * their concerns, needs and personal agendas
★ Make personal contact with some or all of your future audience
★ Uncover local references to people, events, or issues
★ Clarify the amount of audience time available
★ Discover if people are willing to participate actively in the presentation
★ Firm up numbers attending
★ Ask who is presenting before you, and consider how this might affect subsequent reactions to you
★ Discover how you could surprise and delight this group of people
★ Get specific: what can you reasonably expect the audience to do next?

I never let them cough. They wouldn't dare.
   ETHEL BARRYMORE (1878–1959), ACTRESS, 1956

Compelling reasons

The strategy of large-scale or 'mega' bidders is usually to focus on identifying a relatively small number of potentially high-value customers. Rather than attempting to give formal presentations to a wide-ranging audience, instead the aim is usually to identify

★ Who are the major players?
★ What are these players' important issues?
★ What do we know about them?
★ Which players might be for us and which against us?
★ What are the major pressures on that customer?
★ Is there a compelling event sparking off the need for action?

The qualifying process

Major bidders and contractors have sophisticated operations with dedicated and secure preparation rooms for creating multi-disciplinary teams to devise important proposals and presentations.

Before embarking on the elaborate and costly process of responding to requests for proposals, these presenters first subject a project to an elaborate qualifying process. 'Deciding what business we're going to do is incredibly important,' explains Brian Polk of PWC.

The sort of questions used in the qualifying process include:

★ How important is this opportunity for us?
★ How big is the opportunity?
★ What is the strategic importance of this customer to us?
★ How much does this customer really matter to us?
★ Is there a budget for this?
★ Who can actually sign the cheque?
★ How likely are they to proceed?
★ What's the history, have we had a successful previous relationship?
★ Do we have an offering that can satisfy the need?
★ Could we deliver to the right standards of time and quality?
★ Can we win it and what are the chances?
★ Will it make money and do we want to win it?
★ What impact would it have on our existing customer base?
★ What resources are required and for how long?

These are powerful questions and the answers can save considerable heartache, expense and ultimately wasted presentations. Normally such questions can only be answered through close involvement with the potential customer.

A prudent question is one-half of wisdom.
FRANCIS BACON

As part of the qualifying process of deciding whether to embark on preparing an important presentation bidders often seek a 'compelling reason or event' such as:

★ A major market opportunity
★ Takeovers and mergers
★ Failure to produce new products
★ Supply chain problems
★ Financial crisis
★ Rising IT costs
★ Loss of market share
★ Decline in return on capital
★ Excessive staff turnover
★ New growth/profit targets
★ Changes in legislation
★ The need to change company culture

Though you can't create someone else's compelling reason or event, you can certainly help to articulate it, placing it at the heart of your presentation. No matter how brilliant your performance, if you haven't identified a compelling reason or event you are unlikely to win the argument.

Compelling events are often traumatic, which is why making them the heart of the presentation can be so effective. Doing so allows you to answer with confidence the most worrying issues facing the audience and helps make your overall arguments more persuasive.

The compelling event that you identify, though, may be competing with ones that other people consider to be equally pressing. For example, when CSC presents its case to handle a company's IT services it knows that potentially this is a highly emotive issue. There will be worries at board level about whether vital staff will leave, whether the service can be maintained, what will happen to the remaining staff and so on. However, if the final benefits from such a major change as outsourcing only amount to a 5% cost reduction, what might initially have seemed a compelling reason to change may start looking less attractive.

'As you reach board level and see what's going on in the company, the risk is that people start prioritising,' explains Peter Jackson, CSC's Director of Bids. 'If others have a compelling event and we don't, then what we offer is going to come low on

the priority and is likely to get deferred or shelved. So you've got to have a compelling event.'

It can take time to realise what the compelling event or reason may be. Sometimes this can emerge as something that neither party fully realised at the start of the presentation process. Only by constantly talking and working with your audience can you dig sufficiently deep to uncover the vital factor that makes your final presentation arguments hard to deny.

It also helps to know whether the compelling reason stems from

★ A growth opportunity
★ A problem situation

In a growth opportunity the audience sees a gap between how things could be and how they are currently. Your presentation and proposals will have a significant impact only if they offer ways of closing this gap.

In a problem situation the audience is facing a crisis or something troublesome and wants immediate answers. In this case you are more likely to be well received if you can gear your presentation to acknowledge this reality and provide appropriate advice or solutions.

By contrast if an audience regards the present situation as satisfactory with no particular reason to change, then your proposal, no matter how well presented, may ultimately achieve little impact. Worse, if the audience is complacent about the present situation, then unless you can seriously disturb this passive mood, your presentation will have minimal impact.

For example, when consultants from Maynard Leigh Associates addressed an audience in a major UK supermarket chain the company was then top of the retail league. Complacency and overconfidence permeated the room and the presentation landed with a dull thud. Nothing could dent the solid wall of self-satisfaction. There was in fact no compelling reason for them to do anything. It wasn't until the company results turned sour that once again an invitation came to make another better received presentation.

In complex situations people will therefore respond to your proposals depending on their present state of mind so it pays to find out about it.

Who's the competition?

Whom are you up against in giving your presentation? For instance, you may be appearing before a board of directors just after a rival makes a competing case for resources. Or you may be seeking a salary rise when several others are doing so too.

rivals ⊂   It usually pays to find out who will present both before and after you, and if possible what they will be saying. You can then take this into account in organising your arguments. Those dealing with complex bids, for example, usually know whom they are competing against and set out to discover what their rivals are up to.

'From our knowledge we will identify where our competition is strong and where it'll be weak,' says Peter Jackson. 'And since we want the playing field sloped in our favour, we might want to identify ways in which we would change the shape of the deal, expand its scope, or somehow create a framework for the deal that is to our advantage.'

Most highly organised bidders seek 'win themes', that is skills, services, products or other elements that differentiate them from the competition. Sometimes these prove decisive in the final stages of the presentation. For example, in one major UK defence bid, a contractor distinguished itself from the competition by including in the final presentation several leading figures from the defence industry. It lent the proposal huge credibility, giving it a crucial and ultimately successful 'win theme'. Whenever possible

★   position yourself uniquely

Rubber stamp it

When preparation has been really thorough, the actual presentation itself often becomes less critical. Instead, it merely confirms that the presenter is indeed the one that should be chosen. As one top professional explains, 'By then it should just be rubber stamping of our proposal.'

This is particularly true of internal requests for resources or a

management decision. For example, Peter Hill, Business Development Manager at Rolls-Royce plc, explains that 'it really should be like a marriage ceremony. All the decisions have taken place previously and you don't expect anyone to object by the time you actually get to that stage. I would feel that I had failed if that's where the decision making really took place. It should be a formal approval, stamping all the discussions which have taken place prior to that.'

Building relationships

A successful presentation is ultimately about building a powerful relationship with your audience. The presentation Masters, particularly those seeking major contracts, seldom leave this critical aspect to chance.

'I think there's a lot of focus on the goods and glamour of a proposal,' suggests Brian Polk, Director of Management Consulting Services at PriceWaterhouseCoopers. 'Yet good proposals don't win you business. Bad proposals can lose you the business, but it takes more than a good proposal to win. It takes strong client relationships, developed through a proposal process and often before. You're playing a catch-up game if you're trying to do it during the proposal process.'

'We'd feel uneasy presenting to people we hadn't met and talked to first,' explains Robert Pye, Ernst and Young's Director of Sales. So considerable effort goes into clarifying who is the audience, discovering its influence and power, learning who might be supporters and tracking down who might oppose or prove obstructive.

'We spend a lot of time building the relationship,' confirms Frank Lee, Energies and Utilities Director at Sema Group, one of Europe's leading information technology companies, employing over 16,000 people. 'What you find is that there are gaps and one of the tasks is to go find these people and talk to them, and actually learn what's happening.'

'The more support you've got the better. Interestingly, on these very large bids when we have lost, it's generally not on the rational side, it tends to be that our competitor has gained more support than we have. When we win it's because we've gained more support. The actual presentation delivery becomes less important because you've all got ticks in the boxes.'

Peter Hill of Rolls-Royce plc is equally focused. 'If you want to be the one in five who actually gets the money, the key thing is to identify all the formal signatories and, perhaps equally important, who are the people in the background advising these people. What turns them on? What are their pet initiatives? What do they want to see? What must you do to put a smile on their faces. What do they think about you? Have they any idea what you've been doing recently?'

If you have researched the audience well you should be able to draw up an organisational chart representing all the key people, how they relate to each other and their influence both formal and informal. When you know these facts you can set out to build the relationships.

'We'll try at a fairly early stage to get some of these people involved, invite a senior accountant down, or chief of engineering, or whatever,' explains Peter Hill. 'Get their early input, make them think that their ideas are being taken note of.'

Making it interactive

Presentations can often take the form of interactive workshops. World-class organisations such as the Boston Consulting Group, for example, pioneered the use of seminars to present their message to potential clients.

Information technology group Sema organised a seminar for an oil company and in the preparation stage hired consultants who specialised in creating relationships between companies, customers and suppliers.

The consultants helped prepare the presentation and the workshop, charting out the day. There were lots of contingency plans with over eighty slides that were not actually used but were there as back-up.

'We don't tend to stand up and give a lecture and sit down again,' explains Frank Lee.

Maynard Leigh Associates seldom relies on a straight presentation, nearly always making the experience highly interactive. In one winning boardroom presentation all ten directors had fun discovering new facts about each other that broke the ice and reduced the formality.

Take into account what the audience might want. It is always worth discovering what they had before in the way of a presentation.

Rapport

Whether you call it personal chemistry or rapport, good Master presenters are skilled at putting their attention on other people, rather than themselves. They

★ Gain attention – by *being attentive*
★ Become interesting – by *being interested*
★ Are understood – by *seeking to understand*

Structure

Having researched your audience and firmed up your purpose, it's time to create the presentation structure. This is the framework used for the performance, a route map for taking you from the opening to the ending. In large complex presentations, involving a whole preparation team, the final structure may also determine who should attend.

'We will come up with a structure that has some logic to it,' explains Alex Gethin, Senior Proposals Manager in KPMG. 'There will be a theme to the overall presentation from which we can hang different messages. Only then will we stand back and decide who actually needs to present each point.'

Equally, in some presenting situations who should be there is the first crucial decision, which then determines the nature of the content.

With good research you will probably already have enough material, lots to say and are wondering how to knit it all together. You can't afford to be just like everyone else, you need to stand out from the crowd.

Avoid relying on a standard structure such as the overused: 'Tell them what you're going to tell them; tell them; then tell them you've told them.' This familiar framework is readily recognisable by savvy audiences holding 'beauty parades' and pitches. Just as an audience's eyes glaze over at the sight of yet another PowerPoint presentation with the mandatory bullet points, so people lose concentration when faced with yet another 'tell them' structure.

What will make your business presentation memorable and impactful is

bang
excitement
fun
ideas
imagination
inspiration
magic
music
mystery
new
original
outrageous
props
shock
topicality
unexpected
variety

★ Doing it differently

This means creating a presentation with surprises and ensuring that it is unpredictable. Almost by definition you cannot exactly plan to be unpredictable but you can certainly avoid being repetitive or formulaic.

One reason why some Master presenters refuse to rehearse is they know their material so well that they can concentrate entirely on 'reading the audience', on creating a 'conversation'. Good and enjoyable conversations are seldom predictable.

> **conversation**
> **listen**
> **tuning in**

A presentation is everything you *can't* write down. If everything can fit in a document you don't need to be there . . . send a report!

Be creative!

Two powerful tools for evolving a unique presentation structure are:

★ Branding
★ Story boarding

BRANDING

Once you have a clear purpose and reduced it to a single headline statement, try devising a theme to run throughout the entire presentation and give it unity.

A theme is like a 'personality' that cannot easily be ignored and which tends to be easily remembered. Just about any business presentation can be themed. For example, if you're asking for a pay rise, your theme might be 'adding value'. Throughout your argument for more money you might keep making the case that you have been consistently 'adding value' to the company in recent months or years.

One UK business leader spoke to his employees about what he meant by a winning performance. To bring the idea alive he adopted the theme of 'raising the bar' and showed a video of people winning at world-class sporting events.

Another theme used in a successful business presentation called 'Getting There' was 'we're on our way', acknowledging lots of recent successes while nevertheless focusing on what needed still to be done.

★ Provide a consistently recognisable image and message
★ Make your story memorable
★ Distinguish yourself from competitors

In large-scale pitches bidders sometimes go further, converting the theme into a 'brand', pervading both the formal presentation and the relationship with the potential customer.

'The quality of the presentation is something we take a lot of care about, so we brand it with something that is important to that customer,' explains Frank Lee of Sema. For example, in one large Sema project about integrating and making better use of the potential client's IT investment the preparation team reduced the entire message to a single memorable word. This was transformed by a design company into a neat logo appearing in all communications with the potential customer, including special notepaper, handouts, e-mails, CD-ROMS and so on.

logo ⊂ 'By the time the branding and key messages have been established we will have determined from the customer what it is they want to see in the presentation,' explains Frank Lee.

STORY BOARDING

Another powerful device for clarifying presentation structure is to create a visual story board. You don't need any artistic skill to create this and no one else need see it, apart from you or the presentation team.

Story boards act as a continual reference point and

★ Establish a common understanding of the core messages
★ Show how key aspects of the presentation fit together
★ Clarify who handles different aspects of the presentation
★ Identify areas needing more clarity
★ Reveal flaws in the flow
★ Focus attention on what is important

Most story boards are a mixture of pictures and words.

At CSC the story board is usually 'one page of text and one schematic that describes what our people are going to cover in their section,' explains Peter Jackson. 'There are two purposes. One is an opportunity for the team to understand what every other group is going to be doing, what they will tell us. Second, it enables us to identify any inconsistencies in the messages and whether we are meeting the requirements and whether there are any overlaps or gaps.'

No set structures

Each presentation is unique, that's what gives it impact. Unusual ways to combine and order the material include:

★ Treat the presentation like a TV show – with a strong opener, breaks, key moments and audience involvement

★ Use the Situation, Complication, Resolution framework (explained below)

★ Take your audience on a symbolic 'journey' with varying countryside and stops along the way

★ Tell an unfolding story, breaking at various points to highlight key messages

★ Turn the presentation into a form of quiz, in which the various questions gradually lead to the key message

★ Perform a playlet, in which your key message is hammered home with fun and humour

★ Give the presentation like a major news broadcast, with headlines, an anchor person, 'interviews' with those making the news, commentary and a summary of highlights at the end

★ Devise an interesting dialogue

★ Create a courtroom drama and put an idea on trial

Do these feel risky? If so you're probably on the right track, since the best presentations are always risky, that's why audiences love them. A Maynard Leigh Associates consultant, for example, once structured his entire business presentation around an opening song which he sang with gusto while walking on to the platform.

> excitement
> ideas
> imagination
> inspiration
> new
> original
> subject
> topicality
> variety

> agenda
> frameworks
> message
> mind map
> road map
> speech
> write

Treat your structure as an asset that creates variety in the performance and plays a real part in differentiating you from competitors. Constantly varying structures from one performance to the next helps keep you fresh and a presentation team alert.

For example, if you always begin by explaining in detail who you are and why you're presenting, you'll soon become blasé about it and your performance will suffer. 'How many times have you seen presentations that start off with "this is who we are, this

is our company profile, blah, blah . . ." and already, you have lost the audience, it's crazy,' argues Master presenter David Hughes Solomon, Technical Director of Systems Applications and Products (SAP UK).

So long as your framework makes sense to the audience it can be in any order that creates an impact. It's important to retain flexibility and not allow the structure you've chosen to dictate how you perform. A flexible one drawn from the theatre that works well in business is

★ Situation
★ Complication
★ Resolution

A good play is gripping because the characters face a situation, and want something. However, there's always a complication stopping them achieving their desires. The interest arises from watching how they deal with the complication. When the play ends there is a resolution of some kind.

You can structure business presentations in this way too. For example, suppose you are submitting a tender document and are giving a presentation to decision makers. You might organise your material so that you

★ **Describe the situation** – you reveal how you see the requirements, how these might affect the purchaser's competitive position and your own situation as an innovative supplier in the market place
★ **Explain the complications** – you identify some of the issues that might affect a successful contract and how these need to be worked through jointly, so you both arrive at manageable deadlines and measurable quality standards
★ **Offer a resolution** – you talk about how you propose resolving some of the problems and how your company has special skills or products to arrive at a successful conclusion

This approach is flexible and easily adaptable to most forms of business presentations.

What framework would most serve your client, customer or prospect? Whatever kind you adopt, make it a simple one. Complex frameworks are hard to follow and if you lose your way during the actual presentation they can make it hard to get back on track.

Many business presentations must be done extremely quickly, in response to market and other pressures. A useful five-stage approach for creating an instant business presentation is

Step 1   Get attention – introduce your message with a catchy, grabby opener
Step 2   Relevance – explain the relevance of what you intend saying
Step 3   Core message – summarise your core purpose in a single sentence
Step 4   Give examples – support your case with examples or illustrations
Step 5   Close – end on a striking sentence summarising your speech

Persuasion

What makes a presentation persuasive? Pay particular attention to

★ Facts
★ Logical flow
★ Clear message
★ Relevance
★ Emotional content
★ Effective delivery
★ Benefits
★ Costs

 *Facts*

facts ⊂ 'The trouble with facts is that there are so many of them,' remarked an American writer in some frustration. It is easy to cram presentations full of them in the belief that they will speak for themselves. They don't.

Facts are things you know to be true and you probably already possess far more than you could ever use, particularly if you have done thorough research. An important presentation task is therefore to decide

★ **What facts to include and exclude:** Choose those essential to your argument, rather than 'nice to know' ones

★ **The most and the least important facts:** Identify what the audience 'must' be told and what it least needs to know
★ **The order in which to offer the facts:** Offer the most important ones first, ordering them so they flow in natural support of your argument
★ **What the facts mean and how they can be interpreted:** Facts aren't objective, they support a point of view; the audience needs you to help make sense of the information, otherwise just send a report

Often you already know what message you want to convey but must search for the facts to support it. At other times you have lots of facts but are not sure yet what should be the message. As we have already seen, the Master presenters spend time getting clear about their message, letting the facts take care of themselves.

Lists of facts are boring and don't constitute a logical argument. While in a purely rational world facts alone would win over an audience, the reality is different. To put the facts to work and bring them to life:

★ Support them with examples and case histories
★ Clarify in your own mind what the facts mean and how to interpret them
★ Present facts that enhance your message, acknowledge ones that don't
★ Present facts in a lively fashion, for example, visually or within a story

Normally you would first give the message backed up by the facts. Occasionally, though, it pays to change tack and use a startling fact to grab an audience's attention before launching into your case. For example, one presentation to a retail concern began: (fact) Your management turnover is 30% per year; (message) So within three years nearly every manager currently working for you will have left, so you need help with reducing this attrition rate.

If you have done a lot of hard work gathering facts the temptation is to cram them into your presentation, rather than letting them go to waste. Yet most business presentations are not about pure information giving. Firing lots of facts at the audience usually works less effectively than just a few powerful ones sequenced correctly.

'A lot of senior people are too busy to be able to understand a lot of detailed, technical facts,' argues one Master presenter. 'Some are embarrassed, I think, to show their ignorance so that's part of the problem; the facts have to be very accessible and easy to relate to.'

Part of the skill of using facts is deciding which ones to leave out. Information in presentations is always selective. What sets the Master presenter apart is a willingness to take a ruthless approach about which facts will make a difference and which won't.

'I'm not trying to give them every fact under the sun,' explains Peter Hill. 'I'm trying to give them what I think they require to be able to make a comfortable, well-considered decision; it's a fundamental part of doing any presentation. I have to ask: What is the minimum, essential and accessible information they really need?'

You will only persuade when sure about what you want people to think, feel or do. For instance, do you want them to get excited, take action, agree something, talk to each other, leave in a good mood, accept new information, support your decision, co-operate, or what?

Feelings have as great a part to play as facts. Sometimes they turn out to be even more important than the facts. You sway people as much by their hearts as their heads. Even if you are personally less affected by emotion than most, your audience is certainly collectively influenced by it. To be truly persuasive you need to take their feelings and reactions into account.

BRAINS AT WORK

Brain research shows that people learn in different ways. Some people prefer to say 'show me' while others want to know the whole picture in one go, and still others prefer to be taken through an argument step by step. 'You've got to be very flexible, not just present things or impart information only on the basis that you would feel comfortable learning it that way,' argues Peter Hill.

Studies of the brain also reveal the existence of cognitive dissonance. It happens when someone tries to believe two contradictory facts or ideas simultaneously. This creates internal conflicts that must be resolved. By presenting two conflicting pieces of information you therefore create tension in your listeners that they want to eliminate. This human tendency to want to reduce internal tension can be used to enhance your persuasiveness.

For example, two conflicting pieces of information might be:

★ The computer department believes its users are satisfied
★ Research shows that computer users are unhappy with their systems

These two pieces of information contradict each other and therefore create uncomfortable cognitive dissonance in people's minds. Somehow listeners need to resolve internal tension. Either they must agree that the computer department is fine, or they have to accept the alternative view based on the research evidence.

By causing cognitive dissonance you open up the possibility of persuasion, because people must make a choice – either to accept one state of affairs or the other.

Further reasons why you might seem persuasive include:

★ Your status and role
★ The organisation you belong to
★ Your use of metaphors, stories, analogies and images
★ Your personal credibility
★ How you use language
★ An appeal to reason
★ An appeal to emotion
★ An appeal to self-interest

A good place to start in creating a persuasive argument is to think yourself into the audience's shoes. In constructing a case as to why people should do, feel, or think in the way you want, how would they would reply to the question: 'What's in it for me?' i.e. what does the audience have to gain from

★ Agreeing with you
★ Accepting your arguments
★ Believing your evidence
★ Buying into your emotional appeal?

Logical flow

When receiving information the human brain automatically seeks order and to discern patterns. Arrange your presentation information so that people can easily discern the logical linkages between the arguments.

flow ⊂ Material needs to flow naturally from one point to the next.
mind map Try listing the main points you intend making and see whether
road map they have an easy progression. As part of ordering material consider the logic of what you are saying, which might involve

★ Deductive reasoning
★ Inductive reasoning
★ A mixture of both

Deductive reasoning is when you make a series of connected statements each leading to the next and on to the final conclusion. For example:

★ Our salesmen need training – without training they will be ineffective – if they are ineffective the new product won't reach the shops – if it doesn't reach the shops customers can't buy it – if people cannot buy it the product will fail.

  Thus you *deduce* the final conclusion from the logic of what went before that, unless the salesmen are trained, the product will fail. Deductions firmly based on facts make compelling arguments that audiences find hard to reject.

In inductive reasoning you use disparate and perhaps unconnected pieces of information to *infer* something. For example:

★ The company share price has fallen significantly
★ Competitors have made big price reductions
★ The company has lost market share
★ There are rumours about the company in the financial press
★ There have been some large purchases of shares recently

  Thus you *infer* from these disparate facts that the company is vulnerable to a takeover and needs specialist financial advice. Inference is the commonest form of reasoning in presentations.

The difference between inference and deduction may seem arcane, yet it is really about arguing from the general to the particular or vice versa. It is usually best to choose one approach or the other to support your core message. Muddling the two can make it hard for listeners to follow your reasoning.

Research also shows that people listening to a communication want

★ The most important information first

This is particularly so in business presentations where the audience seldom wants to sit through a lengthy process of building a case. An approach that works well is

★ Numbers

Numbers often play an important role in business presentations. Commonly portrayed as 'facts', their contribution to your

persuasiveness, though, depends as much on how you use them as which ones you choose to present.

figures ⊂
statistics

Most people cannot easily remember more than a few numbers, so use numerical material sparingly and make it accessible and memorable. Typical mistakes in using numbers include

★ Out of context figures
★ Hard to understand data
★ Excess numbers
★ Wrong numbers
★ Lack of pattern, trend or message

OUT OF CONTEXT

Out of context numbers leaves the audience wondering how to interpret them. For example, 'sales rose 12% this year' is meaningless without having something with which to compare it, such as:

★ How sales changed last year, last quarter or in recent years
★ How sales changed for competitors
★ Which particular sales the numbers refer to compared to other types

UNDERSTANDABLE

Hard to understand numbers do your presentation a real disservice and show lack of respect for your audience. Just because you are familiar with the figures does not mean that your audience will understand them. Review the numbers you intend to present carefully and see how they can be

★ Simplified
★ Clarified
★ Eliminated
★ Conveyed by more powerful visual images

Just about any sort of number can be adapted to be audience friendly. For example, round decimal points or fractions to the nearest whole number. Similarly, convert numbers into concepts that an audience can more easily follow such as altering 34% into 'one in three', or change 25% to 'one out of four' and so on.

EXCESS NUMBERS

Excess numbers confuse an audience and therefore make no real impact. A common presenting mistake is to use tables containing, say, five or six columns and rows. No audience can be expected to grasp several dozen figures.

Tables with columns of figures seldom work well and it's better to convert them into a more forceful visual message, such as a chart. Yet sometimes a table of some kind is essential, in which case at least make it easier to read. For example, highlight in colours the particular figure, column or row that conveys your essential message.

With computer-based presentations such as those using PowerPoint it is particularly easy to be seduced into projecting spread sheets on screen that can be instantly altered to make a point to the audience. While this can work with a small select group totally in tune with what you are doing, generally the impact of so many figures that suddenly alter is small.

WRONG NUMBERS

Wrong numbers during your presentation can be seriously embarrassing and undermine your whole credibility. Check everything meticulously before exposing it to public scrutiny and invite a colleague to look for

★ Wrong totals
★ Inconsistency
★ Miscalculated percentages
★ Mistakes in formulas

If you spot a mistake during your performance, point it out before a member of the audience does it for you. Explain the reason and indicate what you think are the implications, for example,

★ 'This does not affect the basic picture of . . .'
★ 'This slightly alters the conclusion but not significantly'

LACK OF PATTERN

The brain's response to encountering a series of numbers is to try to impose a pattern to make sense of the data. Help your audience, therefore, by using this knowledge to find imaginative ways to let them see the patterns or story behind the crude numbers.

Figures, charts and diagrams should tell a story, such as highlighting a trend, revealing an exception, confirming a situation. Just a few, well-chosen numbers can get your messages across, particularly when in picture or chart form.

Clear message

When the Nobel physicist Richard Feynman explained on television what had gone wrong with the Apollo 13 space flight in which several astronauts were killed, he did so in a powerful, memorable fashion. Without confusing his audience with elaborate descriptions of the weakness of the rubber seals that had caused the accident, he simply produced a jug of iced water.

Dipping the offending rings into the water, Feynman then showed how they had hardened and become brittle. He said nothing about the coefficient of rubber expansion or the penetration of negative temperatures into impermeable materials. Yet the audience immediately understood why the faulty O rings had proved fatal.

No matter how complex, difficult or technical your subject, it's vital that your audience understands your essential message. Einstein once claimed that it was possible to reduce any scientific issue to something that a non-scientist could grasp. Coming from the man who discovered relativity, this was certainly a large claim. Yet there is no excuse for hiding behind the complexity of a subject and bamboozling an audience.

Master presenters always find ways to communicate obscure matters so that the audience understands. Metaphors, analogies, stories, drawings, examples and even objects can be used to convey the story.

active voice
analogy
edit
imagery
repetition
sentences

You will never fail as a presenter by making your message clear to the audience, even though some may suggest you are spoon-feeding them.

Review your entire presentation so as to

ACTION

★ Cut verbiage
  ★ Use simple sentences and phrasing
  ★ Avoid multiple sub-clauses
  ★ Substitute short, plain words
  ★ Eliminate jargon
  ★ Use the active voice
★ Reject excess slides or overheads

Sometimes the more you talk the less you say. It is unnecessary to speak the whole time since audiences need time to absorb your message. Deliberate silence can often be highly effective.

Verbiage hot spots

★ **Showing visuals:** Stop talking while showing a visual. Rely on the image to speak for itself. Avoid reading words aloud, except for audiences whose first language is not English.

★ **Scripts:** Having it there in meticulous detail means you're likely to swamp your listeners with extraneous input.

★ **Specialist terms:** Ask colleagues to give you feedback on whether you're being wordy, elaborating unnecessarily or resorting to jargon.

★ **Answering questions:** Don't try and talk your way out of it. Audiences soon detect when a speaker is on unsure ground and this only makes the situation worse. Keep your replies short, the audience will appreciate the brevity.

★ **Getting carried away:** Your enthusiasm is commendable, just keep it sufficiently in check to prevent you going on wordy tangents.

When I think over what I have said,
I envy dumb people.

SENECA, 'ON A HAPPY LIFE', *MORAL ESSAYS*

⊃ foreign audiences

⊃ bluff

Jargon busting

Jargon is a presentation killer. David Hughes Solomon, Technical Director at SAP, can baffle anyone with his knowledge of complicated phrases and terms. Yet as one of the company's top presenters he prides himself on avoiding jargon.

'It's a comfort blanket because it doesn't let anyone else in. The big problem in our industry is that people have almost invented their own language to protect themselves. The only problem is they're not the people spending the money. The ones spending the money are finance directors and people like that, so I use plain English. If you do need to have a technical conversation you can do that as well but be prepared to come back out.'

If one cannot state a matter clearly enough so that
even an intelligent twelve-year-old can understand it,
one should remain within the cloistered walls of the
university and the laboratory until one gets a better
grasp of one's subject matter.

MARGARET MEADE, *REDBOOK* (1963)

⊃ colloquial
jargon
language
slang
vocabulary

Relevance

It is easier to see whether you are staying relevant with your presentation when you are actually in the room, watching your audience watching you. Constructing a persuasive presentation, though, also means ensuring that all material

★ Contributes to getting your message across
★ 'Connects' with the audience

Sound research into your audience allows you to choose material with confidence. Ideally, you are aiming for people to say things like: 'This makes sense to me'; 'You've struck a chord'; 'What you say rings true'; 'This was important'; 'I can use this now'. To choose relevant material keep asking questions such as

★ How will this land with the audience?
★ Does it make sense to these people?
★ Will this seem important to them?
★ What could they do with this information?
★ Is it action-focused?
★ Would this excite them?
★ Why should they care about this?
★ Is it essential they hear this?

It can be tempting to leave out arguments, facts or evidence that undermine your arguments. Audiences soon realise, though, when your line of reasoning is biased and this may not go down well, particularly when presenting business plans or strategies. Make sure you prepare the arguments both for and against every element of the case you are making. Even if you don't include all the adverse factors, at least acknowledge them and make them available if people ask.

Emotional content

For some people this can be the most difficult part of preparing a business presentation. It requires you to answer in depth the single question:

★ 'Why should people really *care* about this?'

To answer it requires an understanding of the people you will be talking to and what moves them. Facts alone won't do it. A logical argument, however well constructed, won't do it. Somehow you need to inject into your material some emotional content.

Why? Surely business people are only swayed by hard facts such as the bottom line, measures of productivity, financial ratios, convincing information and so on? If that were true then all you'd need to do would be to send that report.

It matters *how* you present the facts, the bottom line, measures of productivity and so on. Business people are human and are swayed by emotion as much as anyone else. Material you choose needs to recognise this fact of life. So, for example, if you know that your audience is particularly concerned about customer opinion, choosing material about this issue is obviously relevant. Giving it emotional content, though, means turning raw information into a compelling message.

For example, compare these two pieces of information:

27.85% of all customers surveyed were dissatisfied with product X.
Nearly one in three customers are *unhappy* with *your* product.

We will look more closely at how you inject passion into your presentation during the Delivery Stage.

You know you are staying relevant when you see your audience nodding in agreement or the questions people ask reveal that your message has hit home and raised interest.

SHOW ME!

When Eliza Dolittle in the musical *My Fair Lady* demands that her lover stop talking and 'show me!' she sums up what makes a convincing argument. You can give all the facts and make all the arguments in the world, yet often what sways people is seeing or hearing for themselves what it's all about. It allows them to 'feel' the emotional content.

In Rolls-Royce plc, Peter Hill spends much of his time making internal presentations to obtain investment for multi-million-pound projects. He has found how compelling it is to produce a physical object to put on the table and say 'this is the sort of thing we mean', when talking about a new production technique. Doing this, he is injecting emotional content into his presentation with a simple physical object.

props

'I'd been asked to talk at one of our factories about a recent trip to Japanese factories. I obviously couldn't bring along the factory so I brought in a camera and we talked about what it would cost to make in Rolls-Royce plc. Our people said, "How the heck can they make it for that price?" This really got their attention.'

Whether physical or descriptive, examples always help make a powerful case and provide emotional content. Message, plus fact, followed by an example penetrates an audience's awareness rapidly. Giving them a taste, a feel for the point you are conveying is worth more than endless assertions or arguments supporting your claims.

Maynard Leigh Associates often presents to companies interested in our use in business of ideas drawn from theatre. We could talk till tomorrow about the effectiveness of the methods we use, how they affect rapid change and break through resistance. Instead we simply say, 'Let's show you right now what we mean.' Soon people are laughing and realising through their actions that we have something special to offer. 'Show me' is nearly always more powerful than 'tell me'.

excitement
ideas
imagination
inspiration
magic
mystery
topicality
variety

Examples can take the form of case studies, samples, pictures, objects, film clips, demonstrations, walkabouts and site visits, exercises and interactive experiences. If you are presenting something intangible such as a service, your examples help to bring your arguments to life.

Peter Hill explains that in an engineering company 'there's nothing more compelling than a piece of metal which has been machined and processed or looks like what we are talking about. People can't walk away from that. There's only one thing more compelling and it's if you can find out your competitors are going to do something like it, but hopefully not quite as good.'

PRESENT THE EVIDENCE

To make a persuasive business case you need evidence. Almost anything can be evidence, from personal experience to stories about other companies, from examples to demonstrations.

The evidence supports your case. It can be expert testimony

or pointing to an object. If you give business presentations regularly, open a personal file into which you pour lots of case studies, stories, facts, statistics and general evidence to draw on to make a case. Whenever you make a point in your presentation back it up with evidence.

Telling a story can often be the most compelling form of ⊃ **story** evidence. If you enjoy the story and it's one you relish, your listeners will soon respond to your enthusiasm, which makes you that much more persuasive.

Is the evidence relevant? It's no use bombarding your listeners with great stories that don't support your message. In most business presentations you are there to make a case, not to be an entertainer.

For example, if you are talking to a group who are deciding whether to hire your company to deliver a particular service, don't waste their time telling them fascinating tales of how you also do many other things too. Make the evidence stay on message.

Benefits and costs

To be persuasive in many business presentations you need to offer a clear picture of benefits and costs. People want to know, for example, what's in it for them, the organisation, their division, their factory and so on. The more you spell these out the greater the chance you will have of gaining buy-in.

Having explained the benefits, though, people may be wondering whether these will really be delivered. Will an idea, for example, really work? Clarify for the audience why you are so sure the benefits will happen, perhaps because competitors have already reaped the results of a new technology, or you have delivered on this elsewhere.

Likewise, it is often essential to explain the resources needed to support some particular action. Even if there are no cost implications it makes sense clearly to explain why.

CHAPTER 4

Hit Them with a Visual

'Oh, no! Not another boring pie chart!' It's now so easy to produce impressive-looking visuals that many business presentations are losing their power to hold attention. The response of some presenters is to up the ante and introduce animation, multi-media and even more stunning graphics.

As ever, it depends on your audience. In America, for instance, many business presentations are treated as a form of show, with less attention on content and more focus on whether the performance entertains. In such situations visuals can help play an important role in gaining audience interest.

excitement ⊂
ideas
imagination
inspiration
new
original
subject
topicality
variety

Making it different

Visuals are also an important way of distinguishing your presentation from competitors. One well-prepared presenter, for example, surprisingly lost out to a rival and went back to find out why.

The company explained: 'We were looking for evidence of innovation and creativity, and your way of presenting didn't show that. You could have given us that presentation in any room in the world. You made no use of facilities at your disposal; you could have had big posters on the wall explaining your process and you didn't.

'You could have used other media, one of your competitors used video conferencing because it was a global assignment and they introduced their team in different theatres around the world by video conference. You just flew over one guy.'

By contrast, in Europe an all singing and dancing visual show can prove counter-productive, with the audience feeling distracted and unable really to focus on the issues.

For example, are you risking 'Death by PowerPoint'? This is when you inflict on your defenceless audience endless bullet-pointed slides, keywords and clip art that look pretty, yet cumulatively create a numbing effect and loss of impact.

PowerPoint

A particular drawback of computer-based presentation programmes is the danger of them dictating how you do your presentation. 'How many times have I seen people use PowerPoint slides with things whizzing in from the left or the right, and what that's doing is driving the presentation for you. Because whenever you press a button it automatically programmes what will come up next, even if it is now out of context,' argues David Hughes Soloman, SAP's Technical Director.

Gary Hamel, one of the world's leading business strategists, revels in bombarding his audience with countless visuals that arrive and depart in seconds, leaving everyone feeling breathless. He usually gets away with it because he is extremely adept at making it all look amazingly spontaneous, seemingly playing his laptop almost like a virtuoso pianist. He, not the computer, is clearly in charge of the presentation.

animation
builds
cartoons
clip art
colour
film
graphs
label
overheads
photographs
symbols
tables
television
title
video
video news release

An important role of visuals is to reduce complexity and convey a simple message. The aerospace business is about as complicated as you can get. Business Development Manager Peter Hill at Rolls-Royce plc invented a chart to explain a radical new production process for turbine blades. 'Maybe it's a little complicated if you're not involved in manufacturing but it's an incredibly simple way of understanding the way things could be made, it's much simpler than they've been made so far. That one little presentation has probably been shown round most of the directors of Rolls-Royce. That was the original vision of how we're going to make these parts simply.'

Similarly, Alex Gethin of KPMG is clear about the role of visuals in major business presentations: 'We certainly don't use them as the main thing that drives the presentation, our people should do that. Visuals are there to support your message where necessary. There is often one visual which helps to communicate the whole theme of what the presentation is about. Sometimes you can get gimmicky things with which to make your point – the important job is the signposting.'

★ Visuals need to be visual

bullets ⊂

fonts

lettering

Words and bullet points are not visuals. Holding up a product is a visual, a photograph is a visual and so is a cartoon. Your visuals need to tell a story and save you speaking by punching home your message. Using visuals as a form of diversionary tactic preventing the audience focusing on you though is a sure way to reduce your personal impact.

How can you get the best from your visuals? Apart from making them appealing to look at, select ones that really enhance your message. Clip art and library photos may be enough, though with digital cameras now readily available consider taking your own pictures. Three-dimensional visuals are nearly always compelling, so long as the audience can see clearly what the object is and understand its relevance.

Timing

Whatever image you use to convey the message it needs to arrive at just the right moment during the presentation. This is not just about coinciding with your wording, it's also about ensuring that the image is appropriate at that point in the performance.

A general guideline for judging the value of each visual is that if you have to explain it, the image isn't working. Almost by definition good visuals shouldn't require a verbal commentary. Ideally, select those that evoke a specific emotional response from the audience, such as laughter, surprise, curiosity, concern, relief and so on. If you are unclear what that emotional response should be, spend some time thinking through why you are using it in the first place.

ACTION

Words ain't visuals

★ People listen to words, not watch them
★ Minimise text on each visual: six words per line and six lines per visual
★ Write in upper and lower case; words all in capitals are harder to read
★ Colour code key messages
★ Adopt bold, thick typefaces

Rather than multiple fonts use *italics*, **bold,** and <u>underlining</u>

THE ULTIMATE BUSINESS PRESENTATION BOOK

Win with charts

★ For each chart ask: what does it SHOW, not what does it say
★ Convey only one message per chart
★ Use a sequence of charts rather than one crammed with everything
★ Turn chart titles into action statements, 'Sales rise threefold', or 'The Demand is for Presentation Training'.
★ Create a single visual to convey your main presentation message
★ Use simple rather than abstract or over-realistic pictures
★ Avoid glaring coloured logos in the corner of every image
★ Make the visual balanced and orderly
★ Use horizontal format for slides and overheads
★ If the audience can't read it quickly, don't use it
★ Simplify by removing surplus shadings, excess colours and artwork, technical jumble, distracting backgrounds, grid lines, data points, boxes and vibrating fill patterns such as contrasting lines, wave patterns and criss-crosses unless they enhance the message
★ Use no more than four colours per chart
★ Write words horizontally for easy reading, especially on pie charts

Numbers

★ Use charts to present numbers and data
★ More than two columns and rows can lose attention – use a chart or diagram instead
★ Add coloured rings or shade the numbers you want to highlight – do this to only a few figures
★ Grey out all vertical and horizontal columns except the one that matters

Round numbers are always false.
                    SAMUEL JOHNSON (1709–84)

ACTION

The complexity of the visual needs to reflect the type of audience. Peter Hill's chart of a new way of turbine blade manufacturing, for instance, would make little sense to a group of visiting non-technical investment managers.

Visuals for foreign nationals

interpreters   Many important business presentations are made to audiences
language   whose first language is not English. Visuals for these occasions must be carefully chosen if they are to have the desired impact. Where possible, get the visuals translated into the local language, keeping words to a minimum, relying on the graphics to communicate.

For 'foreign' audiences explain everything in the visual, including how to interpret it. Even if you are talking to a relatively sophisticated business audience it is still best to avoid abbreviated words such as acronyms and only use internationally recognised symbols such as the % sign.

Builds

Builds progressively introduce information, particularly written text, so as to hold the audience's interest. Rather than showing all
builds   the material at once you reveal a portion of it at a time, gradually adding more. Builds can be done manually, as when you cover part of an overhead and then reveal the next portion, or automatically by using presentation software.

Usually the sequence builds, finally to include all the material. With presentation tools such as PowerPoint you can devise animated builds that introduce each new element with a variety of visual devices, such as fades, sentences dropping down from the top or whizzing in from the side and so on.

Simple builds work best. The more complex ones dazzle and are fun to create, yet may focus attention on the show rather than the contents. Some experienced presenters argue that, as a technique, builds are a distraction because they tend to take away attention from the presenter.

The typical build works like this:

ACE TEAMS
☆ **ALIGNED**

ACE TEAMS
☆ ALIGNED
☆ **CREATIVE**

ACE TEAMS
☆ ALIGNED
☆ CREATIVE
☆ **EXPLORING**

ACE TEAMS
☆ **ALIGNED**
☆ **CREATIVE**
☆ **EXPLORING**

Showing the visuals

CRT projectors
electronic white boards
LCD projectors
LCD panels
multimedia
pointers
screen

How you show your visuals can enhance and support your presentation performance. Overheads, based on a computer, for instance, are easy to use though there is more to go wrong at a technical level. More than half a dozen actual overheads tend to look fussy and low-tech.

Slides generally appear professional but the turnaround time for producing them may be unrealistic. Also, they usually require the room lights to be dimmed, distancing you from the audience.

A particularly strong and simple way of presenting your visuals is on large, rigid, lightweight boards. These are easy to carry and have a powerful impact when in full colour. While they also take time to create, the turnaround time can be fast. Chart material is now regularly e-mailed direct to printers and returned the same day.

The attraction of the large board is that it creates it own physical presence in the room. It demands attention in ways that projected pictures do not. It also shrieks at the audience how well prepared you are and how seriously you are taking the task of communicating.

Using computer-generated slides

desktop presentations
PowerPoint

The most commonly used computer program for generating slides is PowerPoint. Anybody who's suffered a series of such presentations can testify to the deadening effect of them. PowerPoint makes it all seem so easy, almost eliminating the need for a live presenter.

If your entire presentation is on PowerPoint, it's the equivalent to running a slide show – just add a voice-over and you might as well not be there. On the other hand, if you can integrate PowerPoint imaginatively into your presentation it can be a valuable asset. Here are some ways to get the best from the technology.

BE CREATIVE

Every presentation, if it is to make an impact, needs to be creative. Adding a visual element makes your message more memorable. There are many sorts of visual aids (props, posters, videos, cartoons, photographs, handouts) but slides are probably the easiest. Putting an image on a screen can be a very powerful way of enhancing your message. Avoid slides with slabs of text or complex charts.

KISS OF DEATH

The worst kind of PowerPoint presentation is when people merely read a speech and have the slides with bullet points going along behind them. The audience might just as well read a document in their own time and not bother to listen to you. These sorts of presentations develop a rhythm, which has brilliant 'sleep' power. With constant slides it's hard for an audience to pay attention.

VARIETY

Like any other visual aid, PowerPoint slides are best used sparingly. They are most effective when intermixed with other visual support, or other completely different aspects of your presentation, such as interaction with your audience, anecdotes, demonstrations, personal experience, audience participation, questions and answers.

KNOW YOUR COMPUTER

There is a lot your computer can do to support your quest for a visual component to your presentation. PowerPoint is a useful resource to generate slides but you need to know your way around the program. Invest time in practising and learning what it can do. You wouldn't drive a car in only one gear, so it's worth knowing the potential of your software.

computers
laptops
multimedia
technology
tools

EFFECTS

PowerPoint offers you various *animations*, *slide transitions* and *text build* effects. These govern how content arrives on the screen. They can be good fun and liven up the presentation. They can also be annoying if overused, or used for their own sake. Really think about whether the information on the slide can benefit by being *uncovered* or *flown in*. The same applies to sound effects. 'Slide-sorter' gives you a good overview and allows you to add and remove slides and change their order.

AUTO-PILOT?

There are some useful automatic functions on PowerPoint.

Auto-layout is a useful way to start your slide design, although it tends to encourage interminable use of bullet points. Try and use the layouts which include charts, graphs or images. *Auto-Design Template* is useful to add an instant and colourful layout. But beware *Auto-content wizard*. It makes it all sound seductively easy but it takes you down a predictable road, which is likely to end in boredom.

CLIP ART

Use images to make your point. But be wary of overused ones, particularly importing from widely used clip art sources. People are increasingly familiar with the selection and they soon lose their effectiveness. These days it's easy to scan an image from other sources and import it into your slide.

pace

pauses

BREATHING SPACE

If, for technical reasons, the projector needs to stay on during your whole presentation, make sure you intersperse it with some blank or title slides. This allows you to set your own pace, be spontaneous and not be driven by the 'slide show'.

RELATIONSHIP

Don't let the computer take over from the essential element of successful presentations – personal relationship with your audience. You are the most important element of your presentation. A projector cannot be passionate, cannot respond spontaneously to your audience and cannot build a relationship with them. Only a human being can do that. It's down to you.

DELIVERY

Talk the message of the slide not the contents. If the latter can't be absorbed by the audience within about ten seconds there's probably too much information. Trust the silence and don't talk constantly through each slide.

Rehearse, Rehearse, Rehearse

There is no absolute rule about how much rehearsal makes a good presentation. You know you have rehearsed enough when you have mastered your material and feel confident about responding to any audience demand.

Far more time often goes into preparing reports, handouts and other distractions than following the three rules of presentation: rehearse, rehearse, rehearse.

Make 'em do it

'It's really hard to get bid teams to rehearse,' complains Brian Polk of PWC. 'Rehearsing is a painful process that involves senior people standing up in front of peers or even more junior people and at times looking ridiculous. If you're wanting senior people to do a presentation, you're talking about people flying from different corners of the globe to wherever you happen to be delivering this presentation and then rehearsing them. My job is to persuade them to rehearse.

'The first rehearsal is always a drawn-out affair that takes two or three times as long as the actual presentation, because you're sorting out what roles people are going to play, where the handover points are, who is going to deliver which messages, working through slide by slide to clarify what people are going to say and what are the key messages.'

The best performers aim is to 'have a conversation' with the audience, which a totally rehearsed, utterly crafted presentation may undermine. 'I know roughly the areas I'm going to speak to,' reveals SAP's David Hughes Solomon, 'but when it's spontaneous, the audience interaction you get is fantastic and they often come up with something that you would never have thought of.

'I've seen many presentations where they've divided up the time so it's like some sort of stage show where people are being pulled on with a big hook and dragged off again after ten minutes.'

An important benefit of rehearsing your presentation out loud is that you gain an accurate sense of how long it will take. One PR company presenting its case for work from Maynard Leigh Associates, for example, had clearly never been through its presentation aloud and ran out of time, leaving no opportunity for a question-and-answer session.

Despite the confidence of the top performers, for most business presentations some form of rehearsal is nearly always justified, even if it is only reviewing the material that will be used and kept in reserve. Generally, the more rehearsal time you devote to the presentation, the greater will be your confidence with the live audience. For some people, though, this works the other way, with each rehearsal only adding to already jangled nerves.

The danger of relying entirely on ad libbing is that in a team presentation there is no cohesiveness. The audience quickly picks up the lack of preparation and may draw the even more negative conclusion that the presenting team's company is badly organised.

Thorough rehearsals should leave you feeling able to drop your entire formal presentation if necessary and instead respond to what the audience is wanting. To rehearse

★ Read the presentation out loud, maybe ten or more times
★ Practice the entire performance in front of someone else and get feedback
★ Try recording your delivery on audio or video tape and review it critically; mirrors don't let you see yourself as others do but in a reverse image
★ Time the presentation by doing it out loud

Who should watch your rehearsals? Ideally, perform it to some of your potential audience. 'I was devising a presentation,' explains Frank Lee of Sema, 'and I sat with the customer's IT director and for three days we put it all together and rehearsed in front of him.'

If you are constantly worrying about remembering the words or what to do next, you need more rehearsal time. Master presenters who do rehearse meticulously reckon they commit up to eight hours rehearsal for a forty-five-minute speech. Practise until you feel you are

★ Confident about handling the material, changing it if necessary
★ Able to eliminate detailed notes and rely on key ideas or words only
★ Ready for just about any contingency

Rehearsals are paying off when instead of concentrating on the words, you start focusing on the ideas and the audience. You can say a word like 'profit' in many different ways. Yet what gives the word meaning and an interesting emphasis is when you are saying it as part of communicating an idea.

While one possible way of learning the presentation is by listening to a complete audio tape of it, it's generally more effective to practise bits of it until gradually it starts coming together as a whole. You seldom need to memorise what you are going to say word for word, unless you are fitting into a multi-media presentation that is calling the shots.

Spontaneity comes not so much from learning your presentation by rote as being utterly familiar with the material.

Team effort

Many major business presentations require a whole team to put the message across. The most elaborate ones may involve several different teams – technical, strategic, behavioural – to make presentations to different groups of buyer influences.

A good team presentation integrates everyone's effort into a smooth-running performance. Each person has a clear role and understands how to contribute to the others in the team. KPMG's Senior Proposals Manager, Alex Gethin explains that within her organisation 'it's important to see how the team behaves together. Experienced presenters can be tempted to leave their presentation

to the last minute. Individually they might be fine but a team performance won't be achieved. This can become particularly apparent in the question-and-answer session.'

A presentation team in KPMG will do several dry run-throughs, one of which is in front of a difficult panel of people who are briefed to act as if they are the potential client receiving the presentation.

The team working together to create a powerful presentation may need to work hard at teaming, perhaps getting together to tackle something jointly that has nothing at all to do with the actual presentation. In some cases the team may literally go into a huddle to get close and build trust and a sense of cohesion.

In working together the team must solve a thorny presentation issue:

★ Where will the audience focus its attention?

The group may need to make decisions about

★ How the team will support the focus
★ How team members will support each other
★ How each person will hand over to the next
★ What each person will do while another is speaking

What colour is your team?

No matter whether it's a small or large presentation, it's always worth reviewing it as you approach the point of delivery. For complex presentations this process is thorough and the Masters talk of red, pink, green and gold team reviews.

The colours refer to the coloured pens used to highlight specific parts of the presentation that may need to be changed.

Pink team review: May look at whether the presentation is following the agreed sales strategy and may be conducted many times.

Red team review: Looks objectively either at the proposal or the presentation, pulling it to pieces and helping the team reconstruct it so that 'if I were the customer, would I understand what you are getting at? You say these are the sales messages, well I don't see them.'

Green team review: Dissects the technical aspect of a presentation to see if it can be fully understood and meets all the criteria laid down by the client.

Gold team review: Asks, 'Is this a viable piece of business? Can we submit this bid?' This review may happen many times and is a continual process of refinement.

Leading the team

Teams for important presentations are usually lead by a senior person in the company. Even if millions or even billions are at stake this person may literally fly into the country just before the presentation to 'front it'.

'If you're talking about trying to persuade one of the world's Fortune 100 companies to spend millions of dollars or ECUs on your business, then they want to know your firm is committed at the highest levels and they want to see some evidence of senior commitment to whatever you're doing,' explains one bid support manager.

'For those really big presentations it is important to bring in someone who's got a global role within the firm to demonstrate commitment.'

It's also essential that the person fronting the team really practises with everyone present, so that the whole group feels at home with the arrangements and the cracks don't show. While this high-level individual may be brilliant, integrating the performance with the whole team's demands practice and true professionalism. Ensure at least one and preferably two full team rehearsals in this situation.

For a potential contract worth many millions IBM formed a strategic alliance with another IT company to pitch for work from a UK government agency. Unfortunately the cultures of the two organisations were very different. While the IT company was used to practising its important bids and drafting in its chief executive, IBM was more bureaucratic and eventually only a senior vice-president arrived to participate in the presentation. He was used to being supported by a cohort of obedient minions and his style was both different and in conflict with that of the other senior executive.

The result was a weak presentation, with conflicting messages in which the chairman of the judging panel remarked that 'you people don't appear to have talked to each other'! The joint effort by IBM and its allied company failed.

We're all in this alone.

LILY TOMLIN, COMEDIENNE AND ACTRESS

Who will lead the presentation team? It's tempting always to put the most senior person in charge of opening the show. Yet this may be a mistake and a better approach might be to allow the person with the strongest presentation style to kick off.

Weak team presenters need to have a specific role and to be placed in the middle of the presentation where their performance will be less critical. Similarly, it makes sense to put on a strong presenter to close the performance.

ROLES

The bigger the presentation team the more important it is to establish clear roles. Issues to resolve include who will

★ Answer questions
★ Be in charge of visuals and ensure they are clear
★ Change the visuals
★ Take notes during the presentation
★ Watch the audience body language for clues
★ Record questions requiring follow-through afterwards
★ Give hand signals to tell the current speaker to speak louder or softer, slow down or speed up, or stop to handle a question

INTRODUCTIONS

Decide how introductions will be made – all at once or each speaker to introduce the next. Make sure also that each presenter's introduction fits in with the others, is relevant and much the same length so that the effect is consistent.

How will each presenter hand over to the next one during the presentation? Will it be a formal handover or a 'smooth as clockwork' performance in which each person knows their part so well they simply take over on cue?

THE CSC RED REVIEW TEAM

There may also be several review teams to help the presenting team put together an outstanding message. At Computer Sciences Corporation, for example, the Red Review team is a small group of people with knowledge of an area, yet with nothing to do with the preparation of the proposal or presentation.

CSC allows a day for its Red Review team to take the material apart. Basically the team checks whether the presentation really does answer the requirements specified by the client. At the end of the review the Red team provides feedback to the proposal and presentation team, who come into the room and receive it. The feedback is usually at a high level, concerned with the overall impact, shape, coherence and win themes.

The Red team has limited authority and cannot insist on change. Nor does it question or validate the technical solution on offer. Instead, it makes observations and recommendations, which the proposal team must then decide whether to accept or reject.

Effective team presentations

★ Appoint a lead person responsible for 'holding' the delivery of the event
★ Allow plenty of time to practise together
★ Consider using an outside coach to enhance the team's performance
★ Give everyone a meaningful and clear role; ask them to understudy each other so as to handle last-minute illness
★ Ensure everyone understands the importance of listening
★ Decide on the different messages and who is best to deliver them
★ Use everyone's creative energy and ideas to devise the presentation
★ Work together to decide how you'll handle various disaster scenarios
★ Clarify the choreography: for example, will everyone enter in the order they intend to speak, how will each person hand on to the next, how will questions and answers be dealt with by the team?
★ Appoint someone to co-ordinate written and visual materials to ensure professionalism and consistency

The impression the group as whole makes is more important than the performance of any one person. While each person presents, individual members need to

★ Pay attention to everything that is said
★ Be interested in each other's responses

Those who are not team players will have to go.
JEANNE GREENBERG, CEO CALIPER,
NATIONS BUSINESS, 1988

If it's a team presentation the energy of the group is an important element that may need attention. 'There's no distinct pattern,' suggests Alex Gethin of KPMG. 'Some teams work well together and create their own energy. If the presentation lacks commitment

and drive then you need to take a long hard look at what you're doing, challenging the motivation, messages and team members.'

BEING CRITICAL

Be particularly careful how you or your team criticise other individuals or rival organisations during your presentation. Apart from avoiding possible legal action, such behaviour leaves an audience with a bad taste in its collective mouth, remembering you for entirely the wrong reasons.

If you must criticise others, avoid naming them and

★ Stick to facts rather than aspects of personality
★ Be sure to substantiate your facts
★ Frame criticisms in the wider context of your overall message

The presentation environment

The more you have thought and prepared for the moment of delivery the more 'at home' you will feel on actually arriving at the location. For example, if you are giving your first presentation to your company's board of directors, try to arrange to sit in the room undisturbed when it is unused. As you soak up the atmosphere, many of your fears may begin to dissipate. Also, you may spot something about the physical environment that could affect the impact of your performance, such as noisy air-conditioning, or the danger of becoming stuck at the end of an excessively long table.

'We pay close attention to the ambience of the environment we're presenting in,' explains Ray Barratt, Industrial Business Unit Manager at SAP. When SAP gives presentations in its own premises careful thought goes into what the audience would prefer in the way of the environment. 'We consider the culture of the prospective customer and whether the people are used to boardroom presentations. If so, we whip them upstairs to our nice dining suite. If they're used to being in a workshop environment we'll take them to the training centre. Where we hold the presentation is always key.'

KPMG is equally thorough in checking out the location. 'We may go there at the actual time of day we'd be presenting to check the sun's not going to be shining in our eyes, and if we want to use any visual aids such as flip charts or projected slides that there is enough room or suitable surface to project onto.'

Presentation scouts of another well-prepared company discovered that sensors automatically switched off the lights if no one made enough body or arm movements. In another the scouts found that the proposed visuals would not easily fit in the room and in another there was going to be no space to exchange business cards and do all the handshaking.

The numbers of people in the room can also influence the type of environment created for the presentation. For example, if you discover the company you are presenting to is fielding a huge team, arriving with only two people won't seem right. Instead, it might be sensible to find ways to bring a large team too, so long as they can have some clear role in the presentation.

Notes and Prompts

There is nothing shameful about needing a prompt. Own up to it rather than surreptitiously hiding it. Your notes can take the form of

★ Outlines
★ Index cards with phrases, keywords and pictures
★ The full script
★ Mind maps
★ Copies of the slides or overheads
★ Mechanical prompts
★ Props and objects

forget
keywords
memory
names
omission
retention
sidetracked

Prompts are reminders, they are seldom the entire presentation. So keywords, simple drawings or even a succession of small objects can often provide enough to guide you through the entire performance. Or a prompt may be a simple card placed where you can see it during the presentation to remind you of something, such as 'stay focused'.

Even in major presentations people accept that presenters may need prompts of some kind. They only become a problem if they start getting in the way of the performance, for example, when someone keeps shuffling papers or dropping cue cards.

While you may never see these vital aids being used by the best Master presenters it could just mean they are discreetly hidden, or they are relying on mental cues rather than physical ones.

Outlines

An outline is simply the headings of your presentation. These should be sufficient to remind you of the main points. Outlines allow you to retain the whole script if you wish, by highlighting the headings in bright colours. These can be enough to trigger your memory of the material; if not, you can quickly glance below at the extended material.

Outlines are usually more than only the keywords and may be whole phrases, rather than a detailed script. You can keep such material in various ways including a full script, a hidden computer screen, a card nearby on a lectern and so on.

Cards

The most commonly used prompt consists of small index cards – A6 size or less – that fit comfortably into the palm of the hand. These contain just a few keywords, phrases or even pictures to guide the presentation.

With practice you'll be able to reduce your entire presentation to one simple card. If you use several, number them sequentially and find an easy way of physically linking them together. Place visual prompts where they can help you deliver a smooth performance without resorting to full notes.

Some presenters reduce their material to basic drawings that sum up visually the points they want to make. These can be perfectly childish, since no one else will see them.

How do you generate a highly condensed prompt to fit on one or more small cards? The easiest way is to practise your presentation until you are really familiar with it and hardly need to refer to the original material. Soon you'll realise which words or phrases best guide you along the way.

The script

speech
write You walk on to the platform and take out your speech, written on a dozen pages. Now the audience knows it's in for a lengthy word bashing. Already some people are becoming bored or restless.

Even talented actors find it hard to sound interesting and spontaneous while reading from a script. Relying on one means you have to read directly from it, which makes you spend a lot of time glancing down, rather than watching the audience. The main causes pushing you towards using a full written script are:

★ Legal requirements – you must communicate very precisely for legal reasons, such as a formal dismissal statement
★ Public relations – you must convey the exact words of someone you are representing
★ Hi-tech presentations – you are part of a complex performance and there are cues that must be followed accurately

The last time someone read aloud to you was probably when a relative was trying to put you to sleep. If you don't want a comatose audience avoid reading your presentation.

Since good presentations are really satisfying 'conversations', relying on a script will affect your ability to built audience rapport. If you must use a script for your presentation,

★ Number the pages clearly top and bottom
★ Colour code key paragraphs
★ Double- or triple-space text
★ Lay out text like a poem showing the phrasing and marking it
★ Print text large enough to read from a distance – 14 or 16 point size
★ Tag or staple pages together
★ Mark passages where you need to alter pace, for example 'slow down here'
★ Run your thumb down the side of the page as you speak – when you glance at the audience and look back, you'll have a rough idea of your place

A full script can sometimes be a useful starting point for learning

your presentation so that you no longer need the complete text when you come to present. However, it is far better and builds more confidence if instead of learning the words you learn the ideas behind your presentation.

Mind map

An interesting prompt that some presenters find helpful is the mind map. This gives a visual overview of the whole presentation with all the links between the different parts. So long as you know broadly what you want to say the mind map provides an easily used guide to the territory. What presenters like about mind maps is that they allow you to be more spontaneous, moving flexibly across ideas rather than being constrained by a linear list of items to cover.

↪ mind map
road map

Slides and overheads

Another form of prompt is to rely entirely on the slides or overheads as your prompt. If each one conveys a key message this may be enough to allow you to elaborate during the live performance, giving it a natural spontaneity that people will enjoy. The drawback of this approach is that you will tend to spend most of the time talking to the visual rather than the audience.

Mechanical prompts

The teleprompt or autocue is a standard item in television studios and at large conferences. It scrolls your script on to a screen that you can see, but the audience can't. The result is that while you apparently look straight at the audience or camera you are able to read the script. A prompt operator controls the scrolling so that it follows at your own pace.

The technology's main drawback, apart from encouraging

you to read your entire presentation, is its reliance on someone else scrolling correctly and at the right speed. It does not roll on relentlessly, though, and a good operator will be as much in tune with the audience as you are.

Some autocue systems are supplied with a hand or foot attachment that you can control yourself. It's hard to be spontaneous with this technology, though, without either abandoning it mid-presentation, or feeling compelled to speed up or slow down to match the scrolling.

Another drawback is that the prompt forces you to look robotically straight ahead, which you would never do if you were talking spontaneously. This is why in some major conference settings there are three autoscript machines so that you can look left, right and front.

Teleprompter tips

ACTION

- ★ Insist on several complete run-throughs
- ★ Meet the person scrolling the script and agree where you might improvise and momentarily depart from it
- ★ Ask the person working the prompt to mark the text so that important phrases appear on the same line
- ★ Highlight all the keywords you want to emphasise
- ★ Know the flow of ideas behind your presentation, so that if the technology fails you can continue
- ★ Keep a written script or notes handy in case the technology fails, though if it fails on page fifteen, you'll probably still be at page one
- ★ To avoid looking robotic, use gestures freely to bring your appearance to life
- ★ Try saying each word as if doing so for the first time
- ★ If you can't actually see a member of the audience, look at where someone should be and make imaginary eye contact

Some hi-tech presenting situations use an audio prompt, concealed within your ear, like a hearing aid. This is the kind often used by television reporters and allows someone else to give you instructions, reminders or specialist information. These devices can be distracting so, again, have plenty of practice before using them live.

Delivery

W hen you reach the presentation location you have, in ⤷ **day**
effect, already begun your delivery. You need to arrive   **staging**
both physically and mentally.

The surroundings

Take care of the presentation environment and it will look after ⤷ **environment**
you. Visit just prior to your actual performance – even if you   **location**
visited more thoroughly on a previous occasion. You may   **outside**
discover a last-minute change, which could affect how you   **technicians**
perform.   **travel**

If you're speaking at a conference, soon after arriving track   **venue**
down the technical staff and enrol them in your intention to
deliver a truly powerful presentation. Don't wait until the last
moment to talk to them.

Encourage these technical staff to see you and them as a
team. Ask for their advice and show that you're listening to their
suggestions. Be assertive by resisting pressure to alter your
presentation because it saves rearranging equipment, lighting,
seating or whatever.

Expect the technology to serve you, not the other way
around. After all, you're the one on the spot, it's your
presentation.

Mental arrival

This means that you are 'here' emotionally, having left behind distractions, such as what's happening back at the office, or what a terrible journey you had to the destination. Master presenters work to ensure that they feel mentally at home in the presenting environment, for example they

★ Do a physical warm-up
★ Alter the seating arrangements
★ Change the lighting
★ Insist on several technical rehearsals
★ Ask the audience to do something, right from the start.

The essence of mental arrival is feeling ready for anything. You are 'in charge' of what happens, you are not a mere passenger as the main event unfolds. Do whatever it takes to get into the right frame of mind.

At some presentations you can find yourself besieged by technical staff – 'we need to attach this radio mic to you', the organisers – 'can we just discuss your handout', and even members of the audience – 'can I just have a quick word with you'. It's important to stay focused and not become distracted. Be polite and explain: 'I have to present in a moment, I need five minutes alone to get myself together.'

Warm-ups

If you play a regular sport you already know the importance of warm-ups and cool-down exercises. Much the same applies to presentations. And even though actors know their lines, they too warm up just before going on stage.

A warm-up wakes up your

★ Mind
★ Body
★ Breath
★ Voice

MIND

You need to be in the right frame of mind to present well. Some simple mind exercises can help you get ready.

★ Recall a favourite place where you enjoy being relaxed, such as by a lake, out walking in hills, cycling downhill and so on. Imagine the experience in as much detail as you can

★ Think of a time when you've felt good about yourself – successful, powerful or have done something worthwhile. Imagine your pleasure at people witnessing this success. Use that mental picture to affect your posture. Hold it in mind, as you walk on to the platform, or are about to start a presentation. Or hold the purpose of your presentation in mind. Or hold a welcoming thought.

BODY

Master presenters build in uncommitted leisure time before each presentation. Rather than yet more practice, they use it to deal with any tensions or nerves about the coming event.

Whether you prefer yoga, swimming, cycling, workouts, or simply watching a film, go for tension-releasing activities so that you approach the actual moment in an alert yet grounded way.

To present well you need lots of energy and Master presenters get themselves fully energised before starting. To wake up your energy do some vigorous shakes and jumps.

Or calm down . . . Do a few simple stretches. Tense and relax hands. Tense and relax stomach muscles – perhaps by pushing or pressing against something. Lift and drop shoulders. Do some head rolls. Push your lips out and make different shapes with them.

Immediately prior to the actual performance spend ten minutes in a quiet room practising relaxation and breathing exercises. This also applies to a whole presentation team. Rather than all sitting nervously together awaiting the call, jointly organise some calming exercises.

★ Sit or lie down
★ Tense all your muscles, face, shoulders, neck, hands, arms, legs and so on. Hold this tension for thirty seconds and then let go. Take slow deep breaths
★ Close your eyes, focus on each part of your body in turn, checking for tension. Breathe in deeply and out slowly, while telling that part to let go and relax

BREATH

If you want to build the energy, try panting.

If you want to relax the energy, then breathe gently. Continue breathing slowly and deeply. Hold in your breath for a count of ten and then breathe out gently, making as little sound as possible. At the end of the out breath hold for a count of ten before breathing in again. Repeat for up to ten breaths.

VOICE

Voice and body exercises loosen you up, making you more at ease with yourself as you step into the limelight. In the quiet place you find just before the presentation

★ Hum gently
★ Make simple sounds such as aahs, oos.
★ Rehearse aloud any difficult words or phrases
★ Rapidly say aloud a tongue twister such as
    * 'I bet he's got a lot of bottle' or
    * 'Red leather, yellow leather'

gargle ⊂ Stay away from smokers and avoid shouting or lengthy talking. If you have a sore throat, take salt water gargles and carry throat lozenges with you.

⭐ Entering the room

The moment has finally arrived. For a business pitch you may have been holed up somewhere in a room awaiting your turn. This can be trying on the nerves and if you're leading a presentation team keep everyone busy with final checks on props, materials, warm-up and relaxation exercises.

A team needs to decide

★ In what order to enter the room
★ Who will sit where
★ Where to place materials for the presentation
★ How to handle introductions

How you walk in to a presentation can have a surprising effect on your audience. If you are erect, head held high and looking

ARRIVAL – QUICK CHECKLIST

Break-out rooms
- ❏ Need them
- ❏ There are enough
- ❏ Know the locations
- ❏ Adequately equipped

Toilets
- ❏ Know the locations

Equipment
- ❏ Can operate it easily
- ❏ Spares, including components such as bulbs and leads, also *availability of additional visual aids*
- ❏ Flip charts
- ❏ White boards
- ❏ LCD panels

Other specified requirements
- ❏
- ❏

Lighting
- ❏ It helps or enhances impact
- ❏ It can be redirected if necessary
- ❏ I/we know how to operate relevant switches

Sound
- ❏ There is an adequate and properly tuned system
- ❏ Spoken with the sound engineer
- ❏ Know what kind of mic it is
- ❏ Can alter mic's height
- ❏ The air-conditioning is quiet
- ❏ Can switch it off
- ❏ Have checked for interference from extraneous sounds (e.g. fire alarm tests, construction work, nearby office equipment such as loud printers, phones and tannoy systems, low-flying aircraft, main roads)

Stage settings
- ❏ They enhance my/our impact
- ❏ Needs flowers or a large prop relevant to the presentation
- ❏ There is a lectern ❏ It is at the right height ❏ It is easy to use
- ❏ There is a platform ❏ It is easy to mount

Seating
- ❏ Suits my/our needs ❏ There is someone to help rearrange it
- ❏ Have sat in the audience seats, everyone can see properly

Refreshments
- ❏ Know the arrangements
- ❏ Know when will these be served
- ❏ There is water handy for our use

Climatic control
- ❏ It is neither too hot nor too cold
- ❏ Can control air-conditioning if necessary

Floor
- ❏ Checked it is in good condition

➲ check list

➲ computer
CRT projectors
equipment
hardware
laptops
LCD panels
LCD projectors
technicians
technology
tools

➲ chairs
lectern
lights
podium
stage

'glad to be here', this communicates energy and confidence. Equally, you won't inspire confidence if you and your people file in looking excessively worried, even if the presentation message itself is a serious one.

★ *Audience arrival*

Part of the process of both you and the audience 'arriving' occurs during the introduction phase. For example, you may be introduced to your audience as a whole, or one by one. 'So many times I've seen introductions along the lines of "I'm this, I'm this, I'm this" and the person on the receiving end doesn't listen to who they are. Yet if you do listen to the introductions and learn what their agendas and concerns are, you discover a huge amount,' says SAP's David Hughes Solomon, veteran of countless high-level presentations.

At this stage you're looking intensely for clues about your audience's state of mind. Do people seem alert, tired, curious, bored, restless, worried, cheerful or what? Can you spot any signs suggesting whether to adjust or adapt your planned performance?

'Often our people go into presentations totally prepared to the nth degree,' says David Hughes Solomon. 'They've rehearsed it, they've done everything possible to prepare, yet after about ten minutes of being in the room I've realised: *If you don't change this now you're going to dig yourself into a big hole.*

'You need to be flexible and see which way it's going. Sometimes I'll say to an audience: "Look, this is what we were expecting to say to you, but now we'll talk about something else." If you do that you usually get most of them on your side because you're identifying with them and what they need to hear.'

When you begin is almost as important as *how* you begin. Rush into the performance and you may lose some of your audience who are still thinking about the previous presentation, hunting for documents, or chatting to colleagues.

Tune in to your audience at this early stage rather than start broadcasting. Senior Maynard Leigh presenters, for example, were asked to pitch for business from a major international airline. When the team entered the room, though, it missed early signs that the audience was distracted. They soldiered on, delivering an excellent, but ultimately irrelevant presentation.

Leave time for your audience to settle down, stop rustling papers, coughing, fiddling with bags, cases, computers, or talking with neighbours. Check out whether people seem ready. Look for a clear signal to start the presentation from the person chairing the session. If necessary, take the initiative and call people to order, then wait and observe.

⊃ **late**
latecomers

★ *Sounding natural*

Now you are face-to-face with your audience, either in person or perhaps electronically in a video conference. Either way, you are definitely 'on-stage'.

What matters most at this critical moment? It is simply

★ Being yourself

From the many training programmes we have run, including innumerable one-to-one coaching sessions, it's clear that many people are both surprised and relieved to realise 'I can just be myself'. Who you are is enough, you don't need to try and be someone else, to act like another presenter or copy what another star performer does. Just be yourself.

When you are yourself you speak naturally. Speaking normally and fluently holds people's attention, impressing even a sceptical audience. Natural speakers are unhurried, sure about what they are trying to say.

You are more likely to sound natural if you aim for some of these objectives:

★ Use simple, everyday language
★ Take your time and enjoy yourself
★ Be well rehearsed
★ Rely only on keywords as prompts, not a script
★ Put your full attention on your audience rather than yourself
★ Allow your personality to shine through
★ Respond to the audience and their moods
★ Avoid being overly slick and word perfect
★ Constantly vary your pace and tone of voice
★ Sound animated

Voice power

accent ⊂
cadence
expression
gargle
pronunciation

★ Clear your voice gently, without a rasping sound
★ Use cool or tepid water rather than heavily iced water
★ Give your voice a rest by altering the cadence and pitch
★ To heighten audience attention occasionally vary your loudness
★ Breathe deeply before speaking, enabling your voice to carry further
★ Speak clearly, pronouncing words completely, especially the vowels (a, e, i, o, u)
★ Put power into your delivery, without shouting

Her voice was sharp and probing, like a needle in the hands of a nervous nurse.
ANN BANNON, *WOMEN IN THE SHADOWS*

Top tips for reading a script – naturally

★ Read it aloud first in private, several times
★ Mark key phrases to be kept together, such as prepositions and nouns
★ Make it sound conversational, as if talking to a friend
★ Keep varying the pitch and tone of sentences
★ Vary the amount and length of pauses between sentences and paragraphs
★ Read ahead to recall the last half-dozen words of each sentence so you can look up, speaking them direct to the audience
★ Find time to smile
★ If possible, occasionally add some of your own words
★ Keep changing the amount of energy you put into the reading
★ Say the material to someone nearby, rather than to a table or lectern

They said you can speak on just about anything and you don't have to be witty or intellectual. Just be yourself.
A. MAURICE MYERS, CEO OF YELLOW CORPORATION, 1996

Nerves

When Microsoft launched Windows 95 in August of the same year, Chairman Bill Gates had a serious attack of nerves. 'You've got the wrong screen set up here,' he snapped to an unfortunate technician. He yelled in disgust when the on-stage computer began to act up and petulantly threw the mouse pad on to the podium floor. 'This video makes no sense!' he shouted at Brad Chase, the Marketing Manager for Windows 95.

    embarrassment
fear
inadequate
panic
uncertain

    Some of the most experienced performers suffer from terrible stage fright, it's nothing to be ashamed about. These nerves surface in various ways that not only affect you, the presenter, but others too. Why shouldn't you feel nervous? After all, something significant is about to happen. If it's not, why bother being there? Send a report instead.

    At an important presentation your body knows you are being risky. Its natural response is to become more alert by sending adrenalin rushing through the system, providing a wonderful source of energy and excitement. Too much of it, though, makes you feel sick, sweaty, or panicky.

    gut
hiccups
stomach
sweating
stammer

    Staying super calm may seem highly desirable, yet nerves can be a great asset. For example, if you're so confident that the presentation seems no challenge, then you probably aren't trying hard enough, risking enough or being sufficiently original.

★ Nervousness is a potent reminder that there is something at stake, demanding your complete attention
★ If you're not slightly nervous or on edge there's probably something wrong

Too much anxiety, on the other hand, can get in the way of preparing and performing. If that happens, invest in a really good presentation skills course. The best courses are highly interactive, offering constant practice, not theory. In a few days you can transform your whole approach to presentation.

    breathing
highway code

    If you're too busy to attend formal training, then one-to-one coaching is an alternative way of tackling nerves. An experienced coach fully understands your fears, even shares them. The best coaches are successful performers in their own right. They know what it takes to handle nerves and how these affect even the most experienced person.

A coach works closely with you, identifying ways to get anxiety under control, so that it contributes rather than detracts from your presentation.

There are many effective ways to reduce the adverse effects of nerves and excessive adrenalin. Start by giving these anxiety symptoms 'permission to exist'. They show you are fully alert. Remind yourself that you are excited, not fearful.

Slow down!

Slowing down is another important way of dealing with presentation nerves. Anxiety can lure you into trying to get the whole experience finished as quickly as possible. Yet hurrying is the exact opposite of what needs to happen.

Take half a dozen deep, even breaths. This slows your heart rate, automatically making you feel calmer. Create a mental picture of the energy flowing through your body and welcome it, directing it towards the audience.

A method used by many experienced presenters is to watch an imaginary film in which you are presenting brilliantly, doing it calmly and with confidence. Keep running this film through your head before the event and just prior to starting your actual delivery.

On our courses we introduce participants to the presenter's highway code:

breathing ⊂	★ Stop
floor	★ Breathe
highway code	★ Look
pace	★ Listen
pauses	

You do this before actually uttering a word. You literally stand there, or sit quietly taking your time, absorbing the atmosphere, making contact with your audience, all without saying anything. The highway code may only last five to fifteen seconds, yet it can have a profound effect on how you come across, conveying poise, confidence and gravitas.

Place a copy of the presenter's highway code where you can see it during the presentation. When you catch sight of these words, let them prompt you to slow down or pause for a few moments.

THE ULTIMATE
BUSINESS
PRESENTATION BOOK

Search for opportunities to relax during the presentation, using these to inject new energy into the next part of your performance. For example, if you get the audience talking and working with each other it allows you precious moments to do a quick relaxation exercise.

★ *Presence*

Our best-selling presentation course, run for over ten years in hundreds of companies in the UK and elsewhere and for thousands of people, is called 'Performing with Presence'. The title is no accident. Presence is what all successful presenters yearn for. They hone this ability, knowing that it's critical for making a strong impact.

acting
charisma
chemistry
contact
ego
insight

Establishing a presence with an audience means being fully 'present' in the moment. That is, you don't think about what you did at the weekend, or wonder whether the rest of the presentation team are worried, or allow anything to stop you being fully alert. It means you are awake and

★ Totally aware of your situation and the surroundings
★ Able to read the audience
★ Ready to adapt to anything that happens

How about right now? Are you aware of sounds in the background, smells, sensations in your body or how you are feeling? When you are fully present 'in the moment' your senses are heightened. For example, you notice the atmosphere in the room and how people look, noises from the air-conditioning, someone's chair squeaking, odd sights like a stain on the curtain, that itch in your palm, a picture slightly askew.

Being fully 'present' in the moment demands a focus on the here and now. Doing so conveys a personal presence, creating in other people an acute awareness of your existence. They become intensely alert to what you might do next.

Presence is not confined to actors or charismatic public figures. You can have a presence too. It is neither magical nor mystical, it's simply being totally 'here'.

What to do about . . .

Dry mouth: Chewing your tongue makes you salivate. Better still, take small sips of water and use steady, deep breathing

sweating **Sweaty palms:** Keep a handkerchief in your pocket, use your hands more actively in the presentation and you'll soon forget them

Shaky voice: Stop, breathe, look and listen. By the time you've done this you'll have recovered your normal manner

breathing **Mind goes blank:** Make eye contact with people so you eliminate
stuck distracting images, breathe deeply, sending more oxygen to the brain. Take your time referring to your notes; the audience will wait. Although it seems like an age to you it passes rapidly for the audience

Palpitations: Establish a calming routine such as doing some isometric exercises that no one sees, where you pit one muscle against another. Press your hands together, pushing hard downwards while counting to ten. Relax and breathe deeply again

Squeaky voice: Can be annoying and hard to follow. Even if you're naturally high-pitched you can lower your voice through slow steady breathing, dropping your jaw and allowing throat muscles to relax. If through tension your voice goes high again, speak more slowly, allowing more air into your lungs by taking in deep breaths

breathing **Fast talking:** Gives the game away to the audience that you're nervous and
gabble want to get it over with. When you stop, breathe, look and listen, you'll
inaudible have slowed down and can start again with new, controlled energy. The
loud more pauses you add, the more measured you will seem
pauses **Legs twitching:** Seldom shows unless you actively jiggle them rhythmically. If you're a leg shaker either stand up and put your full weight on both feet, or move around to let the blood circulate more freely. Without straining, stretch out each leg in turn, as far as it will go. Holding that position for a few moments, let go gently, breathing in and out slowly

Short of breath: Comes from shallow breathing caused by all the excitement and tension of being on-stage. Sometimes you may literally
breathing forget to breathe. Imagine you're a tube of toothpaste with the air being squeezed out like paste. Push all the air out of your lungs and continue right down to the abdomen. If necessary, put your hand on your middle and continue pushing with it. Take in deep breaths when you finish making each point and give yourself permission to pause

fear **Opening terror:** If you don't start you'll never reach the end. Learn your
panic opening idea – rather than the words themselves – until you're confident you can say it in many different ways. Keep a note of the opening nearby where you can see it

> *My stage fright gets worse at every performance. During the overture I hope for a theatre fire, typhoon, revolution in the Pentagon.*
>
> HILDEGARD NEFF, *THE GIFT HORSE* (1970)

highway code

Opener

The opener to any business presentation is nearly always important, establishing the tone for the rest of the event. It's that vital moment when you take charge, gaining people's close attention. A strong opener entices the listeners so they feel unable to escape the rest of the performance.

People tend to remember openers more than any other part of a presentation, except perhaps the closing remarks. You waste a wonderful opportunity if you resort to trivia like: 'Good evening, ladies and gentlemen, it's a great pleasure to have the opportunity to be here today.'

★ You never get a second chance to make a good first impression

bang
excitement
fun
ideas
imagination
inspiration
magic
music
mystery
new
original
outrageous
props
shock
subject
topicality
unexpected
variety
welcome

A powerful opener

★ Hooks the listener into wanting more
★ Makes people think about your purpose
★ Lets people know you're an expert without doing it overtly
★ Cuts to the chase; people hear the main point quickly
★ Presents issues that the audience thinks are important
★ Wakes people up and holds their attention
★ Uses carefully tailored sentences and words to maximise impact
★ Relies on simple phrasing
★ Reaches the particular audience
★ Acts like a headline, summing up the entire presentation

One highly charged opener used by a marketing guru was to be missing when his time came to be introduced by the conference chairman. The latter stood up and announced that the guru was now due to speak but his plane was delayed. Although it had landed he wasn't here yet. Right on cue, the guru yelled triumphantly from the back, 'Hold it. I've made it!' and bounded energetically on to the stage to wild applause.

Nothing is more expensive than a start.
NIETZSCHE, *THE WILL TO POWER* (1888)

No matter what kind of opener you choose – put real passion into it. It's your enthusiasm, commitment and energy that excite people, making them want to hear more.

Having gained their attention, it often makes sense to explain the territory you intend to cover. This is because some people in an audience only feel really comfortable if they know where you're heading. Without a 'route map' they stop paying attention, worrying instead about where all this is leading.

★ Dull stuff

You may also have to find space early on for some housekeeping matters that neither you nor the audience find interesting. With sufficient imagination, though, this can be converted into a creative experience. For example, you could hold up large, colourful cartoon symbols while rapidly explaining

★ Location of fire exits
★ Time of refreshment breaks
★ Switch off mobile phones and pagers
★ There will be time for questions afterwards
★ What will happen next

No matter how apt or clever, someone else's opener is generally less effective than one you devise yourself, reflecting your own personality. This doesn't mean that if you hear a terrific opener you can't ever use it. But find a way to make it your own, adapting it to suit your particular style.

Humorous verbal openers that people have adapted to their own use are:

★ 'If you're wondering if this will be a boring presentation you're not alone. I'm dying to know too'
★ 'I'd like to make three important points. That's the first one. Can't remember the other two'
★ 'They said keep it short and simple, so thanks for listening and goodbye'
★ 'You're thinking, how will I start? Don't. Your real problem is when will I stop?'
★ 'Some of you have heard me speak before. The rest of you

have something to look forward to'

★ 'I've been working on this material for months. Fortunately, last night my cat ate it'

What kind of opener?

There is an infinite variety of possible openers to choose from. Use your imagination and creativity to invent something stunning. You might start with any of these:

★ a poem or rhyme
★ a strange sound
★ a promise
★ a joke
★ a question
★ a request
★ a threat
★ a physical action
★ a quote
★ a drawing
★ a story
★ a personal example
★ expert testimony

★ an analogy
★ a startling statistic
★ a question
★ a magic trick
★ a song
★ a short video extract
★ a slide
★ a cartoon
★ anything unexpected
★ asking the audience to do something
★ an extract from a newspaper of the day

The first blow is half the battle.
OLIVER GOLDSMITH (1728–74),
SHE STOOPS TO CONQUER

Passion and energy

Audiences respond with their hearts, not just their heads. Business audiences are no exception. At Maynard Leigh Associates we are constantly helping talented business people who need to inject sparkle and liveliness into their presentations. Often they have previously received adverse comments on their communication. They may be great on content yet their performance needs bringing to life. How do we do that?

Mostly we do it by showing the power of passion, commitment and energy to transform even the most pedestrian subject into something that an audience is curious to hear. When people find that they possess the ability to convey passion all along, it makes a huge difference to their confidence.

commitment

decision

expression

feelings

impress

orator

pride

respect

risk

success

understate

vulnerable

words

It's easy to ignore the importance of passion in the misguided belief that to sound objective or rational means being bland and unemotive. If you think business presentations should only be about facts, information and hard analysis, think again. Of course these are important and without them even the best performers can fail.

It's passion that gives a presentation its real power, the unique flavour that audiences find memorable. Watch the legendary Jack Welch of GE whose energy and enthusiasm make you forget he has a stammer, or witness Warren Buffet, financial adviser extraordinary, whose enthusiasm is infectious. Both these Master presenters

★ Connect with feelings, not just rational thoughts

Passion is hard to define, yet like love or beauty we know it when we see it. If the word 'passion' makes you queasy in respect of business presentations, think of it as 'absolute commitment'. When you are totally committed you are so fully engaged that everyone senses your energy and aliveness, and above all how you are feeling.

So passion is a mixture of energy, commitment, caring, enthusiasm, excitement, intensity and other signs of strong feelings.

★ Passion is the sparkle separating your performance from other people's

'What I do best is share my enthusiasm,' explains Microsoft's Bill Gates, who presents to more people than many heads of state. When you're obviously excited about your message people respond.

★ First, make contact with your own passion
★ If you don't feel strongly about what you're saying, why should the audience?
★ Discover what you can be enthusiastic about, and make it your cornerstone.
★ Share with the audience *why* you feel enthusiastic

ACTION

★ If you really can't be enthusiastic about something – ask someone else to give the presentation
★ Uncover the audience's emotional trigger point

By analysing an audience's emotional trigger point – 'the compelling factor' mentioned earlier in bid situations – you uncover not merely hard facts but why people are hopeful, worried, anxious, fearful, excited, frustrated or whatever about an issue. Let this drive your performance.

Locating the emotional trigger

★ What aspect of your presentation arouses strong feelings – why?
★ What point would you make if you only had ten seconds – why?
★ What does the audience most care about and want to know – why?
★ How will what you are suggesting improve your audience's daily lives or future?

Everyone's feelings have a front door and a side door by which they may be entered.

OLIVER WENDELL HOLMES SENIOR,
THE AUTOCRAT OF THE BREAKFAST TABLE (1858)

Putting anger to work

Sometimes anger can fuel an entire presentation, for example, if you know that everyone in the audience is equally upset about something, such as the behaviour of a competitor. Allowing your feelings to show through may enable the audience to get in touch with their own.

aggression
anger
dislike
hostility

While anger can sometimes be helpful it is more likely to lead to patronising your audience who are dumped with your emotions. To handle your own anger during a presentation:

★ Stop, look around, take three slow, deep breaths
★ If standing, consider sitting down
★ If already standing, walk around to release some of the tension
★ Use a flip chart to write up information while regaining your composure
★ Think of something that makes you laugh
★ Try to locate where the anger is coming from and what it means. For example, if you are resentful at having to give the presentation, don't take it out on your audience

Dealing with an angry audience

★ Acknowledge people's strong feelings
★ Welcome the anger as bringing issues into the open
★ Only offer sympathy if you genuinely feel it
★ Show you're really trying to understand people's views
★ Don't take it personally
★ Summarise hostile opinions, seeking confirmation of their accuracy
★ Do a reality check: ask the rest of the audience whether they all feel the same way
★ Avoid critical remarks about those being hostile – for example, avoid remarks such as: 'I think that's a stupid idea', 'You're talking rubbish', 'You would say that'
★ Explain how you intend dealing with the situation
★ Defuse and move on
★ Channel the anger: invite those who are angry to meet with you separately to talk about the issue(s)
★ Use the anger to boost your own message
★ Resist allowing their anger to trigger your own
★ Staying super calm may merely infuriate people

People in a temper often say a lot of silly, terrible things they mean.
PENELOPE GILLIATT IN KATHERINE WHITEHORN,
VIEW FROM A COLUMN (1981)

 *Energy*

Successful speakers invest huge energy into communicating, ⟶ attention
though they may be skilled at disguising this fact. Energy can **boredom**
transform a presentation relatively weak on content into a **concentration**
triumph. Speaker energy is not necessarily about loud delivery.
It's your entire demeanour, how you hold yourself physically and
interact with the audience. Because energy is so important, rest
fully before an important presentation.

Ten ways to increase energy levels

★ Alter the pace of delivery
★ Stand up from a sitting position or sit down from
  standing up
★ Move around, rather than staying in one spot
★ Mingle with the audience
★ Pause to breathe and refresh yourself
★ Give the audience and yourself a few minutes break
★ Use humour
★ Use passion
★ Introduce a physical object for people to handle or look at
★ Get the audience doing something, like working in groups,
  standing, going outside, doing some physical exercise

Energy is eternal delight.
                    WILLIAM BLAKE (1757–1827)

Top 10 Tips!

The longer your presentation, the greater the need to keep ⟶ **graveyard shift**
injecting new energy, to hold people's interest. Certain times of **lunch**
the day, for example, cause problems of low energy levels and **last**
therefore loss of attention. The worst is the 'graveyard shift', just
after lunch. The heavier the meal, especially one with alcohol,
the harder it is to hold people's attention. If you're allocated the
'graveyard shift' for your presentation,

★ Try to request a change of timing

★ If you *have* to proceed, acknowledge that 'we may all have
   trouble keeping alert' and do some of the actions shown
   above

Even hardened business people enjoy doing something different
for a while and will often have fun doing a group stretch or a few
vigorous exercises together. If you conduct them with sufficient
confidence, people will usually follow your lead. It may even

fatigue ⊂ make your presentation more memorable.
jaded

Humour

'Humour, stories and anecdotes always bring the presentation alive,' argues Alex Gethin, KPMG's Senior Proposals Manager who advises teams for many of the organizations' major bids and pitches. 'You obviously don't want to use inappropriate humour or use it too early. But if the client's been through four or five presentations that are fairly similar, then showing the human side of your team is helpful, because it reminds them who you are.'

Bid adviser Brian Polk of PWC agrees, pointing out that people want to 'see evidence that you're a living, thinking, humorous human being, so demonstrating enough humour to show you're human is wonderful'.

But humour can go dangerously wrong, he warns, 'especially if the qualities you're trying to convey are commitment and capability. Certainly being funny for funny's sake is destructive in a presentation.'

It's been said that 'humour is the shortest distance between two people' and it certainly has a place in business presentations, relieving tension and further building a relationship with the audience. However, unless you revel in using it as part of your normal way of talking, artificially injecting it into a presentation will probably fail. It's a dangerous myth, for example, that all presentations need to start with a joke.

The best presentation humour stems from drawing on personal experiences that you find amusing. Retelling other people's jokes often sounds contrived and, unless really apposite, can leave you looking rather foolish if no one laughs.

Generally in business presentations what works is wit rather than jokes. You can often more easily adapt someone else's wit to your own use than copy their jokes:

★ Convert the references, situation or people into ones that directly apply to the presentation situation you are dealing with

★ Integrate the wit into your speech, not the other way around

anecdotes
gag
joke
story

Choosing how to be witty is rather like selecting facts for your presentation. With good research you will soon be spoilt for choice. First plumb the depths of your own experience. Perhaps you can find out something amusing about the audience or their company situation. Ask around and see if you can pick up something that you can make your own.

As a last resort there are scores of books of contemporary wit available, many of them aimed at specific presenting situations, including, business pitches. You can even download material

web-sites
from the Internet.

How Master presenters use humour

★ Draw on personal experiences
★ Use humour only when you feel naturally funny
★ Don't force yourself to start every presentation with a joke
★ If the presentation is being simultaneously translated into another language keep humour to a minimum
★ Stick to short stories, not long rambling ones
★ Be sure that the audience will understand a particular joke
★ Tailor humour for a specific audience
★ Avoid racist, sexist, ageist references or other slurs
★ Use jokes only if they fit the presentation
★ Jokes are funny because of timing and how they are told; both need plenty of practice and feedback
★ Wait for the laughs
★ Don't insult or blame the audience if no one laughs
★ Learn the punch line

It's hard to be funny when you have to be clean.

MAE WEST

Humour is a wonderful antidote to problems during a presentation, particularly when you personally mess up. Audiences love it if you can laugh at yourself and your predicament.

★ Turn the humour against yourself, rather than someone else

Off the cuff

Audiences really appreciate a presenter who allows humour to shine through in a natural, unrehearsed way. Spontaneous humour becomes easier when you are used to thinking on your feet. Ad libs, for example, work best when they are drawn from the same moment that everyone experiences. So the best speakers carefully rehearse their ad libs.

For instance, if you regularly use a slide projector there are various predictable problems such as bulbs failing, images out of focus or foils askew. Why not develop a series of quips to handle these events that you can draw on when the time comes?

Similarly, suppose you are presenting to a board of directors. You may discover that one member of the audience has a reputation for interrupting or firing difficult, embarrassing questions. Have some possible responses up your sleeve. Your 'comebacks' appear spontaneous because you drag them out only when needed, and adapt them to suit the moment.

Damage limitation

If you're in the middle of an important business presentation and your humour fails, it's like an actor dying on-stage, extremely painful. Your audience may be acutely embarrassed too. Have a fall-back strategy for how you'll recover from such situations, without undermining the rest of the performance.

Faced with an obvious failure to amuse, it's usually better simply to shrug your shoulders, adopt a wry expression and move on.

Humour tends not to travel well. Check that your wit really does transfer to another culture and that audiences whose first language is not English will understand the references.

Having chosen a funny remark or story, ask yourself, 'Would I tell it to . . .

gender
innuendo
interpreters
offence
political correctness
religion
sarcasm
satire
sexism
taboos

- ★ My mother or grandmother
- ★ An audience on television
- ★ A rabbi, priest or some other religious leader
- ★ Everyone in the company restaurant'

To avoid a laughter black hole

- ★ Memorise the punch line so you get it right each time
- ★ Keep it short – the best jokes are usually the ones that take the least time
- ★ Wait for the laughs – audiences need time to absorb a joke
- ★ Enjoy the moment – don't hurry or talk over the laughs
- ★ If there are no laughs, know in advance how you will respond

It is a difficult thing to like anybody else's ideas of being funny.

GERTRUDE STEIN,
EVERYBODY'S AUTOBIOGRAPHY (1937)

Laughter is a useful way of communicating a difficult or controversial message. It can make the seemingly unacceptable palatable and the unthinkable worth considering. Playing a business audience for laughs, however, is risky and best left to comedians.

Get 'em nodding

In many business presentations you want to gain the audience's agreement. Signs that you are doing this successfully is that some people are nodding, laughing or even saying 'yes'. Frowning, shaking heads, looking down and doodling, are all warnings that you have not reached your audience, either emotionally or with hard facts.

Just because people are laughing though can prove misleading, lulling you into a false sense of security that your presentation is right on target. Indeed, in some situations and cultures these encouraging signs may be merely indications of politeness.

If you suspect that you are being led astray by laughter and nodding signs of approval, ask directly: 'I see you're nodding. Does that mean you all agree with me?'

Ways to get people nodding and saying 'yes' include:

★ Present a powerful fact that you know people believe to be true
★ Make a statement with which you can expect most people to agree
★ Pose a closed question to which the answer is either yes or no ⟳ affirmations
and is likely to be yes

hits
opportunities
rhetorical questions
visualisation
win

CHAPTER

9

Image

eyes
hands
posture

*T*he image is so carefully presented that the new McKinsey consultant is trained in how to behave with his or her clients. Where to keep the hands during a presentation is crucial (not in the pockets and always above the table when seated). Eyes being the mirror of the soul, the McKinsey consultant always keeps that crucial visual contact, but never to the point at which it makes the target uncomfortable . . . McKinsey's people are always being watched, first by the client, who will be solicited for comments that can make or break a new consultant's career, and then by superiors, who participate in what must amount to the most excruciating, intensive performance reviews anywhere. James O'Shea and Charles Madigan, *Dangerous Company*, (1999)

You hardly need to be a McKinsey creation to realise that image is a vital element of your business presentation. You'll be watched closely during it and the impression you make plays an important part in whether your performance is a success.

So what kind of image do you or your team convey and how would you like to come across? For example, as an honest broker, a guru, a super professional, a joker, a winner, a go-getter, a thinker, an ideas powerhouse, a safe pair of hands and so on. Being specific about your image can help enhance your overall message from the moment you enter the room.

Try summing up the image you want to portray in one or two words, for instance,

★ Class act; dynamo; thinker; doer; professional, critic, outsider; competent; ideas person

What are the implications of these? For example, what would you have to do or say to confirm that impression? Image is not a single item, such as clothes or looks, it's a complex mix of

★ Appearance – physical characteristics, clothes, grooming
★ Body language – mannerisms, posture, gesture, territory, positioning
★ Reputation – visibility, track record, experience, qualifications
★ Communication style – how you speak, write, listen, think and present
★ Presence – charisma, confidence, self-assurance, self-esteem

Ten reasons why image matters

★ It's the first thing people see
★ Personal style influences decision makers
★ People believe what they see
★ A busy audience relies on instant information
★ You're selling yourself, your profession, your team, your organisation
★ How else can people spot star quality?
★ Looking good is good for you
★ Non-verbal signals are more important than just words
★ It's an important way of indirectly conveying your message and who you are
★ It supports the rest of your credentials

Everybody wants to be Cary Grant. I want to be Cary Grant.

CARY GRANT (1904–86)

Body Shop founder Anita Roddick has became renowned for her dishevelled hair, it's almost a trade mark. Richard Branson's open shirt and sweater misled British Airways into thinking they needn't take him seriously as a competitor. Business guru John Harvey Jones's famous loud kipper ties work for him, yet would probably undermine anyone else.

personality
style
yourself

There are no rigid rules for what can make or break an image during a business presentation. Anything, including your perfume, a style, a colour, how you laugh, can become a trade mark. For

anyone else these may become an image killer. It also depends where you are. In Texas, for instance, if you wear a cowboy string tie with a silver clasp probably nobody would notice, yet it might look pretentious if you are English and presenting in London.

For most business presentations it is sensible to pay careful attention to your image. This doesn't mean that you necessarily have to do what people expect. UK Government Minister Gordon Brown wore a lounge suit, instead of formal evening wear, to the 1997 annual Mansion House dinner. Despite his informality, people paid close attention to his performance, mainly because he was the newly appointed Chancellor of the Exchequer.

If you're highly skilled it may hardly matter what you look like. In the glory days of IBM, founder Thomas Watson insisted that all male employees – and in those days it was mainly men – were clean-shaven and sported the mandatory blue shirt and grey suit. After sharing an elevator with a bearded individual in slacks the irate Watson demanded the man's immediate dismissal. 'I'm afraid we can't do that,' apologised the anxious minion.

'Why not?' insisted Watson.

Back came the disconcerting reply: 'Because he's your chief computer programmer.'

You can also afford to be less conventional with your image if you're rich, powerful, incredibly beautiful, or knowledgeable.

★ *Physical appearance*

cosmetics
feet
glasses
grooming
hair
mannerisms
mouth
wig

As part of your overall image, physical appearance can enhance or undermine your presentation impact. For instance, dirty hands, face, nails, or even messy, badly cut hair can distract an audience and reduce personal credibility.

A sense of personal space is important to most of us, although what we require varies considerably across cultures. Try standing close to a potential new customer in Japan, for example, and you may be perceived as impolite and the rest of your presentation will probably die. Such closeness may matter less in Italy.

Touch, too, can prove an important way of conveying who you are. For instance, a good business handshake makes a favourable impression, while a limp one silently conveys the opposite. Try your handshake on colleagues and ask them to comment.

Tips on enhancing your appearance

★ Your image is a trade mark. Consider what message it conveys. For example, if you're talking about quality will the audience see it in how you look?

★ Take your audience into account when planning your appearance. For instance, if you dress casually when people are anticipating the opposite it may obstruct your message

★ Select comfortable clothes, not just stylish ones

★ Choose clothes that build your confidence

★ Details count: well-ironed shirts, wrinkle-free dress or suit, stain-free materials, no buttons missing or hanging by a thread, clean shoes and so on

★ Avoid audience distractions such as hair in front of eyes, keys or money jingling in pockets, over-heavy make-up, pocket flaps askew, wispy hair covering bald patches

★ Tinted glasses may prevent the audience seeing you as a person, while heavy frames may fixate an audience and detract from your impact

It is only shallow people who do not judge by appearances.

OSCAR WILDE, *THE PICTURE OF DORIAN GRAY*

⊃ glasses
grooming
hair

The business handshake

★ Eye contact
★ Direct, unforced smile
★ Lean forward

★ Dry palm
★ Firm grip
★ Not too strong

Her handshake ought not to be used except as a tourniquet.

MARGARET HALSEY,
WITH MALICE TOWARDS SOME (1938)

⊃ eyes
hands
handshake

Smile

Want to know the favourite technique of most Master presenters? They insist on smiling at their audience. Though it's an obvious winner, less experienced presenters often completely ignore it.

A smile, though, is relatively easy to fake. For example, ventriloquists, salespeople and sophisticated liars tend to smile more than others. Excessive smiling during a presentation becomes tedious for the audience. Instead, try to allow your natural smile to come through because you genuinely feel like doing it.

If you use the presenter's highway code (see p. 72) you can also take several moments to look around and smile at as many individual members of the audience as possible. As you pass from one person to another, mentally say something like 'I'm really glad to see you', 'Welcome', 'Glad you're here', 'Thanks for coming'.

When people enthuse after a presentation that 'I thought the speaker was talking to me personally', it's often because at some point the performer actually did look straight at them and smile.

Unless your audience is in hundreds, it's possible, while presenting, to work your way progressively along to each person and make eye contact and smile. This may sound excessive, yet it works, and your audience will really appreciate your efforts. With large numbers, talk and smile at specific individuals in different parts of the room.

For example, talk to the person in the middle of the furthest row at the back, then to another on the far left halfway back, then another closer still on the right and so on. Let your momentary contact be random, not like a radar scanner going from left to right, which makes it monotonous and artificial.

★ Only smile if you feel comfortable doing so; it needs to be natural and unforced

Image killers

Badges with slogans
Toupees
Trainers
Distracting hair ornaments
Transparent fabrics
Excessive perfume or
  deodorant
Strange body odour
Shoes needing repair or
  polishing
Hair in need of cutting
Pens and pencils in top
  pocket
Creased trousers, particularly
  at the crotch
Total black
Suede trousers
Heavy sweaters

Flowery frocks
Laddered or holed tights
Vulgar tie
White blouse over black bra
Huge belt buckle
T-shirts with slogans
String vest under a nylon
  shirt
Suit and trainers
Badly shaven face
Dandruff on collar
Chipped nail varnish
Poor complexion
Bad breath
Dated clothing
Light socks under dark
  trousers

She looked like a million dollars, I must admit,
even if in well-used notes.

ANGELA CARTER (1940–92),
WISE CHILDREN

cosmetics
feet
glasses
hair
mannerisms
mouth
wig

The well-groomed presenter

Your presentation may be brilliant, your résumé impressive, the proposal a persuasive marvel. Yet all this can be negated by the wrong grooming. Although the importance of grooming might seem obvious it can vary in different cultures. For example, if you turn up in a smart suit and tie for a presentation in parts of the EMAP organisation, the recipients will see you as slick and Establishment.

Personal factors such as bad breath, badly cut and wispy hair, grooming

ragged cuticles and so on can all undermine your presentation impact. Why spend all that time on your presentation and then look like a loser? Excuses such as 'I'm too busy to worry about these things', 'People must take me as they find me', 'I don't want to appear vain' won't work. If you regularly give business presentations you need a systematic grooming strategy to keep you to the highest standards:

CLEAN

Start the day with a shower, bath or thorough wash, including teeth and mouthwash.

SMELL

Though you can't help perspiring you can do something about it. If you sweat a lot, particularly when anxious about your presentation, use an antiperspirant. Otherwise a deodorant may be enough to remove odour. Clothes worn two days running can smell fine to start with and then deteriorate as the perspiration from the previous day becomes active when warm.

HAIR

Cut, colour and condition all send a message about your personal hygiene and habits. Keep hair clean and well-cared for, even if you have to go regularly to the hairdresser. If you're male with a bald patch, keep your hair short and avoid using long hair to try and conceal it, the result always looks contrived.

Designer stubble may sometimes be appropriate, yet in most presenting situations it's preferable to be clean-shaven. In some occupations, such as accountancy or sales, you could lose credibility looking hirsute. This may not be so in countries where beards are a sign of religious commitment.

HANDS AND NAILS

Bitten nails are a give-away, as the UK's Chancellor Gordon Brown discovered when enlarged pictures of his chewed fingers appeared in several national newspapers. Disapproving headlines wondered what these ill-kept nails indicated about his state of mind and, by implication, the economy.

During any presentation your hands are extremely visible and people will certainly notice if they're grubby, stained or unkempt.

TEETH

People with bad teeth tend to smile less and cover their mouths more with their hands when speaking. This habit conveys lack of confidence and may even suggest shiftiness.

Make sure your teeth are in good condition with no traces of food or lipstick on them.

FACE

No other part of your body receives so much attention during a presentation. It's important that you have a healthy complexion that looks cared for. Lack of regular exercise may leave you looking washed-out and grey.

Professional women usually look best with discreet make-up, particularly when presenting under powerful lighting.

SHOULDERS

Check for dandruff, dust and loose hairs. Give yourself a good brush before leaving for your presentation and as you enter the room. Consider keeping a clothes brush handy if you do lots of presenting.

CLOTHES

Your clothes speak even before you do. Today there's a more relaxed attitude in business towards what people wear. Casuals are now quite common and some companies have edged into this territory by having one day a week on which people are encouraged to wear less formal attire.

As a presenter, be sensitive to what is required. If you arrive impeccably dressed for a business presentation to a company that dresses down, you may look out of place and feel uncomfortable. Likewise, arriving in casual clothes where a traditional dress code prevails may immediately place a barrier between you and your audience.

The quality of your clothing matters too. If you regularly appear before impeccably dressed senior managers, you need to look at least as well appointed as they are. Otherwise you risk them seeing you as somewhat 'downmarket'.

In Europe, rather than California's Silicon Valley, for the more serious occasions such as interviews, pitches, conferences and so on, invest in formal clothes such as a business suit.

Clothes take several days to 'recover' from a day's wear and this permits bacteria to die, for the fabric to hang properly and creases to drop out. So you need enough garments to allow a gap between wearing the same item again.

Conduct a regular maintenance review of your business

clothes to see that items are clean, well pressed, and without tears or missing buttons. Make sure that there are no loose hems, unravelling buttonholes or hanging threads.

UP TO DATE

Wearing fashionable clothes won't necessarily improve your presentation impact. But if you've lost touch with current fashion people may assume that your thinking has gone the same way.

What's the image of the shop you buy from? For example, do you come across as a Designer person, an M & S fan, an Austin Read junky, a Boss person, or an Armani type?

Ways to make your business wardrobe more effective include:

★ Identify the top ten items you wear regularly and decide what makes them so popular, that way you learn to make fewer mistakes

★ Identify the items you wear least or not at all – what lessons do they offer?

★ Conduct a regular, six-monthly clothes sort-out

★ Before buying something new, use the rule of three
    Will it go with three things you already have?
    Can it be worn for three different kinds of event?
    Could it be worn for three seasons?

★ Check your wardrobe for the cost per wear factor (CPW).
    For example, if you buy a suit for £300 and wear it twice a month for a year the CPW is £300/24=£12.04.
    By contrast, if you buy a silk shirt for £40 and only wear it twice you're paying £40/2=£20. Aim for a CPW as low as possible

★ Don't be afraid to have alterations done, the cost will only be a fraction of the purchase price and it can make such a difference to how you look

★ Cut your losses: don't let items sit around making you feel guilty or waiting to come back into fashion

Remember the City never forgives casual clothes. Whenever so-and-so's name comes up, people don't mention the quality of his thought or the pungency of his prose. They say, 'Wasn't he the fellow who wore suede shoes to the Bank of England'?
L. D. Williams, City Editor, *Daily Mail*.

On-Stage

Four common problems that regularly undermine otherwise effective business presentations are:

★ Poor body language
★ Distractions
★ Freezing
★ Misuse of visuals

Body language

Your body is an asset in any presentation. How you hold yourself and the hidden, and often not so hidden, messages of body language, are essential ingredients of being a powerful presenter. The two main myths of body language are:

Myth no. 1: It's all jargon-filled rubbish and a bit of common sense and carefully listening are all that's needed to understand people.
Myth no. 2: You can tell more about people through eye contact, foot tapping and odd gestures than anything they say.

Both of these are wrong. We communicate by language, which uses complex and subtle ideas. But we are also creatures of passion, anxiety and fear. We like to display ourselves to others. Not only do we consciously send and receive non-verbal messages, we also 'leak' the truth about our emotional state.

It is hard to fake body language since there are many less obvious signs that transmit tiny signals to others, which are also picked up unconsciously. Non-verbal behaviour sends impressions and helps people decide whether or not what you are saying is true.

Signs you're not being entirely truthful

Linguistic distance: You tend not to say 'I', but talk in the abstract: 'One might believe . . .'

Slow uneven speech: As you think through a lie – this may not apply where people are speaking in their second language or have an ethnic background where slow speech is normal

Too eager to fill in the silence: Liars keep on talking when it's unnecessary

Excessive rises in voice pitch: Instead of speech dropping at the end of a reply, it lifts, as with asking a question

Too much squirming: Shifting around may suggest you don't want to be there

Increase in comfort gestures: These include self touching, particularly around nose and mouth

Increase in stuttering, slurring of verbal slips

Loss of voice resonance: Voice tends to become flatter and more monotonous

Ethnic and cultural differences may well explain some forms of body behaviour, rather than attempts at misleading.

When you want to fool the world, tell the truth.

OTTO VON BISMARCK.

Important though body language is, your attention during the actual performance needs to be 'over there' on the audience, rather than 'over here'. When you take the attention off yourself and put it on to the audience it helps you relax.

Since you cannot control your body language completely, the best you can do is to ensure you make the best use of it for presentation purposes:

ARMS AND HANDS

★ Ignore artificial rules such as 'no gesture should be wider than your body' or 'keep hands always in repose'
★ Allow your natural creativity to dictate your use of arms and hands so that they enhance your performance ⊃ hands
★ Speaking with your arms folded could just mean that you are cold, but if you stay that way for a long time it may signal that you are unduly defensive

POSTURE

★ Standing straight tends to convey more authority than slouching
★ A tense upright position usually signals anxiety ⊃ posture
★ A really laid-back posture as of the film director on a chat show could signal you are a show-off and even too confident

EYE GAZE

★ It's the amount of eye contact that counts ⊃ eyes
★ Too much and you signal aggression, too little and you may glasses seem distant and unfriendly
★ Ideal amount depends on distance, the situation and the relationship. Extroverts do more looking than introverts

FACIAL EXPRESSION

★ Smiling is the most obvious signal but also the easiest to fake

Since you can seldom fake body language convincingly, instead, ⊃ acting
try discovering what you are doing so that you can tackle root personality
causes and find new forms of expression. For example, positive walking
gestures with hands:

★ Enliven your performance
★ Give audiences something to look at
★ Help you express yourself
★ Convey your strength of feeling

Use any gesture with which you feel comfortable and which the audience will understand and feels is appropriate. Unless you are constrained by space considerations, such as appearing close up on television, avoid limiting your movements.

Beware some body habits

Looking small: 'I'm five foot four, but I always feel six foot one, tall and strong,' claimed Yvette Mimieux in Popcorn in Paradise (1979). It's not a matter of size. Think Danny De Vito. If you're small avoid puffing yourself up to look bigger. Similarly, if you are tall don't slump down trying to hide your height

Tilting your head when you talk: If you are an excellent listener you may tend to tilt your head without even realising it. This can make you look less authoritative. Instead, keep your head up and chin forward, relax your shoulders back

Voice rising at the end of sentences: This habit makes you sound as if you are asking a question, rather than making a statement. It may explain why your suggestions are overlooked or ignored during business meetings. The lower your voice the more credible it tends to sound

Introducing yourself too soon: In the first few seconds of meeting someone new, people don't usually register what is said. They're checking you out visually, which explains why we forget names so quickly. Instead, try explaining first what you do, then the company you work for and finally your name

Fidgeting: Studies show that when some people enter a conference room they make around twelve movements while others make nearly thirty. This includes adjusting clothes and jewellery. Keep your movements to a minimum

The body says what words cannot.

MARTHA GRAHAM, DANCER (1894–1991)

The gestures that help in a business presentation are those stemming naturally from your enthusiasm and a need to express yourself. Hand and arm gestures, head movements, turning at key moments, walking and sitting can all be effective ways to emphasise a point or convey your personality.

When you have a really clear intention or purpose behind your presentation the body and gestures usually take care of themselves.

★ *Distractions*

THE ULTIMATE BUSINESS PRESENTATION BOOK

Do you have any nervous verbal habits such as using 'er' or 'um', or repetitive phrases like 'well' or 'my next point is . . .'? Try filling the space instead with pauses. Likewise, mumbling can kill a presentation quicker than shouting.

> disruptions
> distractions
> sidetracked
> stuck

Stick to your message and avoid wandering off on some story that seems entertaining yet is totally irrelevant. If you are part of a presenting team have someone ready to signal if you seem to be diverging from the points you need to make.

A good discipline is to keep summarising, offering regular recaps. This forces you constantly to return to the main thrust of your argument.

The more you know or care about the topic, the easier it becomes to be sidetracked, either by your own actions or those of your audience. You can reduce the chances of divergence if you

★ Have clear aims for your presentation
★ Keep your prompts in a clear sequence with key points highlighted
★ Stick to a maximum of three points in a fifteen-minute presentation or five main points in a longer one
★ Give short answers to questions, offering to deal with side issues later

Once you have left your chosen path it may take a while to realise that you have indeed been distracted. How do you refocus?

★ Pause to gather your thoughts – gives your audience thinking time too
★ Admit you are lost and summarise
★ Use humour to defuse the situation and buy time
    For example: 'Some of you may feel that I have strayed from my main point. You are absolutely correct'
    'As you can see, I am so passionate about this I've gone off at a tangent'
★ Ask the audience for help in getting back on track
    For example: 'Does anyone remember where I was before I got so carried away?'
    'If anyone is taking notes, could you tell me where I got to, please?'

★ Look around, breathe deeply and take in your surroundings
★ Say nothing, let the silence build as you give yourself time to think
★ Be honest, for example:

'Sorry but I've completely lost track of where I was. I'm just going to take a few moments to sort myself out'

★ Say nothing, simply take a few moments to consult your notes
★ Gain time by asking for questions
★ Have the audience do something, while you get yourself together
★ Call a coffee break so you can ask someone what you have said so far
★ End the presentation now with a short summary of your message

Freezing

It happens to the best, even the Master presenters. Freezing is a ghastly experience and some of the most experienced actors admit to being anxious about it. The symptoms are:

breathing
distractions
sidetracked
stuck

★ You don't know what you are doing here
★ You forget what comes next
★ You find yourself unable to utter a word
★ You go completely blank about what you have already said
★ You have a desire to rush away but are rooted to the spot

While such moments are genuinely scary, the worst part is imagining they might happen to you. In fact, they are relatively rare and usually occur because you are

★ Excessively tired
★ Emotionally distraught
★ Under-prepared
★ Sidetracked into an irrelevancy
★ Haven't previously warmed up physically

Freezing temporarily blocks your ability to think straight and only a natural instinct for survival, knowledge of calming techniques and good preparation really help. Often, though, an

audience never even realises that you have frozen. If you take a few moments you will probably get your thoughts in order again.

As with other distractions, the most useful response to freezing it to gain time to think and unwind. For instance, get the audience talking to each other about what you have been saying while you gather your thoughts.

Visuals

Let's assume that you have chosen some wonderful visuals. They may have taken weeks to prepare. It can therefore be tempting to linger lovingly over them during the actual presentation. The reverse problem is equally common: giving people insufficient time to absorb the message.

For example, one of the world's Master presenters loves to dowse his audience in a deluge of visuals and sometimes his enthusiasm gets the better of him. The images come and go at a mind-numbing rate, leaving people impressed yet unsure what they have seen.

Allow your visuals to 'land', but not long enough to bore people. Around ten seconds should be enough for most simple images. Occasionally some charts may need longer at around thirty seconds. A visual that requires more than half a minute to absorb is almost certainly not working.

★ Stay silent while people absorb your visuals
★ Reading material that people can see for themselves can be patronising and irritating

FLIP CHARTS

Are you a flip chart freak? Many business presenters can't resist the lure of flip chart scribbling. This can soon turn the session into a talk-and-chalk event, leaving the audience as passive, and usually bored, observers.

A flip chart gives a sense of immediacy if you are recording current material drawn directly from the audience. Generally, however, writing while actually presenting is a distraction, since you cannot look at people any longer and it wastes time. Instead, either prepare your flip charts in advance or ask someone else to do the writing.

Making the best of flip charts

★ Put the stand where you won't inadvertently knock it
★ Make sure the stand is stable and straight
★ Ensure there are sufficient blank pages for your needs
★ Talk to the audience, not the board
★ Lettering size:
   An audience up to 10 metres away needs 5mm lettering
   10–15 metres away needs 10mm lettering
   15–20 metres away needs 55mm lettering
★ Print neatly and legibly
★ Use different colours for page headings and primary points
★ Avoid pastel colours, unless you outline them in bold
★ Put the marker down when not using it
★ Stick to 10 or less lines per page
★ People at the back may not be able to see if you fill the page to the bottom
★ Post important papers on the wall
★ Check with the venue about posting finished charts on the wall
★ Avoid writing on pages posted on walls in case the pen bleeds through the paper
★ Use prescored pages for easy tearing, or score them in advance
★ For complex pages prepare ahead in light pencil, tracing with a marker when going live
★ Use the top corner to pencil in your notes, if you write small no one will notice
★ Where possible use symbols, images and pictures, not words

Good communication is as stimulating as black coffee and just as hard to sleep after.

ANNE MORROW LINDBERGH,
GIFT FROM THE SEA (1955)

Relationships

Master presenters build a strong relationship with their audiences. While there's nothing mysterious about this process, it does rely on some subtle forms of communication. For example, you need to be sufficiently well prepared so that you concentrate on the audience rather than yourself. The moment you focus on yourself or the words, you become self-conscious and commit less attention to building bridges with your listeners.

Relationship building occurs when you

★ Meet and research your audience
★ Enter the presenting environment looking around in a friendly, confident way
★ Take time before launching into your performance, absorbing the atmosphere and making visual contact with people
★ Tell stories that tap into people's feelings
★ Share personal information that reveals your human side
★ Involve your audience

expectations
listen
tuning in

Showing your human side, particularly your vulnerability, is an important and powerful way of contacting people. And if throughout your entire presentation you are consciously building or maintaining the relationship it will sustain you whenever you make mistakes.

Participation

A powerful way to build relationships is through involving your audience in some way. Switching during a straight presentation to an interactive session changes the dynamic and requires the

audience to use energy. This automatically increases their attention and interest.

Audience participation also creates unpredictable situations and these tend to provide opportunity for humour and spontaneity. These in turn help build a bond between audience and presenter.

Interactive presentations are a terrific way to gain audience buy-in. For example, when Maynard Leigh pitches for new business we often explain that it's hard just to describe how we work with people. So instead we ask if we can give a demonstration on the spot. Before long, people are up and doing, experiencing the very approach we are hoping to persuade them to adopt, and there's usually much laughter and joking. It then becomes much easier to argue our case for using our services.

A motor manufacturer pitching for an important hire contract might know that the audience has already seen the vehicle. Yet inviting everyone to leave their seats and troop outside for an unexpected sight of the very latest model, driven by a well-known personality, creates an entirely different and involving atmosphere.

When we trained British Airways cabin crews who were presenting the launch of the airline's new business class Cradle Seat, we encouraged them to let the audience try it out.

Promoting participation

There are many ways to encourage audience participation. Like presentation openers, you are only restricted by the limits of your imagination. Here are some methods you might use:

START A QUESTION-AND-ANSWER SESSION

The moment when a presentation comes alive is often when you stop talking and hand over to the audience. In many business presentation situations the best strategy is to turn the entire session into questions and answers.

ACTION

CONDUCT AN INSTANT SURVEY

questionnaire
quiz

Warren Bennis, a world expert on teams and leadership and a superb speaker, has given literally hundreds of business presen-

tations around the world. One of his favourite audience involvement methods is to pose a 'pop' quiz in which he asks people to guess the answers to apparently simple questions, such as 'Who painted the Sistine chapel?' Most people choose Michelangelo, only to find the correct reply is a whole team of painters recruited by the master.

GET EARLY ARRIVALS DOING SOMETHING

Rather than wait for important players to arrive for the presentation, start things moving immediately by issuing a challenge, such as solving a problem. This makes people feel important and valued. Those arriving late miss the fun but not the important parts.

CREATE SMALL GROUPS

You can often create an effective change of pace and alter energy levels by breaking a large group of people into several small ones to work on something together. Whatever you ask them to do, make sure it is crystal clear and won't take so long that your overall presentation time runs out.

> conversation

POSE A PROBLEM

Present everyone with an immediate, live issue and invite people to suggest ways of solving it. They can talk among themselves or offer information direct to you. If the problem you pose is close to their hearts you're continuing to build the relationship.

> discussions

VOTING

Ask the audience to vote on some issue, such as the priority for discussion, or what they think is the most important issue facing the organisation. You can be creative in how people exercise their votes; for instance, you could write the issues on a flip pad and give everyone different coloured sticky stars to put next to the items they value most.

> questionnaire

BRAINSTORMING

Create a situation in which people look for unusual ideas and solutions. For example, you might challenge your audience to work in pairs, inventing as many ways as possible to use your product or service.

ALLOCATE ROLES

Give members of the audience specific roles such as keeping

track of the time, distributing material, handling roving mikes, writing on flip charts, collecting material produced by other members of the audience and so on.

LINE-UPS

Ask everyone to line up in some interesting order that gets people off their chairs and moving around. For example, the two founding partners of Maynard Leigh Associates once worked with senior members of a UK regional health authority and invited them to form a long line with the longest-serving chairman at one end and the newest at the other. This caused much hilarity and drew attention to the diverse experience in the room, and built a sense of involvement.

POST-ITS

Issue the audience with Post-it notes on which they write some issue or concern, and get up and place them on a wall. Then they start to rearrange them by sorting and ordering.

MAKE IT TWO-WAY

boredom
concentration
dull
sleep
snore
yawn

Business presentations don't have to be dull stand-up affairs in which one or more people talk at a dutifully silent audience. One-way presenting can prove entirely inappropriate, making it harder to build a relationship.

David Hughes Solomon, SAP Technical Director, argues that the main thing is to 'try and get them interacting and understanding what you're saying. I've sat through many technical presentations and seen how people are at the end. It's quite clear

conversation
discussions

that many haven't understood the last half-hour at all. That tends to happen with a bigger audience, typically a seminar to multiple organisations at the same time.'

USE VOLUNTEERS

Another indirect way of building relationships is to use volunteers from the audience. These willing individuals contribute a new energy to the performance and the audience can identify with those carrying out the role.

How do you get people to come forward? First, explain that you won't be asking them to do anything embarrassing. Second, rather than pressurising them, only use those who genuinely want to assist.

In certain cultures volunteering is unusual and you may need to be more directive, or tolerant of a lack of volunteers. When

you ask the audience to participate, start slowly and build up. Rather than immediately requesting everyone to stand, for example, make the first activity something they can do sitting down. For instance,

★ Seek a show of hands
★ Get people talking to the person next to or behind them
★ Ask them to write down something

As you progress through your presentation you can make greater demands. It can be scary as a member of an audience to find yourself involved in someone else's presentation. You may, for example, be presenting to an audience of people engaged in private wars with each other, with low levels of trust, or lack of mutual respect. You probably won't know quite what to expect, so show understanding if people hesitate to come forward. Let them know what they're in for. Rather than say 'I need a volunteer', ask

★ 'Could someone help me distribute these notes?'

USE HUMOUR
Occasionally humour can reduce an initial resistance to volunteer:

★ 'I learned my handwriting from a doctor, so could someone please come up and write legibly on this flip chart for me?'
★ 'Anyone have a watch with a second hand? Great. Would you be willing to keep track of the time for me?'
★ 'Anyone here do regular weight training? Fine, do you feel strong enough to come up here and help carry these notes round?'

CLOSING
How will you leave your audience? If you have succeeded in ⮌ building a relationship during the presentation your closure is a critical moment of consolidation.

applause
closing
conclusion
end
stop
thanks

Research into audience attention levels reveals that it tends to rise in the last five or six minutes, especially when people realise the end is close.

Closure

★ Signal the coming close with relevant remarks
★ Remind people of the key message they should take away with them
★ Be specific about what you want them to do next
★ Finish on a memorable note such as a picture, a story, a single word, a fact, an appeal, a demand, a poem, a full motion video which you freeze-frame at some point
★ Show that you have finished, perhaps with a nod or a thank you, then move from the centre of attention
★ In the final moments of your performance add extra energy to your delivery
★ State that you are available to people afterwards
★ Ask for feedback to learn what they thought of you and your presentation, what they learned, what they felt was missing

That's all there is, there isn't any more.

ETHEL BARRYMORE, *CURTAIN CALL*, 1904

In a business presentation such as a pitch you don't usually expect applause. If you have made a powerful impression, though, there may be a period of silence while people absorb the fact that you have finished and process the information. If that happens, stay calm and patient. Simply wait for a reaction. Eventually someone will speak, either with a question, a thank you or some other indication of what will happen next.

★ It's your responsibility to create the space for what happens next, for saying, in effect: 'Over to you.'

Handling Presentation Disasters

*W*hen faced with a crisis put a little spittle on each earlobe and inhale deeply through the nose. Then break a chopstick. All nervousness will disappear instantly. This is a secret matter. From the seventeenth-century Samurai manual *Hagakure*

When Shell proposed to dump the Brent Spar oil platform in the North Sea it unleashed a tidal wave of opposition. The environmental group Greenpeace spent over £300,000 on its highly visible and successful campaign to oppose the company's intentions.

Shell faced an image and presentation crisis, as well as a serious problem of what to do with an enormous chunk of redundant metal. Its carefully laid plans to dispose of the platform ended in shambles after the presentations justifying its actions failed to convince.

With continuing outside pressure and insiders expressing unease that the company had lost sight of its wider community responsibilities, Shell conceded defeat. It agreed not to sink the platform in the sea. The crisis had a major impact within the company.

When Intel was first approached by an obscure professor claiming that its latest computer chip had a mathematical fault, the company at first denied it, downplaying the issue. In its public presentations the company came across as only grudgingly offering replacements and even then solely to selected customers. The company's public presentations were a disaster, nothing but a total climbdown worked. Eventually it

promised replacements to anyone who wanted one.

A public crisis such as those faced by Shell or Intel puts a company's business presentation skills to the ultimate test. The task for Shell challenged the company's entire culture. Intel's crisis lesson taught it the value of acknowledging problems early and dealing with customers generously. Such crises make huge demands on individuals to communicate with impact.

A crisis can threaten either a company's survival or some vital aspect such as credibility, image, brands or reputation. Often actions speak louder than words, as when Perrier withdrew its entire stock of bottled water to preserve its reputation for purity, or more recently when large numbers of tinned chopped tomatoes were withdrawn from Tesco supermarkets. In such situations, business presenting acquires a whole new dimension. It becomes vital to clarify the nature of the threat to avoid overreacting or failing to see the build-up of true dangers.

Give us the facts

An inescapable pressure during a crisis is the demand for information. Yet it's not always possible to give it, which poses a difficult presentation challenge.

facts ⊂

In the late 1980s a British Midland Boeing 737 crashed on to the UK's M1 motorway in Leicestershire. Forty-seven people died and as the terrible facts emerged there was huge pressure on the airline as TV, radio and newspapers made frantic efforts to meet deadlines.

Within an hour of the crash, British Midland's boss Michael Bishop was on television being interviewed. He shared everything he knew, including the arrangements his team had already made to inform relatives of the known facts and fly them to the East Midland Airport. Bishop's handling of the presentation was masterly and the immediate media response was sympathetic and favourable.

It was later reported that bookings for British Midland's scheduled services had increased by 10% in the period immediately after the disaster.

Adapted from Michael Barratt, *Making the Most of the Media*, KOGAN PAGE (1996)

Name your crisis

★ Yet another company restructuring
★ An environmental accident or decision
★ Product failures or sabotage
★ Seriously adverse publicity
★ A hostile takeover
★ Terrorism
★ Major court action
★ Major financial problems, including filing for bankruptcy or protection
★ Wholesale sackings
★ A top management clear-out
★ A vital business pitch goes seriously wrong
★ Investor disillusionment

No blare of trumpets announces a modern crisis. In these matter-of-fact times, a telephone call will do.

ELIE ABEL, *THE MISSILE CRISIS* (1966)

Business presentations during a crisis require intensive preparation, although often there simply isn't time. Once it's clear there is a crisis, many companies assemble a special project team. You know your business best and although outside advisers such as PR companies and lawyers can offer technical advice, how you present your message remains your responsibility.

A crisis raises the stakes so the normal presentation preparation questions become even more critical to answer:

★ Who is the essential audience and what does it need to know?
★ How do we reach this audience?
★ Who needs to be told first and what is the order of communication?
★ What is the story and how shall we tell it?

In preparing your story, develop a plan for reaching the different constituents such as the media, trade unions, stockholders,

regulatory bodies and so on. Each may require a separate form of presentation and an experienced spokesperson able to handle the unpredictable.

Ten presentation tips on crisis management

★ Make personal contact with key players such as board members, major shareholders, trade union leaders, employees, important media people, other stakeholders

★ Communicate early and often, particularly to employees, and through regular press briefings

★ Look hard for ways to turn the situation to your advantage

★ Consider creating hot lines for people to ring

★ Use special mailings such as faxes, express letters and e-mail to underpin verbal messages

★ Choose a credible spokesperson who comes across as capable and trustworthy

★ Use symbolic communications, such as the CEO travelling to a trouble spot

★ Don't issue hostages to fortune; the ex-UK minister who tried showing that British beef was safe during the BSE crisis by eating a burger in public has seen that discredited video clip replayed countless times

★ Stay visible – don't go to ground leaving the troops to field all the answers

★ Once the crisis is clearly over, say so and offer the evidence

We don't get offered crises, they arrive.

ELIZABETH JANEWAY, *CROSS SECTIONS* (1982)

Few actual presentation disasters are life threatening. However, they can certainly undermine personal credibility and seriously threaten business prospects. When presenting to City analysts, for example, if a presentation goes awry the result may be a large drop in the share price. Similarly, when a conference appearance is a duff one you may not be invited back, or elsewhere.

Yet even when a presentation does go wrong there are often ways to retrieve the situation. You can only start doing that, though, when you

bluff
challenges
mistakes
objections
pitfalls
stuck
trip

★ Accept that something has gone seriously wrong

Denial usually makes matters worse. Pretending that everything is fine might work for minor slip-ups, but for anything serious you need to take positive action to put things right:

★ Stay calm and alert
★ Smile – if appropriate, use humour to relax the situation
★ Avoid looking worried or fearful
★ If necessary, call a break to consult with your team
★ Decide what you want to happen next and start trying to make it happen

Often in a disaster situation you can make real gains with the audience by how you handle it. Few audiences actively want to see the presenter fail. If you take care of things with confidence you are, in effect, looking after your audience who may be every bit as anxious as you.

In business pitches potential customers have little to gain in seeing you get it really wrong. If you make a serious miscalculation in your presentation this may not be the end of the road, provided you recognise the situation and take immediate steps to rectify it.

Pitch problems

Pitches are some of the most unnerving places in which to experience a presentation disaster. Some situations are more common than others and there are some viable retrieval strategies:

decision
impress
success
win

★ **The key decision maker fails to arrive** – *Solution*: Treat the stand-in person as a reporter. What do you want this person to say to the absent decision maker? Be highly specific and use this statement several times at the start and at the end of the presentation

Dealing with the unexpected

★ **Be prepared:** The more prepared you are, the more freedom you acquire to cope with the unexpected

Top 10 Tips!

★ **Clear your mind:** Concentrate on the three key points you want to convey. Write them on a cue card in case something does go seriously wrong. It's easier to return to an idea that you want to convey than to a single word in a script

★ **Focus on purpose:** The more you concentrate on the overall purpose of your presentation, instead of trying to remember everything, the more you will be able to say and do what's needed

★ **Trust:** We are all capable of spontaneous invention. Allow your natural creativity to take wing. Humour is often a great saviour, frequently flowing best under pressure

★ **Stay present:** Be aware of what's happening around you. Stay alert and 'in the moment'

★ **Build relationships:** True creativity often flows from unexpected relationships with people

★ **Breathe:** Take your time. Don't rush. Breathe and allow yourself the space for invention

★ **Tell the truth:** If a disaster happens – don't pretend it hasn't. Acknowledge what's going on. The more you are able to handle it, the easier it is for your audience

★ **Ask the audience:** If somebody tries to deliberately throw you – ask for clarification. Be curious. Try and understand your audience's motives

★ **Risk:** Every presentation is a risk and there are no guarantees of success. If you have been thrown by a situation, acknowledge what's gone wrong and make sure you learn from it

Surprise is the greatest gift which life can grant us.

BORIS PASTERNAK,
ON MODESTY AND BOLDNESS (1936)

★ **The decision maker leaves before you have finished** – *Solution*: Get all key points across right at the beginning and if you have a visual use it to punch home the message. Don't save the most powerful point till last. Before the person leaves ask politely if you can sum up the basic message in thirty seconds – most people will stay for that long

★ **You are told you have ten minutes not the forty you expected** – *Solution*: Start by assuming that you have half the time you were allocated. That way you'll be prepared. Don't try talking fast to cram everything into the reduced time. Decide how much to reallocate to each part of your presentation and keep a careful watch on the time as you perform. Have a written summary available for distribution afterwards

★ **You are asked a question you intend to deal with later** – *Solution*: Explain you will deal with this, but not right now. If the questioner is the key decision maker, offer a short answer and ask if that will do till you return to it later

★ **You forget where you have reached in the presentation** – *Solution*: Every other human being has lost their train of thought at some time. Allow yourself to be vulnerable. Smile, explaining that you need a moment to compose yourself. Start again at a point where you feel confident to continue

★ **You've handed out a report and people are rushing ahead of you at their own pace** – *Solution*: If the decision maker is pressing on regardless, suggest a break to allow people to go through it for themselves. Keep referring to the page you are dealing with so that people don't go off in different directions. Generally make it a habit not to distribute reports and documents in advance, unless you can give the recipients plenty of time to do their homework

★ **The decision maker is confusing you with one of your competitors** – *Solution*: Start the presentation by announcing who you are, using a visual to emphasise the point. Mention the name of your company frequently

★ **You have prepared your pitch for three people and find fifteen people in the room** – *Solution*: Rejoice. You have an opportunity to build a relationship with even more people. Decide what needs to be done to cope with this influx. For example, ask someone to make extra copies of handouts, abandon any idea of working in as much depth as you planned; ask for a flip chart and use this to write up key points

★ **You arrive to pitch and are offered a seat in a deep, soft sofa** – *Solution*: First consider the underlying message. Could you have misjudged the situation? Maybe the decision maker wants not a formal presentation but a more intimate form of communication. Check the person's expectations. If it's for a formal pitch then either do it standing up, explaining that you would prefer it or ask for a hard, straight-backed chair from which to perform

★ **In the middle of the pitch several people start a side conversation** – *Solution*: Enquire pointedly if there are some issues worrying this group. Ask if there's anything they would like clarified. If that fails, move physically closer to them while continuing your delivery. If you can't stop them talking ask the decision maker if it might be better to take a break or reschedule the meeting

★ **You drop your overheads on the floor** – *Solution*: Be glad you numbered them. Apologise for your clumsiness, pick them up and quietly reorder them

★ **The decision maker keeps quoting your competitors** – *Solution*: Refuse to knock the other party, focus instead on what you will do and why you offer something special

★ **You are a non-smoker and the decision maker is puffing away furiously** – *Solution*: Politely ask the person if they would mind not smoking just while you are talking as you need to protect your throat

★ **A member of your presentation team gets something spectacularly wrong** – *Solution*: Don't overreact. Check the audience to see if people have realised the error. If they have, but no one interrupts with a challenge, quietly brief the next person to make a correction. Alternatively, save the correction till the final summing-up. If the audience challenges on the error the presentation team leader may need to intervene and support the misguided colleague

★ **You present a price and the recipients react in total horror** – *Solution*: Could be a sign you have seriously misunderstood what you can charge, or that the other party is signalling the first shot in a prolonged negotiation battle. Don't start bargaining in the middle of the presentation. Instead, acknowledge the potential difficulty with a remark such as: 'Seems we may have a problem on that front, let's come back to it later,' or 'Price is clearly a critical issue; we'll have to work hard to get this part right.'

That embarrassing moment

Occasionally you find yourself saying or doing something that is a real *faux pas*, a mistake that makes you, and perhaps your presentation team, cringe with embarrassment.

foreign audience
names
offence
political correctness
religion
sarcasm
satire
taboos
trip

Presentation *faux pas*

★ Arriving unacceptably late
★ Leaving an important article of clothing unzipped
★ Continuously forgetting the names of people or the company
★ Showing slides upside down
★ Using inappropriate language.
★ Noisy bodily functions
★ Falling over
★ Upsetting a whole jug of liquid
★ Misjudging someone's intentions
★ Questioning someone's integrity
★ Making an unintended racial or sexual remark

The man that blushes is not quite a brute.

EDWARD YOUNG (1683–1765),
ENGLISH POET, *NIGHT THOUGHTS*

Such moments may pass an audience by completely, so before rushing to apologise assess whether anyone has really noticed or even cares. If you need to offer an apology do so gracefully and with good humour. Then move on swiftly.

late
mistake
pitfalls
stuck

Avoid dwelling on what happened, that is, don't keep returning to it. For example, if you have arrived unacceptably late, having apologised once, avoid mentioning the same subject, except where you can realistically convert it into a running joke at your own expense.

Sometimes a slip of the tongue can upset a smooth-running presentation and in those situations use a phrase that makes it clear you realise you have erred:

'I just can't believe I said that! I'm sorry let me rephrase it . . .'

'That came out entirely wrong. What I meant to say was . . .'

'Sorry, can we rewind the tape. What I was trying to say was . . .'

'Hey! That was nonsense! My brain just slipped out of gear . . .'

Venue disasters

Do a full reconnoitre of the venue days or weeks before you are due to speak, or otherwise allow several hours before your actual performance for a check. Be on site at least an hour before the event.

While careful preparation, including the use of the Arrival Check List (see page 67) can eliminate many potential disasters, some may still arise to upset your performance, including:

checklist ★ Insufficient chairs or room for the audience
environment ★ Sound system failures
outside ★ Accidental damage to computer cables
technicians ★ Unscheduled fire alarm tests
venue ★ Flooding
★ Fused lights
★ Extraneous noises
★ Audio-visual failures
★ Doors slamming
★ Insufficient materials
★ Inadequate photocopy facilities
★ Fewer breakout rooms than expected
★ Interpreters have mislaid the translation of your speech

It's not much fun coping with these sorts of problems and audiences tend to expect you to solve them without undue fuss.

In team presentations, allocate one person responsibility for spotting these hazards and resolving them, preferably before the audience realises there is a problem.

If you are on your own, make sure you know whom you could call on to help retrieve the situation. That leaves you free to continue giving your full attention to the audience.

Handling a major venue snag

★ Smile and try not to look rattled

★ If appropriate, apologise and share the problem with the audience

★ Call a break while you solve it

★ Use humour to reduce the tension

★ Take responsibility, don't blame the organisers

★ Call an emergency meeting with the organisers to discuss measures to sort out the problem

★ Resort to your back-up arrangements; for example, using overheads instead of slides or handing out copies of visuals because the presentation equipment has failed

★ Cut short your presentation and promise to send everyone copies

★ Rearrange to repeat your performance, for instance, later during the same day or evening or at an alternative venue

If you can keep your head when all about you are losing theirs, it's just possible you haven't grasped the situation.

JEAN KERR, *PLEASE DON'T EAT THE DAISIES*

Follow-Through

Y ou have delivered your carefully prepared presentation, held people's attention and finally sat down. Is that it? What should happen next?

Follow-through means continuing to build a relationship with your audience. This can happen in many ways, even as you leave the room. For example, if there are only a few in the audience you might go round shaking everyone's hands, thanking them personally for their attention. This might also be a good time to hand over some further information, a sample, or a personal visiting card.

Q & A

interviews press conferences

The commonest form of follow-through is a question-and-answer session. Many people dread these, usually because the event is unpredictable. Anything can happen and often does.

Handling questions well can be critical to the success of many presentations. 'If you waffle on the first couple of answers then you may be doomed,' argues one Master presenter.

The question-and-answer session is an opportunity to excel. You'll be confident about these if you understand the essentials.

PREPARE

Murphy's Law
prepare

★ Think about the questions you may be asked
★ Play devil's advocate

★ Research your audience
★ What's the worst question they could ask you?
★ How could you answer it?

ENERGY

It takes more energy than usual to come over well in these situations. You need to concentrate at all times, so be

• alert • involved • enthusiastic

TALK TO THE AUDIENCE

Talk directly to the audience. Address the person who has asked the question, then open it out to everyone.

A SATISFIED CUSTOMER?

Having finished an answer, try the occasional, 'Does that answer your question?'

YOU'RE 'ON' AT ALL TIMES

Even when you are not answering you're communicating actively using non-verbal signals, so

★ Don't slouch back in your chair
★ Appear ready to answer the next question – it's no good trying to disappear
★ Listen attentively – with eyes open

'What often wins proposals for us is the way we behave in response to questions not simply how we behave during the formal part of the presentation,' says Alex Gethin of KPMG.

WHAT'S IN A QUESTION?

Behind many questions is really a statement. Remove the query part of them and you often unearth a particular point of view. For example:

> 'What is your market share?' might really mean 'I don't think you're as successful as you claim.'
> 'Can you explain how you'd meet our June deadline?' might really mean 'You probably don't have the resources to deliver on time.'
> 'Have you met any handover problems with this technology?' might really mean 'I bet we'd have lots of problems making this equipment work.'

'Is your system based on validated research?' might really mean *'I think your system is arbitrary and probably unreliable.'*

'Please clarify what you meant by saying that this method of data handling is less vulnerable to error than the old one' might really mean *'I like the old method and the new one isn't cost effective.'*

No matter how difficult the issue thrown at you, uncovering the implied statement enables you to fire it back so as to regain control. If you suspect that the person is posing the statement disguised as a question so as to embarrass you or make themselves look clever, then giving an honest factual reply such as 'No we don't have such problems' won't necessarily deal with the issue.

You don't need to know all the answers, just to understand the question. Audiences would rather you said 'I don't know' than give misinformation or be excessively vague. Since you often can't know what lies behind a query why try and answer it immediately? It may be better to do some digging. A good way of doing this is to respond with some questions of your own such as:

★ 'What prompts you to ask that question?'
★ 'Do you have any reason to think we do have such problems?'
★ 'Could you be a bit more specific about why you think that's an issue?'
★ 'Would you please explain a bit further what you mean?'
★ 'Could you clarify how that point relates to what we've been dealing with?'

This tactic often gives the other person permission to state openly what they are thinking, rather than hiding behind the question.

STATING THE GROUND RULES

So long as you know some of the essential techniques, handling question-and-answer sessions can be fun. Even if you cannot control the entire process you can make sure that it serves you well. For example, you could set the tone by posing yourself a tough question and propose some helpful ground rules such as:

★ How long the session will last
★ One question per person until everyone has asked one
★ Questioners identify themselves
★ Don't pull your punches
★ State a definite information goal for the session
★ How unanswered questions will be dealt with – e.g. information sent within three days

Keep to a consistent presentation style. For instance, there's no point in being animated during the presentation and becoming leaden once question time arrives. Similarly, if your formal presentation is pedestrian and you suddenly come alive during the questions and answers it suggests that you weren't particularly interested in the presentation itself and were probably nervous.

No matter how weak or irrelevant the question, treat the person posing it with absolute respect. Find a way to make them look good, rather than wrong or stupid. People ask questions to

★ Learn more
★ Seek clarification
★ Challenge you
★ Make things awkward for you
★ Make themselves or you look good
★ Get across their views

Treat all questions as if they are for the first two reasons. Prepare twice as much material as you need so you have plenty left for questions. If you regard questions as simply a great way of re-enforcing your presentation message then there's no such thing as a hostile or unanswerable one, only another opportunity to hammer home your arguments.

If the acoustics make it hard to hear the questions and there's no roving mic, repeat them so that everyone can hear. Or invite people to submit their queries in writing. Give them enough time to do so and either collect the material yourself or use a volunteer.

REPEAT QUESTIONS

For less experienced presenters, one of the most disconcerting moments is someone posing a question that has already been fully answered, perhaps minutes previously. Why do such repetitions occur?

Repetitive questions either mean that something was

genuinely unclear or unconvincing and was unresolved by previous answers, or that the audience is being deliberately provocative. Should you say 'We've already had that question' or try and answer it all over again?

The best tactic is patience. Summarise your previous reply and invite the person to come and discuss it further with you afterwards. This may also reduce the person's embarrassment if they realise their error in repeating a question already dealt with.

DIFFICULT QUESTIONS

Truly difficult questions can initially seem irrelevant or even incredibly obvious. 'The person who'll ask a silly question is always the most senior person in the room,' claims David Hughes Solomon of SAP. 'If it's a board of directors, always without fail the senior person will ask what everyone else has been wanting to ask. You can see the relief on the rest of their faces. They have been sure that everyone else knows the answer and they're too embarrassed about looking silly.'

When faced with a really tough question, congratulate the person on their astute enquiry. Take a little time to summarise their point and check that you have really understood it, even if you have no ready answer. This gives you extra time to think and you can then

bluff
challenges
examples
objections
stuck

★ **Give a direct answer:** Keep it short and simple

★ **Admit ignorance:** 'Difficult question! Right now I don't know the answer, let me have a note of where to contact you and I'll get back to you in a couple of days.' In a large audience ask the person to write down their difficult query with their address, or on the back of a visiting card

★ **Hand on:** Pass the problem back to the audience: 'What do the rest of you think about that question?'

★ **Redirect:** 'Good question. John's an expert on that. Any comments you'd like to make, John?'

★ **Throw back:** 'Nice question. Would you like to elaborate a bit on that?'

★ **Redefine:** 'Could you perhaps rephrase that question?'

ACTION

Some presentation teams have a laptop computer connected to a phone line accessing various information sources. Even if they can't provide the answer on the spot they can offer to produce it later.

THE ULTIMATE BUSINESS PRESENTATION BOOK

Humour can defuse tricky questions

★ 'Could you rephrase that, preferably into something that I can answer!'
★ 'Glad you asked me that, only trouble is I haven't the faintest idea'
★ 'You've asked the right person and my answer is I don't know'
★ 'A well-thought-out question which deserves a well-thought-out reply. Call me in a couple of weeks'
★ 'I'd love to know the answer to that too. Next'
★ 'Bet you write crossword puzzles for a living'
★ 'I knew they shouldn't have let you in!'
★ 'That's a good question for you to ask, not a wise one for me to answer'

There aren't any embarrassing questions – just embarrassing answers.
CARL ROWAN, *THE NEW YORKER* (7 DECEMBER 1963)

NO QUESTIONS

It can be a disconcerting moment when you invite questions and no one stirs. As part of your preparation you could plant some questions in the audience to help get things going.

Lack of response might be because people are:

★ Still absorbing your presentation and aren't ready to ask questions
★ Too shy to ask questions in public
★ Fearful of looking foolish
★ Exhausted from your performance
★ Unsure what to ask

Faced with silence or in cultures where questioning the speaker is frowned upon, you could pose a question yourself: 'A question you might like to think about is . . .'

You may need to become more directive and put people in pairs or small groups, asking them to discuss your presentation and identify issues they'd like to explore. Visit the groups in turn and deal with their questions on the spot, rather than in a plenary session.

Score on handling questions

Top 10 Tips!

★ Use thorough preparation to anticipate possible questions
★ Ask colleagues to give you practice by posing difficult questions
★ Announce in advance whether or not you'll be taking questions
★ Before answering, summarise the question to show you've understood it, and to win extra thinking time
★ Avoid signs of irritation at irrelevant, repeated or aggressive questions
★ After a question has been posed, be seen to give it some thought
★ Ask the person or the audience what they think
★ If you don't know the answer be honest and say so
★ Summarise long questions before replying
★ Invite the person to say why they're asking the question

The 'silly question' is the first intimation of some totally new development.

ALFRED NORTH WHITEHEAD

If there are questions that you didn't handle at the time you may need to contact people again or mail out additional information. In pitching for new business maybe there are mini-presentations to pursue, additional showcase opportunities to follow up and so on.

Assume that while people have liked your performance, they will quickly forget your key messages and essential facts. Where appropriate, follow up with written material, further calls, invitations to other sessions. For example, if you present at a conference, get hold of the names and addresses of everyone in the audience and thank them for coming to hear you. Ask if there is any further information they might want about your topic or company.

If you promised to supply information send it out promptly and if there is any delay call or let the recipients know when they can expect the material.

Types of questions

★ **Yes or no questions:** Need either a straight yes or no with a chance for you to elaborate further, or a challenge such as: 'What lies behind that question?'

★ **'What if . . .' questions:** Show they are raising a hypothetical point. Rather than accept their assumption you return to re-enforcing your existing message

★ **Laundry list questions:** Consist of a series of perhaps disconnected questions and the questioner may not even expect a response. Don't attempt to answer all of them. Instead choose one you can deal with well

★ **Legal or personal questions:** These could leave you vulnerable in some way, either in a court of law or personally. Handle with care – it may be best to explain that the issue is sensitive and not suitable for this particular forum

★ **Stupid questions:** Usually these are ones that you struggle to make sense of and where you can see no connection between what you have been saying and the nature of the enquiry. Handle these by treating the person with total respect, perhaps suggesting that you'll have to 'give this one some real thought and what is the next question please?'

★ **Technical questions:** Often come from someone with specialist knowledge that you cannot match. Acknowledge their mastery and act on behalf of the rest of the audience by asking them to put it a simple way that everyone, including you, can really understand. If necessary, invite them to come and discuss it in depth afterwards, or to meet with your own technical people to explore it further

'How many husbands have you had?' You mean apart from my own?

ZSA ZSA GABOR, AMERICAN TV, 1985

Negotiation

Some of the trickiest follow-through situations are when the formal business presentation ends and turns seamlessly into a

negotiating session. One minute you are making your play, the next you find yourself answering pointed questions. Finally, you realise that it's become a bargaining session.

If you have prepared well for the main presentation this development is at least a welcome sign that you've made a real impact. You are now entering territory where the purpose is to reach agreement in which both parties leave, feeling that they have won.

On balance, though, it is better to separate the presentation process from the negotiation stage. This may require you to find tactful ways to refuse to answer certain questions that are clearly concerned with specific bargaining points and refer them to an alternative forum.

'We caution bid teams not to negotiate in a presentation,' reveals Brian Polk of PWC. 'Negotiations can suck up tremendous amounts of time. It's generally not a good place to negotiate as there are too many people in the room who could be embarrassed by taking certain positions in front of their peers, colleagues or subordinates.'

If you spot the drift from presentation session to negotiation stage you can deal with it tactfully with responses such as:

★ 'It would be best if we dealt with that in a more detailed session'
★ 'Let's schedule a meeting to look at these issues of implementation'
★ 'If you're suggesting we now proceed, we'll need to cover your points and various other issues. Shall we fix a date for these discussions?'
★ 'I think that point needs to be dealt with in a separate negotiation session'

negotiation ⊂ If the presentation team is the same as the negotiation team, be fully rehearsed in who can say what. For example, the lead presenter may no longer be the person who ideally fronts the negotiating team or has the authority to vary terms and make concessions.

Anticipate how you will handle disagreements among the team since some people may see a concession as capitulation or weakness, while others view it as smart tactics.

THE ULTIMATE · BUSINESS · PRESENTATION BOOK

Top negotiation tips

★ Build in regular recesses and meal breaks to allow the team to rest, review its position and enable people to share disagreements

★ Prepare meticulously for the negotiation, if necessary conducting simulated sessions with others playing the role of your adversaries

★ Identify the other side's strengths and weaknesses

★ Decide on your fall-back positions

★ Begin with easy-to-handle issues

★ Don't underestimate the other side

★ Use inclusive language not words creating a 'them and us' atmosphere

★ Express disagreement in an open-ended way to encourage further discussion – for instance rather than saying: 'Impossible, our price is already rock bottom', try 'How could we close the gap between us on this one?' or 'That seems too low for us, but we'd still like to do business with you'

★ Avoid posing confrontational yes-or-no questions

★ Use specific numbers rather than quoting ranges: if you quote a delivery price range or a variety of delivery dates you force the other side to push hard for the most favourable figure, so stick to realistic figures and have no more than two fall-back positions

★ Don't concede something without gaining something in return

★ Resist, if faced with a demand, to concede something in return for something

★ Stick to the truth. Exaggeration and posturing seldom enhance a business negotiation; deliberately trying to bluff or confuse will make mutual agreement harder

★ Don't gloat if you're winning – remember you're seeking agreement not victory

★ Watch for the non-verbal signs from the other side, including fatigue

★ Keep control of emotions – ranting or haranguing just makes a solution harder

Let us never negotiate out of fear.
But let us never fear to negotiate.

JOHN F. KENNEDY, ADDRESS TO UN ASSEMBLY, 1963

What next?

Having made the presentation is that it? Do you just sit around wondering what happens next?

The professionals seldom hang about consumed by anxiety. 'The thing we dislike most is silence,' explains one bid support manager. Rather than waiting for something to happen they get right back to the customer and ask what they thought of the presentation, whether a decision's been made, what will happen next and so on.

If you have a 'coach' among the audience this person can usually tell you within hours whether you have won or lost. 'We would make calls at all levels,' explains one bid support manager. 'So the programme manager would call if he's built a relationship, the salesman would ring one or two people suggesting a meeting, maybe a forum, a visit to an existing client, generally asking if there's anything else we can do.'

The extent to which Master presenters invest in follow-through can be surprising and explains why they make things happen. For example, Frank Lee of Sema explains: 'We continue to put in effort to drive things through. We make contact to ask if there are any outstanding issues that we need to address.' The aim is always to stick in there and continue to influence the decision.

An important aspect of the follow-through is to learn what's happening. It is not saying to the customer or audience: 'What can I do for you next? Can we give you more information on this area or that?' Instead, it is about keeping the customer involved with you, maintaining the relationship and therefore helping to move things forward.

'Because we've invested a lot of time and effort in a big proposal clients are generally willing to talk to us,' says Brian Polk of PWC. 'They recognise that they've asked us to jump through hoops. You get the occasional client who will say "I don't want to talk to you" or "I had a five-minute conversation with one of your senior people when I told him 'no', isn't that enough?" In general it's good practice to go and talk to your clients after the process.'

'Almost every presentation has some requirement for follow-up, so you must do it,' says one Master presenter. 'It's just naïve to believe that senior management will make the right decision

or understand or assimilate all the information one has given. Most people are coming at it from their own work view perspective and the presentation may or may not have fitted into it. They might easily latch on to the wrong end of the stick.'

Look for an angle to get you back in again, rather than waiting for news about your presentation. At CSC, says Peter Jackson, 'presentations will potentially include examples of where we've added value with similar clients. We would normally offer in the presentation the opportunity to go and visit whenever a potential client wants to check it out. So that's another hook to go back.

'We normally assume arrogantly that we've made a good presentation,' he explains. 'If we've made a bad one then we're in recovery mode. It's all about talking to people about what can we do? How can we demonstrate? Do you have any issues? Anywhere that we haven't quite hit the mark?'

Another hook is to trigger some new correspondence that also leads to continuing the dialogue. For example, one company asked its president of Europe to write a letter to his opposite number in the potential client's company suggesting a meeting. This was after the presentation and prior to the negotiations.

A phone call is another follow-through that may break a significant logjam. After one complex CSC business presentation, both parties left saying 'there's no deal' because neither seemed willing to move on various issues. In such situations there is also an element of pride that can get in the way, with no one prepared to take the first step to a solution. In this particular case the experienced presenter went back in again and started a new dialogue, and the differences were eventually resolved.

'I would probably phone one or two people I know best and say "how did it go",' explains Peter Hill, who steers many internal requests for capital investments. 'I'd ask did it really go well? Were there any issues that came out of it? If someone said there was a problem on the finance or IT side, for instance, I'd phone them up and have an informal chat. I'd want to get them into a situation where they felt free to talk about it. A lot of it comes down to networking.'

Other follow-through techniques applicable to all kinds of presentation situations include holding seminars, quasi social events like taking people to sports matches, theatre visits, sponsoring seminars and so on. These are all ways of keeping the dialogue going.

Debriefing

Immediately after the presentation, sit down and review what you remember about what went on. 'We just dump what's in our heads,' is how one bid support manager puts it.

As part of the capture process, large-scale presenters often use a formal review system to discover:

★ What have we done that has been good?
★ What's been bad?
★ Why did we win/lose the business?
★ What did they like about us?
★ What did they dislike about us?

If the reason for losing the business is stated as 'price', the mega bidders refuse to take no for an answer. Instead, they press to unravel what part of the price got in the way, or at what point price became the sole criterion. 'I refuse to accept that price is an answer, because price is very rarely an answer,' explains Sema's Frank Lee.

Feedback

Few people enjoy criticism, yet Master presenters are always hungry for ways to improve. Whenever you give a presentation, make it a continual learning process, otherwise you'll keep making the same mistakes.

One way to collect opinions is to ask your audience point blank: 'Did you get what you want?' Or you could hand everyone an evaluation form, which asks people to tell you what worked and what didn't, what they liked most and least, and so on.

'We do a lot of debriefing – talking to people after we've done the tenders to find out whether we've won or lost,' says Alex Gethin of KPMG. 'We always try to go out and interview the decision makers, once the result has come in.'

For example, once the result of a presentation is known, KPMG will send someone independent of the bid team to uncover the lessons to be learnt. For a major bid the de-brief may be done by someone who is entirely external to KPMG.

Try to arrange for regular presentation criticism from friends and colleagues. First, though, give yourself some feedback – what do you think went well, what didn't and why? What have you learned from the recent event? Once you have arrived at your own conclusions you can compare them with what other people tell you.

Debriefing questions

★ What went really well or badly?
★ What had impact?
★ What was memorable?
★ What was confusing or unclear?
★ Where did I gain or lose the audience's attention or interest?
★ What did I do that annoyed, irritated or distracted?
★ How did I come across?
★ How would you describe my manner and tone?
★ Did I have vocal richness and variety?
★ Did I seem well prepared?
★ Could you hear everything I said?
★ Did all the visuals succeed?
★ Did I seem to care about what I said?
★ Was the length of my presentation OK – too long or short?
★ What would you say was the main point I was trying to convey?
★ Was I authoritative?
★ What suggestions can you make for improvement next time?

The knowledge of ourselves is a difficult study,
and we must be willing to borrow the eyes of
our enemies to assist the investigation.

HANNAH FARNHAM LEE, *THE LOG CABIN* (1844)

Be hungry for information about your performance. The more feedback you acquire, the easier it becomes to identify weaknesses and work on them. Likewise, you can focus on building on your strengths: are you assuming that one of your assets is your sense of humour? Test it out with friendly colleagues to see whether they agree.

feedback
observer

Obtaining personal feedback

★ Quiz members of your audience after a presentation
★ Ask colleagues to note down helpful comments
★ Issue questionnaires to your audience
★ Use video or audio recordings
★ Attend a presentation course
★ Get one-to-one coaching
★ Use a self-assessment log systematically to record impressions over time
★ Invite a presentation coach to attend your live performance
★ Ask a whole presentation team to share their views
★ Commission an independent person to research in depth

Top 10 Tips!

You are always the arbiter as to what is useful and what isn't. But, if there's unanimity of opinion that you would be more effective if you changed something about your appearance, manner or delivery, it's worth paying attention. As the Irish say, 'If two people tell you you're drunk – lie down!'

The unexamined life is not worth living.

SOCRATES (469–399BC), *APOLOGY*

⭐ *Follow-through seminars*

Seminars are a great way to follow through on the presentation, extending it in various ways by creating a more interactive experience. They continue to build relationships, they inform, stimulate, show you off, and re-enforce your message.

Occasionally, a seminar becomes a straight substitute for a formal presentation. For example, Maynard Leigh Associates runs an annual coaching seminar as a way of indirectly presenting to companies the benefits of our coaching service.

Seminars add value to the business relationship, acting as showcases and providing clients with a chance to network, to gain new ideas and further identify what their business

prospects want in the way of information, services, products or solutions.

Getting people to attend your business seminar is all about good marketing. It may take three or more 'hits' or contacts, before someone decides they will attend your session. Direct mail, personal phone calls and special enticements can all play a part in persuading people to attend.

For instance, when Maynard Leigh Associates ran three seminars in Bristol to drum up business there, we mailed and telephoned everyone twice. We also tempted them with a free copy of one of our books on presentations and communications. We presented on the three topics of Presentation, Inspiration and Transformation. Each session began around 12.30 and included a buffet lunch. We never made a sales pitch, instead merely showing people how we work and get results. It was a business presentation by another name. Within a few weeks we had contracts with two of the largest companies in the region.

Showcases are when you have the chance to show off, to demonstrate who you are and what you represent. It's a precious presentation opportunity and worth preparing for carefully.

A showcase tends to be a 'sell' situation, however well it's camouflaged. There's probably a greater element of entertainment than in a traditional business presentation. Ways to make the most of showcases are:

★ Discover how much time you can commandeer and stick to it
★ Discover who'll be there and their special interests
★ Put important messages and information at the start, not the end
★ Begin with a bang and end memorably
★ Offer follow-on material for when you finish
★ Get people involved early by doing something
★ When you spell out what you want to happen next avoid making it into a big 'sell'

Attractive business seminars

★ Clarify exactly what's in it for those attending
★ Identify when would be the best time for people to come
★ Determine precisely who you most want to come
★ Get creative – find an amusing, eye-catching, memorable way of inviting people
★ Choose a simple memorable message for the event
★ Find a way to give an experience of your service or product
★ Rehearse so you are confident and able to focus on the audience
★ Get people talking in groups about issues you have raised and to identify questions they want to pose
★ Send a thank you for attending
★ Call people to ask for feedback on how you could do it better next time

People seem to enjoy things more when they know a lot of other people have been left out of the pleasure.

RUSSELL BAKER, *NEW YORK TIMES* (1967)

Lessons from the Masters

R esearch into what the Masters do to produce outstandingly successful presentations has important lessons for
both individuals and organisations. Whether making
internal presentations, talking at conferences, addressing
groups of employees or making a sales pitch, their
experiences offer useful guidelines for most sorts of
business presentations.

ACTION

1 **Invest heavily in understanding and, if possible,
   contacting the potential audience.** The Master
   business presenter turns out to be extraordinarily persistent
   about knowing the audience and discovering what people
   need to hear. Meeting some or all members of the actual
   audience is also a high priority.
2 **Create a ruthlessly honest review situation.** The Masters
   jealously guard their time and resources, systematically
   assessing the desirability of each potential presentation. They
   are equally analytical about the effectiveness of each presentation: how it went and why. The desire for constant improvement drives the Masters to seek out and accept tough
   feedback using a variety of means, including third-party
   neutral observers.
3 **In a team presentation, invest significant time ensuring the
   group works together seamlessly.** Driven hard by the Master
   presenters, great presenting teams strive to integrate their
   performance, including how to handle different possible
   scenarios. Most successful ones consist of people whose
   skills complement each other and who build a performance
   around their respective strengths.
4 **Disaster plan.** Master presenters can cope with just about

any contingency arising before, during or after the actual presentation. Even the most resourced and rehearsed presentation can go seriously wrong but what matters is knowing how to handle the worst-case scenarios.

5 **Struggle hard to be different.** In many cases competitors or rival presenters will be trying to be different too. So the presentation Masters often take considerable risks to create a unique angle or approach that sets their performances apart.

6 **Turn question-and-answer sessions into a presentation triumph.** This is where many of the Master presenters shine, revelling in the opportunities that an unstructured situation presents to re-enforce their message. Presentation Masters get tough critics to view the presentation before it happens and to highlight areas where difficult questions could arise.

7 **Be willing and able to instantly change the entire presentation.** Presentation Masters are highly adaptable. They are keen observers of the audience and are constantly evaluating whether what they are delivering is hitting home. It takes courage and nerve to abandon a well-rehearsed presentation at the last minute, but the Masters do it without hesitation whenever they see that an audience wants something different from what was planned.

8 **Bring it alive.** The Masters make a feature of introducing examples, objects, samples, stories, metaphors, real people such as existing satisfied clients to demonstrate credibility. The aim is to involve the audience by complementing the basic ideas with powerful images and experiences.

ACTION

9 **Use visuals sparingly.** The Masters usually concentrate on a few visuals to deliver major impact. They know that they are the presentation, not pictures on a screen or a report. They therefore select visuals extremely carefully to enhance their performance.

10 **Keep it short. Master presenters always leave you wanting more.** They know that you don't need to be lengthy to be effective, since audiences have an extremely brief attention span. A typical business presentation will last around twenty minutes.

11 **Know what action you want the audience to take.** The Masters follow a definite ground plan for deciding what should happen next, spelling it out clearly to the audience.

12 **Follow up the presentation.** Nothing is left to chance by the

presentation Masters. Once the immediate performance is over, they devise ingenious ways to stay in touch with some or all of the audience.

13 **Be fully present in the moment.** When the Masters present, their attention is entirely on the situation, away from themselves and completely on those listening. Nothing is allowed to distract them from building a relationship with their audience.

14 **Invest passion and energy in your performance.** What separates the Masters from the run of the mill is the extent to which they are willing to share their emotions, show they find the experience rewarding and energise both themselves and the audience.

15 **Treat everyone in the audience with respect.** No matter how irritating the questions, or annoying the individual, the Master presenters convey a deep sense of respect for their audience, which is consequently reciprocated.

If giving a terrific business presentation were easy we'd all do it, nor would we need any help. The reality, of course, is different. It takes practice and a commitment to develop continually. Most of all, it means having a go, getting out there and performing – learning by doing. So keep practising and . . .

Good luck!

A–Z

A

Ability (see main body of text on pages 2–3)

Knowing what you cannot do is more important than knowing what you can do. In fact that's good taste.

LUCILLE BALL (1911–89) US ACTRESS.

Accent (see also PRONUNCIATION)

Presidents Lyndon Johnson and Carter both had strong Southern accents and people paid more rather than less attention to what they were saying. Despite his strong German lilt, few would presume to ignore Dr Kissinger.

Business presenters often feel a pressure to tame their accents. There is a curious belief that a standard form of speech – 'mid Atlantic' – is essential, being neither too American nor too English. It is far more important that you are fully understood, articulating clearly, rather than adopting a homogenised, all-purpose accent:

★ Never apologise for a regional or 'foreign' accent
★ Be proud of your difference
★ Accents give a presentation colour and help bring it to life
★ Your accent is the authentic you
★ If talking to a non-English-speaking audience, check with a local national that your pronunciation of a word won't cause a major misunderstanding

An accent can give you a positive advantage with an audience, making you more memorable; for example, an American-born trainer working for Maynard Leigh Associates uses 'y'all', which makes people smile. Some accents even sound more reliable: a Scottish accent is regarded by many as conveying reliability.

*I can do Irish, Welsh, Manchester, Liverpool, Birmingham,
Cockney and New York Jewish lesbian.*

JULIE WALTERS, BRITISH ACTRESS

Acting (see also PRESENCE)

The art of acting consists in keeping people from coughing.

RALPH RICHARDSON (1902–83), BRITISH ACTOR

Acting is the art of being yourself in public. To some degree great
business presenters are actors. They are concerned with gaining,
holding and affecting their audience emotionally in some way.
You don't need to become an actor, though, to present well.

Acting does not mean trying to be something you are not. It
is about the actor's skill of building a relationship with your
audience. Those skills are learnable and include:

★ Clarity of intention
★ Systematic warm-ups before a performance
★ Intense focus on the audience, rather than yourself
★ High energy when delivering
★ Commitment to communicate well
★ Readiness constantly to learn
★ Willingness to rehearse, rehearse, rehearse
★ Staying open to frank feedback
★ Respect for the audience
★ Ability to vary the delivery to make it interesting

All these are the result of practice. Now is the time to start.

Active voice

The grammatical 'active voice' gives your communication a sense
of immediacy. For example, this sentence uses the passive voice.

★ A report is being written by John Jones
  While this sentence uses the active voice:
★ John Jones is writing a report

To create active sentences place 'the doer', or the person doing
the action in the sentence, before its verb. Here are some
examples with the active verbs underlined:

★ The Chancellor <u>intends</u> the economy to grow
★ I <u>travelled</u> to America
★ Companies <u>are</u> cutting costs
★ He <u>needs</u> clear feedback

If you are starting your presentation by writing out a full script, check for passive sentences using your word processor.

★ Active verbs generally sound better than the passive version

Ad libs (see main body of text on page 85)

When you know your text, that's when you can improvise.
JODIE FOSTER, ACTRESS

Affirmations

Affirmations are a way of reminding yourself about your presenting power. They are phrases, words and names that help create confidence by counteracting any natural tendency towards negativity or a sense that you might fail.

Affirmations may seem close to prayers, yet they needn't be particularly spiritual. Simply by constantly repeating phrases to ourselves we help to 're-programme' our brain into accepting that we can influence outcomes positively.

Choose an affirmation with which you feel totally comfortable, one you are happy to repeat to yourself on many occasions. Assume the presentation is already happening and the affirmation applies to it. Examples might be:

★ 'My presentation is an outstanding success'
★ 'The audience absolutely loves my performance'
★ 'I am doing brilliantly'
★ 'I am a terrific presenter'
★ 'Everyone enjoys my delivery'
★ 'I am having a huge impact'
★ 'I am totally confident about my performance'
★ 'There is no reason why I cannot be brilliant'

It helps to imagine someone you admire saying the affirmations to you. Even if you have never met them, picture them talking to you, saying something really encouraging about your actual performance.

Close your eyes and do some relaxation exercises. First say the affirmation out loud, so you hear the words and gain a feel for them. Second, keep repeating your affirmations throughout the day, as many times as possible and last thing at night.

★ Affirmations have a slow, yet cumulative effect

Agenda (see Route Map, in main body of text on page 23)

Some people in a business presentation will only feel comfortable sitting through it if you have first set out an agenda – the route map for where you are taking them. You may need also to clarify how long you are going to take, when there's going to be a break, how you'll handle questions and so on.

Since this can take up precious time during the actual presentation it often pays to send a brief outline of what will happen in advance.

Aggression (see also ANGER)

Never go to bed mad. Stay up and fight.

PHYLLIS DILLER

Though naked aggression seldom plays well in business presentations, it may work when talking to colleagues and employees about dealing with the competition. Generally, as a presenting style, aggression quickly becomes tedious.

Aims (see main body of text on page 5)

The secret of success is constancy of purpose.

BENJAMIN DISRAELI, SPEECH, 1870

Alcohol

The choice is whether you start sober and end drunk, or start drunk and end sober. The former is much better, both for the health of the speaker and for the effect on the audience.

OSWALD MOSLEY, BRITISH FASCIST LEADER

You don't drink before driving for the same reason that you avoid drinking before a presentation. No one ever ruined a presentation through drinking water. You need all your senses fully functioning, so avoid alcohol before you enter the limelight, or while in it. You need to be fully alert.

★ It takes about an hour for the body to absorb the alcohol from any kind of drink

While you can prevent yourself drinking too much before an important business presentation, what about the audience? Plan your appearance so as to minimise the chances of your audience arriving hung-over. For example, if you are presenting to the board and know that they have a tendency to imbibe, try to arrange your appearance early in the morning.

Alcohol acts as a sedative and dulls the mind, so people don't process information properly. Arrange only light wine or non-alcoholic drinks during long breaks in a lengthy presentation. Serve plenty of snacks with high-fat, protein and starch contents like cheese crackers as these help reduce the impact of alcohol.

Drinking alcohol also makes people thirsty, so ensure there are plenty of tall cool glasses of water with limes or slices of lemon. Often people will grab these instead of the alcohol. If you detect that your audience is suffering the effects of alcohol:

★ Cut short your presentation
★ Start your presentation later in the day
★ Don't try to involve people interactively too much

Alertness (see PRESENCE in main body of text on page 73)

It was if I had worked for years on the wrong side of a tapestry, learning accurately all its lines and figures, yet always missing its colour and sheen.
ANN LOUISE STRONG, *I CHANGE WORLDS* (1935)

Amnesia (see MEMORY in body of text on page 117)

I never forget a face, but in your case I'll make an exception.
GROUCHO MARX

Analogy (see also METAPHORS, IMAGERY, SIMILES)
This is a figure of speech that helps bring your arguments to life. Analogies are 'as if' stories. They substitute powerful imagery for what might otherwise be an uninteresting message.

For example, suppose you are explaining how you see an organisation coping with change, you might say that you feel it resembles a 'motor cyclist leaning into the curves'. Of course, the organisation isn't a motor cyclist, but the phrase is a useful analogy that enlivens your argument.

Anecdotes (see HUMOUR in main body of text on pages 83–87)

Humour is by far the most significant activity of the human brain.
EDWARD DE BONO

If you're talking about team work you could expound at length on how teams usually perform better than individuals. Or you could tell the story of the Canadian geese which fly 70% longer when they fly in formation rather than individually.

Anecdotes are a great way of enlivening a business presentation. These really work when they come from the heart and your own life experience.

Peppering a business presentation with anecdotes, though, can be distracting, especially if every member of a presenting team does it. Use anecdotes strategically to make a crucial point, alter the atmosphere, perhaps to reduce tension, or give a complex issue more colour.

Anger

> *Anger is loaded with information and energy.*
> ANDRE LORDE, 'THE USES OF ANGER' (1981)

Few business presentations gain from a great show of anger. It is not that there is no place for it, only that it seldom works as a way of involving an audience and building a relationship.

Containing your anger during a presentation can be vital to success. For example, if you are rigorously questioned and people seem to be challenging your word, don't take it personally. Treat all such attacks as merely a search for greater clarity.

If you find yourself becoming angry during a presentation either call a break or change the dynamic. For instance, get people talking about the issue in groups.

Animation (see also VIDEO, MULTIMEDIA and POWERPOINT)

Animation is increasingly popular in business presentations. In some companies if you don't have it you are regarded as old-fashioned. Good animation grabs an audience's attention but only if it really supports your performance.

Too often, animation gets in the way of the presenter coming across with the basic message and is a distraction.

You can add animation to your visuals in numerous ways, such as using clips within programmes such as PowerPoint and by using ordinary video material including film.

★ Use animation sparingly
★ Choose relevant items
★ Keep the amount of animation short
★ If you have to explain what the animation is about it is isn't working
★ Know what you'll do if the technology fails

Anxiety (see NERVES in main body of text on pages 71–73)

I have a new philosophy.
I'm only going to dread one day at a time.

CHARLES SCHULTZ, PEANUTS CARTOON

Aphorism (see QUOTATIONS)

The aphorisms of one generation become the clichés of the next.

LILLIAN DAY, *NINON* (1957)

Appearance (see IMAGE)

You've no idea how much it costs to make a person look this cheap.

DOLLY PARTON, *MS* (1979)

Applause

Will the people in the cheaper seats clap your hands?
All the rest of you, if you'll just rattle your jewellery.

JOHN LENNON

Applause in business presentations tends to be rare, unless you are talking to a conference. Unlike an actor, as a business presenter applause usually isn't your goal. If it does happen,

★ Accept it graciously
★ Express your thanks aloud
★ Don't hog the limelight; if part of a presenting team, point to the others
★ Avoid looking smug

If you are expecting applause and it doesn't happen what do you do – slink away in shame, bury your head in your arms or look distraught? A lack of applause sometimes happens only because an audience is unsure whether it is meant to show appreciation or that you really have finished. If you expect applause, make it clear to everyone that you have reached the end.

In some countries, silence is the equivalent of a standing ovation.

Apprehension (see NERVES in main body of text on pages 71–73)

Don't panic. It's the first helpful or intelligible thing anybody's said to me all day.

DOUGLAS ADAMS, *THE HITCHHIKER'S GUIDE TO THE GALAXY* (1979)

Argument (see main body of text on pages 28–31)

Her arguments are like elephants. They squash you flat.

RUMER GODDEN, *THE BATTLE AT THE VILLA FIORITA* (1963)

Arriving (see main body of text on pages 66–9)

Success is 95% turning up.

WOODY ALLEN

Asleep (see ATTENTION)

No matter what time it is, wake me,
even if it's in the middle of a cabinet meeting.

RONALD REAGAN, US PRESIDENT, 1984

Attention (see also main body of text on page 81)

You are confidently in your stride when you notice people asleep. Maybe even snoring! This is certainly telling you something about your presentation, even if they have been up the whole night partying or have just flown in from another continent.

Use the new information to

★ Wake yourself up
★ Wake up the audience
★ Ask if people are finding the room stuffy
★ Detail someone to open a window
★ Call a five-minute comfort break
★ Start putting more energy into your presentation
★ Walk around the room
★ Change the pace of your presentation
★ Make a sudden noise
★ Loudly ask the audience a question, without waiting for an answer
★ Make a joke about the need to keep people awake – ring a bell, twirl a rattle, bang a drum
★ Invite the audience to stand up for a group stretch, or a quick jog around the block

Research on an audience's attention span suggests that it starts high, falls slowly in the first ten minutes and rapidly reaches its lowest point after about thirty minutes. If you announce that you are nearing the end then the attention level starts rising steeply again.

The implications are:

★ A presentation of twenty-five to thirty minutes will maximise attention

★ Communicate your most important points early in the presentation

★ After the first ten minutes it really matters how you vary tone, voice and content to retain interest

★ Signal the approaching end, for example by saying 'and finally' and mean it

> *Attention is a silent and perpetual flattery.*
> ANN-SOPHIE SWETCHINE, *COUNT DE FALOUX* (1869)

Audience (see main body of text on page 4, 123)

> *There is no director who can direct you like an audience.*
> FANNY BRICE, *THE FABULOUS FANNY* (1952)

Audience Size

This affects how you approach the presentation.

★ 1–10 people: Establish relationships rapidly with an informal approach, try to engage each person and make eye contact, occasionally use their names during the presentation

★ 10–30 people: You need a more formal approach. Talk standing up, use large easy-to-read visual aids, be well prepared for questions and how you will handle these

★ 30–100 people: Hard to approach and build relationships with so many, so be meticulously well prepared; presentation aids should be faultless and well rehearsed, consider using a microphone

★ 100+: This is more like theatre: plan for issues such as décor, lighting, large-scale and possibly hi-tech visual aids, have a formalised way of dealing with questions

Audio tapes – for rehearsal (see also REHEARSAL, VIDEO)

Audio tapes can be a useful way of rehearsing your presentation. Record it while you practise the entire delivery. Listen to results critically. Does it excite you? Are you bored at any point? What needs to change?

Give the tape to family members or work colleagues and ask for their feedback.

As you refine the presentation, record it again for wasteful

phrases and excess verbiage. This also helps you memorise the contents. You won't need to know everything word for word. Play the tape in the shower, when you are in bed, in the car, on the way to the final performance.

Audio tapes – for the audience

The drawback of using audio in a business presentation is that people have nothing to look at while they are listening. If possible, back up the use of sound with some kind of visual, which does not need to change while the tape is playing.

★ Ensure the audio contents really enhance your presentation
★ Check the tape is rewound and at its starting point
★ Adjust the volume in advance so that all participants can hear
★ Use a high-quality machine to avoid distortion
★ Explain the purpose of the tape and identify the speaker(s) on it
★ Carry a back-up in case of failure
★ Keep the playback short, around a maximum of two or three minutes

Audio-visual (see EQUIPMENT)

Authority (see PRESENCE, in main body of text on page 73)

I don't mind how much my ministers talk –
as long as they do what I say.
MARGARET THATCHER, *THE TIMES* (1987)

B

Bang (see also OPENERS in main body of text on pages 75–77)

Just because it's a business presentation doesn't mean you shouldn't aim to start with a bang. Not literally a sudden sound, though that too can sometimes work. Choose something that grabs the audience's immediate attention, otherwise it may soon begin to wander. Your bang can be:

★ How you look
★ A provocative statement
★ A dramatic silence
★ An important announcement
★ A humorous anecdote – not necessarily a joke

★ Some kind of audience participation such as an instant survey with a show of hands

★ An audio-visual hook, such as a slide, video, audio sound and so on

★ An object such as a prop, a model or some other physical item

★ An action such as a demonstration, a quotation, a mime, a conjuring trick, the entry of someone or something unexpected

Closing bangs leave the listener with a clear message and could be based on any of the above.

Barrack (see INTERRUPTIONS)

> *Interruption is a form of contempt.*
> LUCILLE KALLEN, INTRODUCING C. B. GREENFIELD, 1979

Bathroom (see TOILET)

Psychiatry's chief contribution to philosophy is the discovery that the toilet is the seat of the soul.
ALEXANDER CHASE, *PERSPECTIVES* (1966)

Beard (see IMAGE in main body of text on pages 88–96)

You know it's hard to hear what a bearded man is saying. He can't speak above a whisker.
WOLF J. MANKOWITZ

Beginning (see OPENERS in main body of text on pages 75–77)

> *Beginnings are apt to be shadowy.*
> RACHEL CARSON, *THE SEA AROUND US* (1950)

Bluff (see also QUESTIONS in main body of text on pages 125–129)

People always overdo the matter when they attempt deception.
THOMAS WOLFE, *THOMAS WOLFE'S LETTERS TO HIS MOTHER* (1943)

Bluff is the last resort of the unprepared presenter and seldom works. Audiences have an infallible mechanism for detecting a cover-up. Honesty is always a powerful card to play in situations where you are unsure or don't know the right response.

Body Language (see main body of text on pages 97–100)

Books (see also References)

Books are good enough in their own way, but they are a mighty bloodless substitute for life.

ROBERT LOUIS STEVENSON, SCOTTISH WRITER

Books on giving presentations are a rich mine of stories, tips and techniques. Followed wisely, they can enhance your own performance. But you cannot become a brilliant business presenter just by reading, any more than you can learn to ride a bicycle that way. It's practice that counts, plus honest feedback.

From the scores of 'how to present' books there are rather fewer focused just on business presentations. However, there is a growing amount of easily accessible material on the Internet. Additional source books abound on quotes, apt comparisons, euphemisms, clichés, synonyms, English usage, slang, jokes and so on.

Books you might find useful include:

★ *Wooing and Winning Business*, Asher, Sping and Chambers, Wicke, John Wiley (1997, ISBN 0-471-25370-7)

★ *Making the Most of the Media*, Barratt, Michael, Kogan Page (1996, ISBN 0-7494-20375 5)

★ *Say it with Power and Confidence*, Collins, Patrick J., Prentice Hall, (1998, ISBN 0-13-614280-X)

★ *The New Strategic Selling, Heiman*, Stephen E. et al, Kogan Page (1998 edition)

★ *The Complete Idiot's Guide to Successful Business Presentations*, Kroeger, Lin, Alpha Books (1997, ISBN 0-02-861748-7)

★ *The Perfect Presentation* Leigh, Andrew and Maynard, Michael, Arrow Books (1993, ISBN 0-7126-5536-0)

★ *The Image factor: A guide to Effective Self Presentation for Career Enhancement*, Sampson, Eleri (second edition) Kogan Page (1996, ISBN 0-7494-2101-0)

★ *Sharp Guide to Presentations: The Complete Guide to Audio Visual and Video Presentations* (1994)

★ *What to Say When . . . You're Dying on the Platform*, Walters, Lilly, McGraw Hill Inc. (1995, ISBN 0-07-068039-6)

You can sometimes make quite an impact during a business presentation by handing out copies of a book, especially if it's one you've written. Generally, though, avoid asking your audience to delve into books while you are presenting. This

disrupts the flow and takes away attention from you and your message.

Boredom (see also ATTENTION and PASSION)

You can kill, you can maim people, but to be boring is truly a sin. And God will punish you for it.

BURT REYNOLDS, FILM ACTOR

Few presenters want to be like American ex-president George Bush who asked plaintively: 'What's wrong with being a boring kind of guy?' Boring an audience of fifty people in a ten-minute presentation means you have wasted the equivalent of eight hours of people's time. Or, putting it slightly differently, you have bored the equivalent of one person for a whole day.

Business presentations generally don't have to be showy entertainment but they do need to avoid boring the audience.

Because most of us are convinced we are fascinating talkers we can easily fail to see the obvious signs that the audience has lost interest. These include:

★ Coughing
★ Shuffling feet
★ Talking to each other
★ Not looking at you
★ Eyes closed
★ People leaving
★ Rustling papers
★ Yawning
★ Slumping in chairs
★ Rummaging in briefcase
★ Head in hands
★ Doodling
★ Fiddling with pens, glasses, etc.

The secret of never boring your audience is not being bored yourself. If you believe that what you are saying is dull, your audience will certainly agree with you. Your own disinterest instantly communicates and since the signs are involuntary body language, they are almost impossible to hide.

Selectivity is an important way to avoid losing an audience's attention. Make your material strictly relevant to your particular audience. As Voltaire pointed out back in the nineteenth century, the secret of being a bore is to tell everything. Experienced speakers who worry about being boring work extra hard to

ensure that they interest both themselves and the audience:

★ If giving a business presentation seems boring – hand over to someone else
★ Find at least one part of the presentation about which you feel strongly and use it to focus your thoughts and sharpen your performancc
★ Show your passion and commitment to conveying the basic message
★ Don't speak continuously, introduce plenty of breaks and pauses
★ Avoid reading your presentation verbatim from a script
★ Vary your voice to avoid a monotone
★ Speak without mumbling
★ Stick to simple words and phrases
★ Use lively visual aids
★ Practise till you eliminate hesitancy
★ Don't ramble, stick to the point

I don't mind people looking at their watches when I'm speaking, but I strongly object when they start shaking them to make certain they are still going.

LORD BIRKETT, BRITISH HIGH COURT JUDGE

Bravo (see Applause)

I want to thank you for stopping the applause. It is impossible for me to look humble for any period of time.

HENRY KISSINGER

Breaks

Anything over half an hour is a lengthy business presentation. Some people may be anxiously wanting to leave. The longer you intend speaking the more necessary it is to allow them short breaks to:

★ Visit the toilet
★ Smoke
★ Process the information
★ Discuss your message
★ Stretch
★ Get some fresh air
★ Have a coffee
★ Make an urgent phone call
★ Check their e-mail

If you're addressing a conference or a large number of employees arrange for help with encouraging people to get back to their seats on time. You could have a whistle, a musical chime, or some other loud instrument or signal that it's time to return. Set clear expectations about the nature of the break. Explain:

★ How long it will be
★ When you will restart
★ You'd like everyone back on time

Breathing (see also NERVES in main body of text on pages 71–73)

Proper breathing reduces nerves and helps project the voice.

★ When you are about to present – stop and breathe
★ Breathing out is just as important as breathing in
★ Take a deep breath, without heaving your chest or raising your shoulders
★ Gently let out the air through slightly open lips, as if blowing a candle to make it just flicker

While you are breathing at the start of your performance look around at the audience in a friendly, interested way. Nod at people you know and smile; meanwhile keep breathing. Soon you will be ready to begin your presentation.

Measured breathing helps you handle tricky situations, such as an aggressive member of the audience, or an awkward question. When you take time to breathe gently you feel more able to assess the situation and consider your response.

Brevity (see main body of text on page 140)

> *To be brief is almost a condition of being inspired.*
> GEORGE SANTAYANA, *LITTLE ESSAYS* (1920)

Briefing

In the mid-1990s an industrial survey asked managers to nominate the most effective way of communicating with employees. Over half (57%) chose team briefings.

Briefings for teams, colleagues or others are a special form of business presentation but they too demand the usual time for preparation.

★ Good briefers make it a dialogue not a monologue
★ Decide the main headline you want them to remember

★ Start with an overview of the whole message
★ Early on, explain the purpose of your briefing
★ This is not a chance to chastise people
★ Reduce the message to no more than seven points
★ Explain what will happen next
★ Restrict the presentation to half or two-thirds of the time, the rest is for allowing a break and for people to start talking
★ Start and finish on time
★ Take careful notes of what people say

Builds (see VISUALS in main body of text on pages 40–48)

Builds progressively reveal visual information, rather than showing the whole story at once. Presenters keen on electronic presentations systems usually love builds since the technology can create amazingly subtle and visually attractive effects.

Text flies in at angles, pictures drop into place as each point is made, fade-ins and fade-outs and wipe effects abound. As so many other people are now using these kind of builds shouldn't you perhaps be doing something entirely different?

Bullets (see also VISUALS in main body of text on pages 40–48)

These are the balls, stars and boxes that mark off each item of text instead of presenting the material in lists. The trouble with bullets is that there are usually too many of them – they can quickly kill off a business presentation. Nobody ever lost a business deal because they didn't have enough bullet points.

Bullet points are not visuals. There is no substitute for a picture, or a graphic presentation.

Butterflies (see NERVES in main body of text on pages 71–73)

Everyone has butterflies.
It's the professional who gets them to fly in formation.
TOMMY COOPER, COMEDIAN

C

Cadence (see VOICE in main body of text on page 70)

Cadence is a mixture of changing the pitch of your voice and the rhythm you inject into your speaking. Outstanding public speakers like the late Lord Birkett have extraordinary cadence.

THE ULTIMATE · BUSINESS · PRESENTATION BOOK

They use it like a musical instrument to give their sound an attractive, almost mesmeric quality.

Changing the pitch of your voice is essential in any business presentation. It helps inject new energy into what you say and provides variety for the audience.

To practise altering the cadence of your voice, first try humming a set of scales gently, listening to how each part varies from the next. Now say a short sentence that follows the same 'tune'. Then do it in reverse. This is an exaggerated version of how cadence is used in speaking to give the sound more variety.

A good presentation coach can provide you with help in how to use cadence.

Caffeine

A cup of coffee sounds just right before a presentation and if it's part of your routine, enjoy it. Caffeine, though, can

★ Make you twitchy
★ Act as a diuretic, draining water from the body, leaving your mouth dry and making you need toilet facilities right in the middle of your performance
★ Increase your heartbeat and sometimes blood pressure, creating the same effect as nerves, making you speed up and be less articulate

Before performing minimise your caffeine intake.

Calm (see Nerves in main body of text on pages 71–73)

> *There is no joy, but calm.*
> ALFRED LORD TENNYSON, *THE LOTUS EATERS* (1842)

Cartoons (see Visuals in main body of text on pages 40–48)

Cartoons drawings and figures, whether still or animated, enliven a presentation and can effectively re-enforce your key messages. You can find a rich source of cartoon figures in the better graphics packages, such as Corel Draw. You can even animate them, adding your own backgrounds, sets and props.

To make the best use of cartoons ensure they

★ Are relevant
★ Integrate into your material
★ Move the presentation on in some way
★ Look professional

★ Support the points you are making
★ Can be readily understood – if you have to explain them they've failed

Avoid adding lots of distracting, tacky, aggravating figures that do little to enhance the message. Where possible, use original cartoons rather than obviously clip art ones.

It can be tempting to use a cartoon just to liven things up even when it is not entirely appropriate. Some business presentations, for example, may appear unduly flippant by using too many cartoons.

Caterers (see Interruptions in main body of text on pages 120–1)

Everything you see I owe to spaghetti.
SOPHIA LOREN IN JOHN ROBERT COLOMBO, *POPCORN IN PARADISE* (1979)

Celebrity speaking

Want to become a celebrity business speaker? It's not as difficult as you think. Celebrity speakers differ from 'experts', though may be experts in their own right. While people ask experts to speak because of their specialist knowledge alone, they invite celebrities to present because of who they are.

Celebrity speakers are often used to bolster a business presentation by adding additional credibility or interest. If you are a celebrity speaker in your own right this can usually only enhance your formal business presentations, for example, if you have become a well-known industry spokesperson.

Here are some tips on how to get known as a celebrity speaker adapted from the experience of a member and past president of the US National Speakers Association.

Rise above your industry
Hard work will ensure that you know your own industry well and may allow you to talk regularly about it to the media and at conferences. To become a celebrity speaker, though, you have to rise above the industry, providing it with information and opinions that it won't receive from anywhere else. Rather than become the 'industry expert', aim to stay detached. That way people will see you as 'bigger' than the industry and therefore beyond the role of narrow specialist.

Raise your profile
You need to get into print, with books, articles and releases about

what you have said elsewhere. You also have to be seen and heard on platforms and programmes. Yet achieving this means you require a profile in the first place, a sort of Catch 22. Why otherwise should a magazine, for instance, want your stuff? The solution is to push material out continually with ruthless persistence, regardless of setbacks.

For example, when you do speak, record it, get it transcribed and commission a freelancer to write two articles from it. Then fax them to the industry. The articles have to be hot and real issues.

Own the language

The celebrities in any industry own and hone their own terminology. If you call it what everybody else does, you won't control it. The authors of 're-engineering', for example, literally invented the phrase so they could 'own' the language.

Once you have grabbed possession of some idea people begin associating it with you.

Use live issues

Draw on contemporary themes in society to enliven and title your material. If the world is worrying about recession then your output has to reflect that in your issues and subject titles. If the biggest movie hit is about a world plague, incorporate the idea somehow into your material.

Get help

You may be a blindingly fast writer but to be a celebrity speaker you probably can't do everything yourself. Hire a freelancer to help you extend your reach. Work to a regular schedule, with the freelancer coming into your office to produce articles that you mail regularly to the press. Once you find publications, conferences and other media that like you, look for similar ones to target.

Leverage it

If you present to a pharmaceutical industry conference, immediately afterwards send information to other relevant associations. Send a note to each association before you speak, then within two days follow it up with an article written from your speech. That gives you momentum. It heightens your importance. Create visibility around an event.

Systematically bombard

Never let them forget you exist. Consider targeting two dozen speaker organisations, two dozen major companies and the same number of associations close to your industry. Keep reminding them of who you are and what you talk about.

Using e-mail, faxes and other means, every few weeks contact half a dozen people from each of these places so they can't forget you. Yes, you'll make a nuisance of yourself, but guess whom they will turn to when they do need help and a speaker?

Focus yet extend your reach

Keep extending your reach in a focused, targeted way. For example, choose one topic you intend speaking on that you like and where you think you can add value. Limit your exposure so that you do not become narrowly concentrated on one organisation.

Use market hit strategy

Marketeers know the importance of a series of hits before they start making an impression and eventually a sale. A speaking engagement is only one hit. How can you reach that audience both before and after the engagement? Tell the industry about your upcoming speaking engagement? A speaking engagement is just the start of a relationship. What else could you do? Can you get the editor of a trade publication to sit down and interview you when the event is over? Can you provide something to that publication every week or every month?

Become an industry spokesperson

Stay close to major clients and visit their premises and make contact with top people when on site. You'll pick up ideas and issues and contacts that will enable you to speak about the industry in a really informed way. This becomes self-sustaining – people know of you, welcoming your visits. The more you speak and comment, the more you collect in the way of feedback and the ability to give out more opinions.

Chairs (see also VENUE)

Where will people sit during your presentation? Chair arrangement seems an innocuous issue till one realises this can radically affect how you interact with your audience. For example, your relationship with the audience will be very different if you remove tables and have people sitting in a circle.

Although in many cases you are stuck with an existing seating arrangement, which seems as though it cannot be altered, it can be surprisingly easy to make changes by explaining your particular presentation requirements.

When you can influence the seating arrangements consider

★ The aims of your presentation

★ Size of audience
★ Sight lines that could affect others such as pillars, other furniture, window alcoves
★ Whether you want people to work in groups and if so of what size
★ Different shaped chair arrangements offer you different audience opportunities:

U-shaped

pros: with two ends you gain flexibility to relate to either
cons: slightly formal and can create feeling of 'us' and 'them'

Circle

pros: informal and everyone sees each other
cons: unsuitable for really large groups and makes it hard for you retain sufficient control

Semi circle

pros: encourages general participation
cons: you either have to join the people sitting and present from there, which may be tricky, or place yourself in the centre and face a wide spread of people to contact

Theatre style

pros: puts you firmly on stage, up front
cons: formal, obstructs audience rapport, suggests a lecture or teacher

V-shaped tier

pros: audience can see more of each other
cons: can be hard to handle well as a presenter, as people at the back may be hidden or partially obscured

Clustered in groups

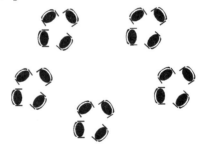

pros: good for audience participation and discussion
cons: may encourage groups to talk over the speaker, some people may have to adjust chairs to see you

Fish bowl

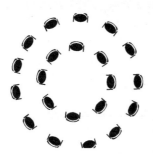

pros: you are high profile in the middle of the circle and everyone can see you
cons: you are completely surrounded and a presentation is hard to handle this way as you always have your back to someone

Check whether the audience's chairs are comfortable and silent. You don't want to talk over creaking sounds from all over the room.

Challenges (see also QUESTIONS in main body of text on pages 125–129)

Challenges can arrive at any time during a presentation. While pitching for new business you may be stopped in your tracks with a direct challenge. You need to be well prepared and know how to deal with most likely confrontations. Audience challenges can take the form of direct observations:

★ 'I absolutely disagree with that statement'
★ 'You've got your facts wrong'
★ 'This doesn't add up'
★ 'Our shareholders won't stand for that'

Or they may arrive in the guise of questions such as:

★ 'How do you justify that?'
★ 'What evidence do you have to support that claim?'
★ 'Why weren't we consulted on your suggestion?'
★ 'Isn't there another way of looking at this?'
★ 'How do you know sales will hit that level by June?'

People may challenge because they genuinely want enlightenment or because they want to sound good in front of others, or show they have power.
   Tips for handling challenges are:

★ Acknowledge the challenge

★ Listen carefully to the person and don't interrupt
★ Look the person straight in the eye
★ Pause and take time to think
★ Welcome the challenge, make the person look good
★ Treat the challenge as another chance to drive home your message
★ Where necessary, ask for help from the audience
★ Give a straight, sincere answer

Charge (see also Fees)

If some one outside your organisation approaches you to give a business presentation at a conference ask: 'Is there a fee?' Even if you decide not to charge, this at least shows you value your ability. Anyone offended by the question probably shouldn't be seeking speakers in the first place.

Charisma (see also Presence in main body of text on page 73)

It has very little to do with looks and nothing at all to do with youth . . . it's an expression in the eyes, or an aura of being in control, and responsible, or something easy and powerful in the stance, or who knows.
LUCILLE KALLEN, INTRODUCING C. B. GREENFIELD, 1979

Ronald Reagan had it, George Bush didn't. Charisma is that indefinable something for which every speaker yearns. If you could learn it instantly you wouldn't be wondering about it now.

Charisma is really a presence, an aura of great charm and consequently it often inspires. You cannot bottle charisma but the mystery is not quite so deep or out of reach as it may seem. Ways to develop your charisma for presentations include:

★ Be really relaxed and enjoy delivering your presentation
★ Be utterly yourself
★ Be totally physically and mentally 'present'
★ Be willing actively to use your personality
★ Be prepared to be different, surprising or even outrageous

Charm (see Presence in main body of text on page 73)

Charm is a cunning self-forgetfulness.
CHRISTINA STEAD, *HOUSE OF NATIONS* (1938)

Charts (see Visuals in main body of text on pages 40–48)

Try reducing your entire presentation to one solitary chart. The

very act of trying forces you to clarify the message, honing it down to a simple and communicable image.

Check list (see VENUE CHECK LIST in main body of text on page 67)

Presentation check lists can help build confidence by reassuring you that you haven't forgotten anything important. A simple venue check list, for instance, can keep you suitably busy rather than worrying about the forthcoming start of the presentation.

Just about any aspect of a business presentation can have its own check list, from preparation and visual aids through to equipment and venue. Keep the list short and manageable or you probably won't use it when it really matters. Although there are numerous check lists for presentations that experts have devised over the years you will find it more rewarding and useful gradually to develop your own, as your experience increases.

Chemistry (see also PRESENCE in main body of text on page 73)

Personal chemistry unfairly accounts for many successful business presentations. People simply get on with each other, there's a rapport that builds and builds. When the chemistry is right, almost anything can happen.

Is there any way to influence the chemistry? Up close, it turns out to be a mixture of:

★ Personality factors
★ Specific behaviour

leading to a feeling of rapport.

While you may not be able to alter your personality, you can certainly change your behaviour. You start creating chemistry and building rapport when you

★ Actively demonstrate you are listening
★ Don't constantly interrupt
★ Build on people's ideas
★ Avoid saying 'yes but'
★ Share personal feelings
★ Show your vulnerability
★ Demonstrate respect for other people
★ Clearly enjoy the company of the people you're with
★ Do something challenging together
★ Convey empathy

Children

I love children especially when they cry, because then somebody takes them away.

NANCY MITFORD, *THE TOURIST* (1959)

Few business presentations include children in the audience. Occasionally, though, a working parent brings a child to a meeting or even a conference. Approach the adult to discuss what to do in case the child gets bored and fretful. This tells the carer that you are expecting them to deal with the situation.

Clap (see APPLAUSE)

Every artist loves applause.

ROUSSEAU (1750)

Clarity (see main body of text on pages 4–5)

I hold it a fundamental tenet that...clarity is not the enemy of truth but her most vital ally.

DR R. ZUBRIN,
ASTRONAUTICAL ENGINEER AND AUTHOR OF *THE CASE FOR MARS*

Cliché

Clichés seem to oil the wheels of a presentation yet may achieve the reverse, making an audience feel there is nothing new. Like jargon, hackneyed phrases or opinions can spoil even the best presentation. Some common clichés include:

★ 'What I want to tell you today is . . .' (just tell them)
★ 'People are our most important asset'
★ 'Unaccustomed as I am to public speaking'
★ 'What counts is the bottom line'
★ 'From start to finish . . .'
★ 'Not to be sneezed at . . .'
★ 'I would like to take this opportunity to . . .'
★ 'When the going gets tough . . .'
★ 'And finally in conclusion . . .'
★ 'I now hand over to my colleague'
★ 'To breathe one's last'
★ 'Cry for the moon'

Find original ways of expression rather than overused phrases or sentiments. If in doubt about whether a phrase is a cliché or not, you can consult a standard reference source such as *A*

Dictionary of Clichés by Eric Partridge (1978, ISBN 0-414-06555-0).

Clip art (see also VISUALS in main body of text on pages 40–48, and Web Sites)

Modern clip art collections consist of either drawings or photographs. They offer a huge variety at a relatively low cost and it is comparatively easy to find what you want.

Main-stream presentation packages such as PowerPoint and Corel Draw provide extensive libraries of copyright-free pictures. These resources are usually categorised by subject matter.

There are also separate clip art packages available such as IMSI's Masterclips for Business and more general collections such as Corel Gallery. There is also an extensive amount of free clip art, including photos, on the Internet.

Since everyone else has access to clip art, including your competitors, how will your use of it be different? Many of the best business presenters now avoid clip art because it

★ Looks unoriginal and so obviously 'clip art'
★ Certain pictures are widely used by other presenters
★ May not accurately reflect the tone or content of the message
★ Has an inconsistent style if taken from varying sources
★ Can contain an in-built cultural bias, for example, most large clip art libraries are authored in the USA and reflect that culture

Just because you have a wonderful clip art library does not mean you need to fill your graphics with irrelevant material such as flashy logos and meaningless images.

Clock (see also TIME)

A reassuring sight for an audience is seeing a presenter removing a watch and placing it where it can be seen. The message is clear: 'I intend to take the timing seriously and will try not to overrun.'

Closing (see main body of text on page 109)

> *Great is the art of beginning, but greater the art is of ending.*
> LONGFELLOW, *ELEGAIC VERSE* (1881)

Find an ending that completes your business presentation on a high note. Too many presentations simply run out of steam, leaving the audience let down and unexcited.

A good ending energises both you and the audience and could be a

★ Question
★ Challenge
★ Quotation
★ Sensational fact
★ Story
★ Picture

Clothes (see IMAGE in main body of text on pages 88–96)

Who said that clothes make a statement? What an understatement that was. Clothes never shut up.

SUSAN BROWNMILLER, *FEMININITY* (1984)

Coaching (see main body of text on pages, 71–2, and also TRAINING)

Experienced presentation coaches offer one-to-one support and are usually successful presenters in their own right. They will

★ Visit you if you wish, rather than the other way around
★ Attend when you need help, for however long you can spare
★ Thoroughly assess your needs
★ Show how you sabotage yourself in presenting situations
★ Provide different ways to practise building your skills and confidence
★ Attend one of your presentations and offer feedback
★ Be a resource to consult regularly on your presenting opportunities

To get the best from your presentation coach,

★ Decide in advance what aspects of presenting you want to tackle
★ Prepare a brief presentation
★ Be punctual
★ Keep asking for feedback and suggestions
★ Come ready to experiment
★ Assume the coach is on your side

Coffee (see CAFFEINE)

There was a tiny range within which coffee was effective, short of which it was useless, and beyond which fatal.

ANNIE DILLARD, *THE WRITING LIFE* (1989)

Colour (see also Visuals in main body of text on pages 40–48)

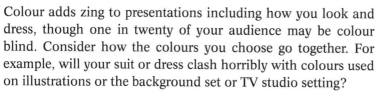

Colours speak all languages.

JOSEPH ADDISON, *THE SPECTATOR* (1711–12)

Colour adds zing to presentations including how you look and dress, though one in twenty of your audience may be colour blind. Consider how the colours you choose go together. For example, will your suit or dress clash horribly with colours used on illustrations or the background set or TV studio setting?

Too many colours on visual aids are a distraction. It is better to use a few that create a sense of harmony and maximise impact. Coloured backgrounds to slides and illustrations are more interesting than plain white ones.

A useful guide to choosing colours for visuals is the *Colour Wheel*.

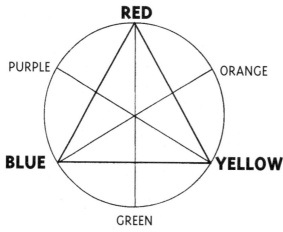

If you want vibrant colours use ones from the opposite sides of the wheel: for example, orange and blue, red and green, yellow and purple.

Warm colours tend to jump at the audience while cool colours recede. To make an image stand out strongly use a warm colour against a cool background.

The shades and tones we use not only affect us on a subconscious level, they also give off subliminal signals about mood.

★ **Red:** Culturally associated with passion, aggression and danger. Red makes a beeline for the brain's adrenal cortex, stimulating the production of adrenalin, the flight or fight hormone.

★ **Yellow:** No one knows how it works but it is a feel-good

factor. It's a welcome colour and wearing it makes people sit up and notice you. However, make sure it suits your complexion as it can clash with a heavy tan, for example.

★ **Green:** A soothing, tranquil colour, which we associate with the countryside and wearing it puts others at ease. Gives off signals of trustworthiness, although many people consider it bad luck.

★ **Blue:** Restful and relaxing but can be cold. Issues no challenges and wearing it gives the impression of being respectable and trustworthy, someone who won't rock the boat.

★ **Purple:** Wild and exciting because of its associations with red and transformation. A passionate colour which is thought psychologically to slow down the heart rate.

★ **Pink:** A loving, caring colour without the danger of red. Too much, though, can suggest insecurity or passivity, sugary sweetness

★ **Black:** Rodin said it took him a lifetime to realise that black is the queen of colours. It can certainly be powerful, demanding, uncompromising and extreme. It also may suggest darkness, brooding, death and doom. If you wear it you'll get noticed but it tends to drain colour from everything else.

★ **White:** Suggests purity, cleanliness, brightness and expense. White clothes make the wearer radiate light, giving an air of youthfulness.

★ **Grey:** Like beige, it denotes indecision and negativity. Floats in the middle of nowhere between black and white. Suggests ambivalence and malleability.

★ **Brown:** Less strident than black but in clothes can give the impression of being staid and stuck in the mud.

Colloquial (see also SLANG)

Expressions from contemporary usage such as 'street cred' or 'cool' have the same drawbacks as jargon. It may make you feel up to date to use them, but will the audience find it useful or stimulating, or merely an irritant?

A few colloquial expressions, on the other hand, can flatter an audience, making it feel up to date and informed.

Comedy (see also HUMOUR)

Great comedy calls large matters into question.

PENELOPE GILLIATT, *TO WIT* (1990)

Commitment (see also Passion)

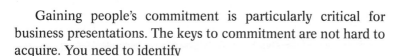

I am committed to non-commitment.

FEDERICO FELLINI, FILM MAKER

Gaining people's commitment is particularly critical for business presentations. The keys to commitment are not hard to acquire. You need to identify

★ Who are the influencers
★ Who are the decision makers

In each case you want to establish who can block what you want to do, who needs to be on your side, what it will take to gain their commitment. Ask yourself for each target person the question they will be asking themselves:

★ 'What's in it for me?'

It is not that people are necessarily selfish, but they are concerned about the personal implications of any presentation. So this means discovering

★ What will people feel?
★ What emotions will be expressed?
★ Who has a stake in keeping things unchanged?
★ Who gains or loses if your ideas are pursued?
★ Who is least likely to like your ideas?
★ What will they dislike most?
★ How will people be likely to react to being hurt?
★ What arguments will they present to counter yours?

Ten ways to gain commitment

★ Demonstrate why the issue is important
★ Show your own commitment to the issue
★ If asking for resources initially seek a commitment for a short period
★ Show how your proposal could achieve the desired results
★ Clarify why what you want to do is an improvement
★ Justify costs
★ Ensure your proposal can be easily grasped
★ Explain how outcomes will be measured
★ Make it possible for others to contribute and develop what you propose
★ Anticipate likely negative questions

> *To act is to be committed,*
> *and to be committed is to be in danger.*
> JAMES BALDWIN, 'MY DUNGEON SHOOK', *THE FIRE NEXT TIME* (1962)

Comparison (see also METAPHORS, SIMILE, SYMBOLS)

Apt comparisons are useful ways of illustrating your point. Comparisons can be images symbols or stories that capture the essence of your meaning. For example, the following are comparisons and their symbols:

Abundant: as the salt in the sea; as the corn in Kansas; as excuses in a traffic court. *Symbols*: cornucopia; cup running over
Balanced: as a man on a tightrope; as a banker's chequebook; as the scales of justice. *Symbols*: juggler; unicyclist
Competitive: as cut-throat capitalism; as baby birds at feeding time; as two prospectors staking the same claim; as three horse traders in a one-horse town. *Symbols*: dog eat dog; price war; sharks in the shark pool
Destructive: as moths in a woollen sweater; as crows in a cornfield; as an erupting volcano; as a force 10 gale. *Symbols*: vandals; hurricane; explosions

Comparisons can also work by referring to their opposites. A reference book of synonyms is a good source for these. There are plenty of comparisons and symbols in *The Speaker's Lifetime Library* by Leonard and Thelma Spinrad, Prentice Hall (1997, ISBN 0-13-496530-2).

Competition (see also RIVALS)

> *Don't knock 'em boost 'em, better still don't mention 'em.*
> ANON.

Computer (see also VIDEO, SLIDES, TECHNOLOGY, OVERHEADS, MULTIMEDIA)

> *To err is human, but to really foul things up requires a computer.*
> ANON.

Computer-based audio and visual effects offer endless possibilities but for presenters the technology can be beguiling. It is easy to acquire a false sense of security that one's own performance hardly matters, so long as the mechanics are perfect.

Creating a really powerful audio-visual presentation using

computers is almost the equivalent of making a short feature film. Allow plenty of time to devise and then practise this electronic performance. A rushed job will almost certainly reduce your impact.

★ Fully rehearse, use the technology until it becomes instinctive
★ Plan for the worst-case scenario where the technology completely fails; for example, have a manual back-up delivery system available
★ Check that the technology enhances rather than obscures your message
★ Unless the room is specially designed for computer-based presentations the equipment may demand a substantial amount of physical space. The audience may then be squeezed into a smaller area and the result can be claustrophobic or oppressive

Concise (see also JARGON and VERBIAGE in main body of text on page 35)

Conclusion (see also CLOSING)

As you wind down your presentation you will be signalling 'the end'. People whose attention might have drifted become alert again and others listen for your conclusion.

Good presenters summarise regularly and end with a conclusion that pulls everything together in one easy to remember message. Fine-tune your conclusion so that it hits home hard and contains the essence of your presentation.

Conference (see also AUDIENCE)

A conference is a gathering of important people who singly can do nothing, but together can decide that nothing can be done.
FRED ALLEN, US HUMORIST.

Conferences generally offer guidelines for presenters about length of speech, use of slides, type of equipment, question handling and so on.

★ Discover the conference rules before preparing your presentation
★ Be willing to break the conference rules if it will enhance your presentation and you can get away with it
★ What is the theme of the conference?
★ Give conference organisers your requirements for making your presentation a success

★ Check the conference acoustics – for example, by sitting at the back to discover how sound carries to the furthest point
★ Check all equipment you intend using
★ Will you be speaking with the lights up or down?
★ If you're speaking in the graveyard slot – just after lunch – consider how you can wake up the audience

Concentration (see also ATTENTION and AUDIENCE)

People's concentration during a presentation can quickly wander. So most business presentations need to be short and easy to follow. The number of points that you can get across successfully is probably no more than three to five.

People will concentrate most intensively when they feel personally affected by what you say. 'What's in it for me?' is a question that each member of your audience is asking, whether consciously or unconsciously.

Confidence (see NERVES in main body of text on pages 71–73, also VISUALISATION)

They can do all because they think they can.

VIRGIL, *AENEID*

Contact (see PRESENCE and PARTICIPATION in main body of text on pages 73, 106–109)

Only connect!

E. M. FORSTER (1879–1970)

Presentations come alive when you really make contact with the audience. It happens most when you really involve people so that they feel alert and interested in what you do or say.

You considerably increase your personal impact when you encourage the communication to be two-way. For example, try to allow people to have a direct influence on what happens during your presentation.

Presentations are powerful when they require an audience to do something active such as interact with each other and the presenter.

Conversation (see main body of text on page 107, and also AUDIENCE)

We do not talk – we bludgeon one another with facts and theories gleaned from cursory readings of newspapers, magazines and digests.

HENRY MILLER, 'THE SHADOWS', *THE AIR-CONDITIONED NIGHTMARE* (1945)

A speech is a conversation between you and your audience, except that you do all the talking. Treat your presentation as if it is a conversation so that you continually put yourself in your audience's shoes.

Convince (see Persuade)

There are two levers for moving men – interest and fear.

NAPOLEON

Cosmetics (see also Image in main body of text on pages 88–96)

Make-up can be a real challenge for women and men too if they are in a broadcasting situation. Intense studio lighting, for example, can do dreadful things to a perfectly normal face by going right through the top layers of skin.

Make-up tips:

★ Use just enough to look good, without allowing people to be aware you're made up
★ With bright lights, use of a foundation to create a layer of colour that reflects light and gives you a normal look
★ Use a modest amount of eyeliner, mascara, blusher or lipstick and other colourants to ensure you retain a healthy look
★ If presenting on video tape or broadcasting, take the advice of the professionals whose job it is to make you look your best
★ Keep lipstick modest to avoid appearing all mouth
★ Make-up that looks fine in small rooms may look wrong in larger rooms
★ Be careful that too much liner doesn't give you circles under the eyes
★ Coloured eyeshadow that looks green or blue can make you look severe
★ Sparkling eyeshadow can be distracting, reflect light and also be fetching

Coughing (see main body of text on page 66)

A cough is something that you yourself can't help but everybody else does on purpose just to torment you.

OGDEN NASH, 'CAN I GET YOU A GLASS OF WATER? OR, PLEASE CLOSE THE GLOTTIS AFTER YOU', *YOU CAN'T GET THERE FROM HERE* (1957)

Courage (see main body of text on page 73)

> *Life shrinks or expands in proportion to one's courage.*
> ANAÏS NIN, 1949

Credibility (see PRESENCE in main body of text on page 73)

Crises (see main body of text on pages 111–4)

> *There can't be a crisis next week. My schedule is already full.*
> HENRY KISSINGER, US REPUBLICAN AND SECRETARY OF STATE,
> *NEW YORK TIMES*, (1969)

Criticism (see main body of text on page 56)

> *I cried all the way to the bank.*
> LIBERACE (1919–87), US ENTERTAINER, REACTING TO HOSTILE CRITICISM

CRT Projectors (see also TECHNOLOGY)

CRT projectors are used for projecting high-quality video and occasionally computer data. CRT (or Cathode Ray Technology) is based on three small TV-style tubes but only the most expensive systems seem to have really good reproduction. The rest look rather grainy or even faint.

The best systems create truly astounding images, especially when several projectors are mounted together to form a huge video wall. You are most likely to come across CRT when it is already installed in a building, though portable projectors are increasingly available.

For most presenters CRT is not a serious choice for regular use unless you use a lot of video as part of your message. Also, newer digital systems are likely to overtake this technology.

Pros	Cons
Fast set-up	Image pixelation at high magnification
Very bright	Seldom adjust for keystone effect
Excellent for video	Often poor on data handling
Highly portable	Top end systems expensive
Easy to use	Usually a weak sound system
Low running costs	
Easy maintenance	

Tips on CRT:

★ There is quite a bit of hi-tech information around on buying a projector – do your research before buying

★ If you don't need projection of computer data and only need video these machines can be good value
★ Use CRT with a dedicated audio system
★ Always see a demonstration, don't buy from catalogues
★ Don't floor-mount the projector if at all possible

D

Day

A useful presentation device is to use a particular day or date to make a point. It's a way of saying that today is important. For example, suppose you are talking on 10 January, you might say, 'A hundred years today ago the Texas oil boom started.' Or 'Today is 10 January and on the same day in 1946 the first man-made contact with the moon occurred.'

References to specific events on selected days in history can be found in various reference books, including birthdays of famous people, both living and dead. Or you could go to a web site such as Ideas Bank.Com and search the history file using key words.

Decision (see also PERSUASION and PASSION in main body of text on pages 26–29 and 77–80)

In many business presentations you're seeking a decision – to make an investment, hire a company, close a factory, start a project and so on. Good presentations make it easy for people to choose by explaining clearly what are the alternatives, the implications of the different choices and what's at stake.

To gain agreement for the decision you want, your presentation needs to enrol people in making the choice. Rather than give a straight presentation it may be more effective to involve the audience in generating the choices and evaluating them, if necessary with the evidence you supply.

If someone tells you he is going to make a 'realistic decision' you immediately understand that he has resolved to do something bad.

MARY MCCARTHY, *ON THE CONTRARY* (1961)

Deductive (see ORDER in main body of text on pages 30–1)

If the world were a logical place, men would ride side-saddle.

RITA MAE BROWN, *SUDDEN DEATH* (1983)

Delivery (see main body of text on pages 63–82)

He speaks to me as if I were a public meeting.

QUEEN VICTORIA IN G. W. E. RUSSELL,
COLLECTIONS AND RECOLLECTIONS (1898)

Desktop presentations (see also POWERPOINT)

The managing director lugged in the projector and spent the next five minutes setting it up, plugging in various leads and booting up the computer. Meanwhile, the audience sat patiently while he flicked through screens, finally arriving at the one he wanted. Four hours later he went through the reverse procedure to pack up. Sadly, though, he had never used the material since the meeting had taken an entirely different direction.

Desktop presentations take time to organize. While you do it you are losing an important opportunity to build relationships with the people in the room. Even if it means arriving unsociably early, try and set up the technology before the audience assembles.

Presentations created on a computer are increasingly popular, offering a huge range of possibilities and many pitfalls. They can replace slides and overheads, and incorporate chunks of video so that all the different media are integrated into one smooth system, controlled by you on the platform or even remotely from around the room.

An obvious gain from switching to this technology is that it allows you to print hard copies, scan in pictures, e-mail the material and use it in ways that a few years ago would have been impossible. In fact, it is the range of options that cause the first major pitfall. It is easy to devise slides, incorporate video and trigger fancy fade or wipe effects that distract you from the core job of giving a powerful personal performance.

Desktop presentations demand considerable practice to integrate them into one's style and ensure that the technology does not dominate. Also, it is not much use having a wonderful computer-based show that projects poorly on the screen. You may therefore need to become closely involved with planning what gadgets to use.

While this technology can be excellent in some informal presentations, it can equally detract from the important task of building a relationship. Laying on a slide show may not be what a client wants or appreciates. After all, if the show is any good why not supply it in advance in preparation for the meeting?

Pros	Cons
Puts power in your hands	Can seriously detract from the impact of the presenter
Inexpensive and likely to be around in the long term	Needs careful practice to use well
Flexible and easy to update	Material needs to be carefully integrated
Templates allow fast creation of professional-looking effects	Requires high-quality design graphics to avoid amateurish look
Portability	Can reduce audience involvement

Destination (see also Location)

> *The trouble with our age is that it is all signpost and no destination.*
>
> LORD KRONENBERGER, 'THE SPIRIT OF THE AGE',
> *COMPANY MANNERS* (1954)

For presentations in previously unknown locations, plan your journey carefully to allow plenty of time and avoid getting lost on the way. In really important business presentations have a dry run by travelling to the destination in advance, just to iron out any possible problems of transport or finding the precise arrival point.

Devising (see Preparation in main body of text on pages 1–19)

There's a considerable difference between devising a presentation based on notice of a few minutes or hours and one you know about days or weeks in advance. Nor is it just about content, that is, what you will say. It's just as much about how you'll behave during the presentation.

Short-notice presentations mean you can't afford to become enmeshed in complexity, there just isn't time. These 'instant presentations' mainly require:

★ A powerful single message
★ A strong opener and closer
★ A lightness of touch
★ A readiness to think on your feet
★ Attention to local situations and events
★ Willingness rapidly to adapt content to changing situations

If such presentations constantly come your way, create an armoury of resources to draw on at short notice: ready-made

slides, standard templates, information files categorised for easy extraction of material, ready-made handouts, standard video clips and so on.

While some of the same requirements apply for presentations in which you have more notice, these particularly benefit from adopting a more structured approach. Devising these major presentations, perhaps involving a whole team of people, can takes weeks, even months of planning. Useful guidelines against which to relate the devising process are the five Ps of presentation:

★ Purpose
★ Preparation
★ Presence
★ Passion
★ Personality

Digital cameras

These filmless cameras capture pictures using computer technology, making it easy to incorporate action shots and other photo images into presentation software.

★ Use a high resolution (at least 1024x768) to create worthwhile pictures for presentation purposes
★ Loading each picture on to the computer for incorporation into slides can be a lengthy process. Allow for this in your preparation planning

Disability

If there are any of you at the back who do not hear me, please don't raise your hands because I'm also nearsighted.

W. H. AUDEN (1907–73), BRITISH POET

If you suffer from a permanent physical disability you will already know the difficulties of getting around and the importance of planning your route. If you have a temporary disability such as a leg in plaster from an accident, you may be unused to taking your temporary handicap fully into account. As part of your preparation, give careful attention to

★ Access problems including stairs, doors, toilets, lifts and platforms
★ Ensuring equipment is positioned for ease of use or access
★ Podiums and unadjustable equipment at wrong height

★ Excessively strong lighting
★ Inadequate microphone support

Warn organisers in advance of your particular disability so that it does not come as a surprise to them. Discuss what arrangements will be required to make your presentation trouble free, such as a blanket, a pillow on a table, extra cushions and so on.

Be alert to some of your audience being disabled. Where possible, discover the nature of these disabilities from your audience research. For example, if you learn that one or more members of the audience are blind explain the contents of charts and diagrams, rather than simply saying 'as you will see from this illustration . . .'

Similarly, be sensitive to how your attempt to involve the audience may affect disabled members. For instance, asking everyone to stand up may be inappropriate if several people are in wheelchairs.

If people in the audience are deaf, check whether someone else will be doing signing to explain your words. If people in the audience rely on lip-reading, explain to the rest of the audience that you realise there are some people with hearing difficulties attending and you will be talking slowly, around 125 words a minute. Where possible, face those who are lip-reading so they can follow your words. This device can often be turned to good account to make a particular point and bring your message to life.

Disasters (see DISASTER PLANNING in main body of text on pages 115–21)

> *No one ever understood disaster until it came.*
> JOSEPHINE HERBST, *NOTHING IS SACRED* (1928)

Discussions

Few business presentations require you to talk continuously. You can't build an effective audience relationship if you just lecture. A powerful tool, particularly during pitches, is to get the audience interacting with each other.

Leading a discussion takes the pressure off you as a presenter. By asking the audience to do something together you force the attention away from yourself, which also helps you to relax. Audience discussions can

★ Create an opener or a closer

★ Buy time while you think or go to the toilet
★ Help you handle a tricky question
★ Wake people up after lunch
★ Introduce a change of pace
★ Re-energise both you and the audience

Tips on leading a discussion session

★ Be clear about the issue or topic
★ Issue instructions on purpose, time limit, procedures
★ Start with people talking in pairs or threes, then move to larger groups
★ Pose open questions for people to tackle, not ones needing a 'yes or no'
★ Paraphrase the answers people give
★ Summarise contributions, usually on to a flip pad or overhead foil
★ Use participants' own words and phrases to show you are listening
★ Give your own views without making other people wrong
★ Get someone else to summarise or collect learning points
★ End by thanking people for their involvement

Dislike

Even if you hate the idea of performing, business presentations are part of business life – whether meetings, interviews, asking for a pay rise, explaining a report, pitching for work and so on.
Often the source of dislike is fear of failure, which in turn stems from lack of confidence. You can't expect to increase you confidence unless you

★ Prepare well
★ Rehearse, rehearse, rehearse
★ Actively use feedback to improve

If you so dislike presentations that you always dread them and no amount of presentation training or coaching seems to make any difference, then perhaps you should bow to the inevitable and let others do them instead.

Ways to avoid formal presentations include:

★ Offer a written report, a fax or e-mail
★ Send a substitute who presents well
★ Hold smaller meetings instead

Some of the best presenters succeed despite their antipathy to the task. They conquer their dislike through their passion for their subject, having an overriding purpose which becomes more important than their fear.

Disruptions (see also DISTRACTIONS and VENUE)

Occasionally one or more members of an audience disrupt a presentation with behaviour such as:

★ Frequent uninvited interventions
★ Repeated, challenging or irrelevant questions
★ Subversive behaviour, such as holding side conversations or phone calls
★ Non-cooperation
★ Arriving late
★ Departing prematurely
★ Rustling papers ostentatiously

Usually such people are trying to impress others, such as a senior person in attendance, or they hate seeing anyone else holding the limelight. It can be tricky dealing with unruly behaviour during an important business presentation and sometimes the only solution is to ignore it. Drawing attention to it merely plays into the hands of the disrupter without necessarily solving the problem.

When the disrupter is the most senior person present it takes a cool head and good diplomacy skills to tackle the delinquent. A useful approach is to

★ Call a break and ask to speak to the person in private

In the private session you politely enquire whether the presentation is meeting their personal needs as they appear distracted or irritated. Usually this will bring to the surface what is happening and allow you to discuss whether to continue or not.

Distractions (see main body of text on pages 101–102)

Anything that puts you off your stride when presenting is a distraction. While you can often anticipate and prepare for typical distractions such as fire alarms, or noisy workmen nearby, some arrive from nowhere to threaten your performance.

There are two main kinds of distractions: those that disturb you but not the audience, and those that disturb both you and the audience.

Distractions that succeed in disturbing you but not the audience can undermine your performance by simply reducing your focus. Instead of concentrating on communicating, you find yourself half listening, looking or worrying about something not entirely relevant. For example, in a team presentation you might see a team member signalling to you unnecessarily, or notice someone in the audience constantly fiddling with an electronic organiser.

These kinds of interruptions are best ignored. Only if they threaten seriously to undermine your performance do you need to deal with them.

Distractions that affect both you and your audience are best dealt with immediately, rather than allowing them to cause increasing irritation. If you can't deal with them then at least acknowledge them, and perhaps ask for the people's understanding: 'Sorry about the noise next door. We'll try and get it fixed, but meanwhile let's continue.' Or, 'We seem to have a separate meeting going on over there. Could we perhaps deal with the issue outside later?'

Dress (see Appearance and Image in main body of text on pages 88–96)

With an evening coat and a white tie, anybody, even a stock-broker, can gain a reputation for being civilised.

OSCAR WILDE

Drink (see also Alcohol and Caffeine)

One more drink and I'd have been under the host.

DOROTHY PARKER, 1930

If you don't want to burp your way through your presentation, avoid drinking carbonated water. Stick to still water, iced tea or fruit juice.

Drink only a modest amount just before your presentation to avoid the need to make an unplanned exit to the toilet in the middle of your performance.

Drowsiness (see Audience and Food)

Sleeping is no mean art:
for its sake one must stay awake all day.

NIETZSCHE, *THUS SPOKE ZARATHUSTRA* (1883)

Dull (see also Attention and Boredom)

Dullness is a kind of luxury.

BHARAI MUKHERJEE, JASMINE (1989)

You can't afford to be a dull business presenter, even as part of a team of excellent performers. However, nor do you have to be the world's most exciting communicator to make an impact. Somehow you need to find that special sparkle that brings what you say to life.

Dull presenters are usually people who have not made the commitment to the actual task. They see the presentation as a chore, a low priority or simply a personal distraction. If presentations are like that for you, either don't give them or it's time to take a different approach.

Each presentation is different, no matter how frequently you convey the same message. To avoid dullness each time you will need to

★ Find new energy
★ Renew your interest in the topic
★ Get in touch with what moves you about the issue
★ Make the experience a creative one
★ Commit to the experience

E

Edit

Written and spoken presentations are very different. Spoken ones are less formal and more colloquial. When developing your presentation you need to edit and refine to

★ Reduce material to the essentials
★ Identify the main points
★ Put most important information first, not last

Doing this will guide you on what to rehearse. It will also reduce the chances of being sidetracked during your presentation.

Writing down your entire verbal presentation will bias it away from a natural speaking style. When spoken, written texts seldom sound easy to listen to without some adjustment. Phrases, sentences and even logical arguments that appear effective on a printed page can prove clumsy when actually spoken.

★ Read the script aloud many times, to test how it sounds
★ Simplify phrases until they come easily in spoken form
★ Remove awkward words or phrases that may trip you up when spoken
★ Use expressions that sound colloquial, rather than formal phrasing associated with written text: for example 'it's', instead of 'it is', or 'can't' rather than 'cannot'.

Read your own compostions, and when you meet with a passage which you think is particularly fine, strike it out.
SAMUEL JOHNSON (1709–84)

Ego (See also PRESENCE)

But enough of me. Let's talk about you.
What do you think of me?'
ED KOCH, FORMER MAYOR OF NEW YORK

Self-importance is a presentation killer. If you're full of yourself there's no room for anyone else, including your audience. Ego also makes it harder to handle a presentation rough patch, preventing you seeing what is really happening. For example, rather than allowing you to cut your losses and end your presentation, ego can cause you to continue, ignoring warning signs, like the audience leaving, talking among themselves, shuffling their feet and so on.

The best antidote to excess ego is to become really interested and focused on the audience. Once the attention is away from yourself, you'll become less self-conscious and more people aware.

Electronic white boards

Electronic 'blackboards' are now common in many presenting environments. They replace the passive 'dumb' board by allowing you to

★ Write, draw, annotate and immediately store, print, e-mail or fax the contents
★ Share material with the audience even before your performance concludes
★ Work in conjunction with projectors, annotating as you go
★ Involve the audience more

Have a colleague or a volunteer helper standing by who takes the output and gets it copied for immediate distribution to the audience. That way lists or comments from the audience need not be restricted to a chart stuck on the wall.

E-mail

Presentations are an expensive time commitment. They therefore need to be dynamic and effective to justify the effort. With all the other mediums of communication available, is a personal appearance the best way of conveying your business message? If all you want to do is impart information, sending an e-mail or something in the post may be better.

E-mail often plays a large role in making large-scale pitches with bidders using it extensively in the run-up to a formal presentation. It can create a useful two-way dialogue between presenter and audience for checking out the main themes of the impending presentation, and altering them right up to the last minute.

It's also an ideal way of adding more 'branding' to presentations by incorporating logos and visual themes. These have a cumulative effect as the image or 'brand message' starts becoming part of everyday correspondence. By the time of the actual presentation the main message is already familiar and visually strong.

Embarrassment (see main body of text on page 119)

Now I am ashamed of confessing that I have nothing to confess.
FANNY BURNEY (1752–1850)

So what is the worst thing that can happen to you? You faint, fall over, vomit on the chairman, make an utter fool of yourself? Even a modicum of preparation will ensure that your business presentation never makes your worst nightmare a reality. In fact, the chances of being truly embarrassed are usually remote.

Embarrassment about giving a presentation often stems from our stubborn self-consciousness. If you are truly paying attention to the audience and what it is doing you'll be far too busy to worry about feeling embarrassed.

Of course, sometimes you may suffer embarrassment when a team member's presentation hits the rocks. The two best solutions are:

★ Retain a sense of humour
★ Don't dwell on it, move swiftly on

Emotion (see PASSION in main body of text on pages 77–80)

. . . a speech can be like an article if you're not careful. So the speech has to have emotional content. To be effective, you have to tap into people's sentiments, feelings and emotions.

FRANO BENABE, CEO ENI, *HARVARD BUSINESS REVIEW* (JULY–AUGUST 1998)

Business presentations need an emotional element because the listeners are human and they therefore make choices both with their hearts and their heads. In theory logic, facts, and information ought to be enough to persuade but they are not. Every successful presentation is a mix of emotion and the harder-edged evidence and arguments.

What you choose to include in a presentation or omit depends on judgement, which is therefore connected with feelings. The order in which to decide to present ideas and information is equally subjective. Similarly, how you speak and which words or phrases you emphasise are also influenced by feelings and emotion. Since emotion in some form pervades the presentation it makes little sense to try to remove it – for example, by speaking in a monotone, or just presenting an apparently 'objective' list of facts.

Instead, put emotion to work to

★ Gain attention
★ Persuade
★ Retain interest
★ Involve
★ Share commitment

End (see main body of text on pages 109–10, and CLOSING)

What we call the beginning is often the end
And to make an end is to make a beginning.
The end is where we start from.

T. S. ELIOT, 'LITTLE GIDDING' (1942)

One of the best ways of creating a presentation is to start with the ending. When you know how you'll finish, and what the final message will be, it becomes far easier to devise not only the entire presentation but to refine the actual ending so that it is memorable.

Few effective business presentations end without indicating the next steps – a decision, a time for reflection, a further meeting, a visit to a site, an expectation of some kind.

★ Take responsibility for ensuring that your presentation ends on a clear note of what you expect to happen next

Energy (see also main body of text on pages 81–2)

Life engenders life. Energy creates energy.
It is by spending oneself that one becomes rich.
SARAH BERNHARDT IN CORNELIA OTIS SKINNER, *MADAM SARAH* (1966)

Enthusiasm (see main body of text on pages 77–9)

You can't sweep other people off their feet,
if you can't be swept off your own.
CLARENCE DAY, A WILD POLISH HERO

Environment (see main body of text on pages 62)

Some presentation environments are thoroughly daunting. For example, large halls, TV studios, imposing boardrooms, global video conferences. The three main ways of handling these testing situations are:

★ Be yourself – at least you control that element of the presentation
★ Visit the environment to gain familiarity with it
★ Rehearsal, preferably on site or via a close simulation

For example, if you are presenting to a board, find a way to visit when no one is there and sit in the CEO's chair. Similarly, if you cannot get into a particular TV studio in advance, ask to visit one that is like it.

Equipment

You are the presentation, not the equipment. Be ready to do the whole performance without anything electronic. If the gadgetry breaks downs, grab a marker pen an use a flip pad to get your ideas across. It will be far more dynamic than a bunch of fancy slides.

As for the equipment:

★ Check it! Nothing destroys presentations faster than unreliable equipment
★ Be sure you know how everything works
★ Know precisely what you will do should specific items fail: for example, what you would do if the computer system

crashes, or someone trips over and breaks a lead, or if you didn't know where the spare set of overhead bulbs are kept

★ The greater your reliance on equipment, the more you need to rehearse and do your research on what happens if . . .

★ The most important part of successful presentations is building a relationship with your audience, not the equipment and what it does

★ It pays to use professional support to help you through the technical minefield of roving microphones, teleprompts, large-scale audio-visual back projections, multi-slide effects, video, film and sound effects

Euphemisms

We use euphemisms because being more direct might be hurtful or hard to receive. For example, instead of talking of someone as bald we may say they're 'thinning'. We may call an ugly person 'homely', or a drunk person 'inebriated'.

Generally avoid euphemisms in a presentation, unless what you want to say is simply too harsh to accept. They tend not to work because they are either not understood, especially by foreign audiences, or they can make you seem less than frank and open.

Evidence (see main body of text on pages 26–29)

> *All necessary truth is its own evidence.*
> RALPH WALDO EMERSON, *JOURNALS* (1833)

Examples (See also QUESTIONS in main body of text on pages 125–9)

Examples are rather like visuals. They can often save you thousands of wasted words and are a good way of dealing with difficult questions or conveying a complicated point in an easy, accessible way.

Examples can take many forms including sample numbers, a word picture, a story or even an object. The more you give examples, the more 'real' the message becomes because an audience starts to fully understand.

Too many examples, however, can clog up a presentation. If you keep inundating people with endless examples it is equivalent to showing them too many slides. People become overloaded with information and unable to absorb it all.

Stick to a few powerful ones that really work, rather than adding another example for the sake of it.

Excitement (see main body of text on page 75)

It is easy to confuse excitement about giving a presentation with fear. The symptoms are much the same: tenseness in the stomach, sweating, dry mouth, palpitations and so on.

It's right that you are excited about the presentation. Why should the audience be excited if you aren't?

Expectations (see also AUDIENCE in main body of text on page 4, and 123 and VISUALISATION)

Do you expect to succeed or fail? If you anticipate failing then you probably will. Expectations – yours and your audience's – have an important influence on the outcome.

Your expectations: Will you excel, or just be competent? There's plenty of evidence from sport and other human activity about the power of creating a mental picture of what you want to happen.

For example, try imagining

★ The audience nodding with approval
★ People laughing in the right places
★ The right questions being posed
★ Prolonged applause
★ People shaking your hand afterwards, congratulating you
★ A phone call from somebody important praising your performance
★ Requests arriving for you to give more presentations

The audience's expectations: Most audiences want a presenter to succeed and have expectations to match. This is both encouraging and a little daunting.

The audience usually wants you to succeed and when you make mistakes will often be extremely forgiving. In particular, an audience usually makes allowances if you are professional and confident in handling difficulties, such as forgetting your words, getting lost in your script, delivering doubtful jokes, making factual mistakes or temporarily losing control of equipment.

Even experienced presenters sometimes misjudge an audience's expectations. However, when you remain totally 'present' you can sense that something is wrong and do something about it.

A useful tactic is to ask people whether they are getting from the presentation what they want.

This suspense is terrible. I hope it will last.

OSCAR WILDE

Experience (see also NERVES in main body of text on pages 71–73)

You should make a point of trying everything once,
except incest and folk dancing.
ARNOLD BAX (1883–1953), BRITISH COMPOSER

When you have little or no experience of presenting it can seem a daunting, perhaps terrifying, prospect.

★ Even the best speakers were inexperienced to start with, like you
★ It gets easier the more times you do it
★ There's no substitute for doing it

The more experienced you become the easier it is to fall prey to complacency and lack of preparation. Treat each new presenting opportunity as a chance to

★ Learn something new
★ Experiment
★ Take a bigger risk
★ Push yourself harder

You can always reach a new level of impact, which puts your experience to work.

Expression (see also PASSION and VOICE in main body of text on pages 77–80, 74, 100)

The more acute the experience, the less articulate its expression.
HAROLD PINTER, PLAYWRIGHT

Turn off the sound of a television set and watch people talking. You immediately start drawing conclusions from their gestures and facial movements. Often you can guess quite accurately what they are saying or feeling.

Expressions play an important part in how you come across. They keep an audience's attention. Without forcing yourself to do anything unnatural, allow your expression to stem from the material you are presenting, adding variety through smiling, frowning, nodding, raising eyebrows, mouth gestures and so on.

Watching your facial expressions tells an audience how to respond. If you deny them expression, for example, by keeping a deadpan face while telling a joke, people may not realise that you are being funny, even if the joke itself is amusing.

Your experience and strength of feeling provide the richest

sources for creating expression. Your concern about an issue, for example, governs how you come across. Eyes, mouth, face, body all convey a message. Feelings relentlessly emerge through your physicality, they can seldom be disguised completely.

★ The best presenters first decide how they feel about something and then use it either consciously or unconsciously to drive their expression

How far should you go in a business presentation to express yourself, either verbally or emotionally? Should you show anger, delight, determination, or whatever? If you are unsure or anxious about reactions to your expression it suggests that you could do more research into the audience. No powerful presentation is entirely risk free; perhaps you're being too risk aversive.

In rehearsals and in live presentations, experiment with different ways of expressing yourself. For instance, try rehearsing your speech in contrasting ways: angrily, dispassionately, cheerfully and so on. Or deliver it like a soap powder commercial or a politician at a rally. Watch how these different moods influence your style and pace of delivery, and also your body language.

Pick out parts of the presentation which might benefit from different levels of energy, a change in style or pace. How much variety of expression can you inject?

Eyes (see also GLASSES)

> *I have the eyes of a dead pig.*
>
> MARLON BRANDO

A terrifying pre-war archive film shows Hitler surveying a vast stadium of people with fanatical attention. Eventually the audience is cowed and falls silent. It is an extreme and disturbing example of a presenter using his eyes to devastating effect.

You don't need to emulate Hitler to use your eyes to enhance your presentation. Ways to do so during the presentation include:

★ Closely observe the audience
★ Survey the surroundings
★ Systematically create eye contact
★ Convey different feelings or expressions
★ Send a smile

How is it possible to make eye contact with a large audience? Strangely, the more people the easier it becomes. Wherever you

look there is someone available to contact. You may only have the briefest interchange, yet this is all that is needed to make people say, 'I felt (s)he was talking to me.'

Skilled presenters swear by the principle that they will never talk unless they can have eye contact with someone. This explains the importance of never reading a script since you cannot sustain eye contact. It's better to use the following steps:

★ Stop
★ Read your notes
★ Collect and deliver your thoughts
★ Make eye contact
★ Then speak

As you make eye contact with people in the audience, try focusing your thoughts around a single question, such as 'what are you feeling right now?' or 'tell me what you're thinking'. Strange as it may seem, the very act of articulating the question helps to bring their answers into your head. Try it.

★ People's expressions often show where you need to go next with your presentation
★ The more you make eye contact the less attention you draw to yourself
★ Good eye contact technique is not a mechanical scanning process. Use it instead to 'talk to' each person

If there are bright spotlights making it hard to see anyone, first try and adjust the lighting to make the audience visible. If you are unable to alter the lighting, imagine the people instead and keep making contact. Fix your eyes on an imaginary person at the back of the room and speak initially to this person. After a while, imagine they have moved their seat somewhere else and catch their eye in this new location.

Eye contact comes into its own in small informal presentations. You can really give everyone attention, building your communication impact. However, not all cultures welcome intense eye contact and you may be considered rude if you stare too much into someone's eyes.

The best way to use eye contact while presenting is to imagine that you are having a succession of intimate conversations with different members of the audience. Skilled presenters make every member of the audience feel they are talking just to them by merely focusing on each person in turn, if only fleetingly. They may smile at one person, raise their eyebrows to another, gesture to someone else, walk towards yet another and so on. Somehow they manage to personalise the eye contact. If you see someone is uncomfortable with eye contact, move on by offering it to someone else.

If you feel your focus is narrowing and you lose peripheral vision, or it seems as if you are looking down a tunnel, you're almost certainly staring. You can counter this tendency if you

★ Keep your peripheral vision active
★ Keep your head still but make yourself aware of the side of the wall
★ Raise your hand so you have to use your peripheral vision

F

Face (see also EXPRESSION)

I think your whole life shows in your face and you should be proud of that.

LAUREN BACALL, US ACTRESS

Facts (see also FACTS in main body of text on pages 26–9, 112)

There is nothing so uncertain and slippery as fact.

SARA COLERIDGE, *MEMOIR AND LETTERS*, VOL.2 (1873)

If you find yourself during a presentation going on at length about facts, it's time to use some emotion. If you find yourself getting too emotional during the presentation it is time to get back to some facts.

Fatigue (see also ENERGY, in main body of text on pages 81–2)

There is fatigue so great that the body cries, even in its sleep.

MARTHA GRAHAM, *BLOOD MEMORY* (1991)

Fatigue is a presentation killer. Audiences soon realise a speaker is tired or lacklustre. If you're due to make an important presentation get plenty of sleep, especially the night before, rather than staying up late endlessly practising.

If, despite your best intentions, you arrive at the presentation location and feel really tired:

★ Keep the presentation short

Faux pas (see also EMBARRASSMENT in main body of text on page 119)

> *I was so embarrassed I could feel my nerves*
> *curling like bacon over a hot fire.*
> MARGARET HALSEY, *SOME OF MY BEST FRIENDS ARE SOLDIERS* (1944)

Doing something tactless during a presentation can happen through ignorance or lack of thought. Since most audiences want you to succeed, recovery from such blunders mainly depends on

★ Realising you have made an error
★ Apologising
★ Moving on swiftly

Fear (see also EXPERIENCE, PRACTICE and NERVES)

> *All the great speakers were bad speakers at first.*
> EMERSON, *THE CONDUCT OF LIFE* (1860)

What are the symptoms of fear? Usually we say:

★ Shallow breathing
★ Sweating
★ Palpitations
★ Muscle tension
★ Eyes wide
★ Mouth dry
★ A sick feeling in the stomach

Many of these also occur when we're excited. Rather than being truly 'fearful' about a presentation instead you may be excited and stimulated. Welcome the feelings of excitement rather than pushing them down out of your awareness. Feel the fear and do it anyway.

★ Acknowledge that you are anxious
★ Rehearse, rehearse, rehearse
★ Refuse to let fear dominate
★ What's the worst thing that could possibly happen – name your nightmare, give it a title a name, describe it in detail
★ What are the real chances of your worst fear actually occurring?

If your fear seems to be getting in the way, get some professional presentation help.

Feedback (see main body of text on pages 134–6)

Good presenters are hungry for feedback. They want to know what worked and what didn't. They use colleagues and questions to actual presentation audiences to discover how they can improve.

Presentation feedback can be tough to take. No one likes to be told they were boring, unpersuasive, or lacking in energy. Yet you can only improve if you have reliable information.

Try making a video of one of your presentations. Take a hard look at the results and be ruthlessly honest about what needs to change.

Feelings (see also PASSION in main body of text on pages 77–80)

Better to be without logic than without feeling.
CHARLOTTE BRONTË, *THE PROFESSOR* (1846)

What do you want your audience to feel? Since people are persuaded not just by logic but also by emotion, you need to inject into your presentation a suitable level of feeling.

Business presentations may have more than their fair share of facts and information, yet these alone won't persuade. The strength of the presenter's feelings also have a great impact and it's essential to share how you feel about what you are presenting with the audience.

Feelings start undermining a business presentation if they dominate at the expense of everything else.

Fees

In every work, a reward added makes the pleasure twice as great.
EMERSON, *ESSAYS: FIRST SERIES* (1841)

If you are invited to speak at a business conference ask whether there is a fee, otherwise it may be assumed you are only too pleased to speak for free.

Travel:

★ Expect as a matter of course to have your travel costs fully paid and clarify when you can invoice and whether it's acceptable to go business class
★ If it's a long journey suggest that you'll arrive fresher if you go business class
★ If travel costs are unavailable think seriously whether this is a worthwhile presentation

Payment:

★ Get the fee agreed in writing, including when it will be paid Some business speakers on the international circuit seek payment immediately before starting their presentation. Asking for payment right after delivery need not sound entirely mercenary. Simply explain that this arrangement avoids any problems with chasing payment or lost mail.

Amount: How much you can charge depends on

★ The market rate
★ Your expertise
★ Importance of the event
★ Expectations about your charges
★ Whether you are belatedly substituting for someone else
★ The amount of work needed for preparation and research
★ Whether you are using a speaker agency

Choose a fee with which you feel comfortable. Demanding a sky-high fee may put you under too much pressure. To the question 'what kind of a fee do have in mind?' your reply might be

★ 'What do you normally pay?'
★ 'As much as possible!'
★ 'My last engagement I charged . . .'
★ 'Give me time to think about that

If you're new to fee payments conduct some private research exploring what you might be worth. For example,

★ What do others charge for doing what you will be doing?
★ Get in touch with other speakers to ask for their advice on rates
★ Call an agency that specialises in supplying speakers to learn about their rates

Experienced business speakers keep testing the market by checking fee rates

Expectations:

★ Clarify what you are expected to do for the fee

You may envisage arriving just in time to deliver your presentation and departing immediately afterwards. Yet this may not be at all what the person approaching you has in mind. They may be expecting you to be available the entire day, even though you are only presenting for part of it.

For the inclusive fee you may be expected to run additional sessions for interested groups of the audience. Or you may find yourself required to socialise late into the evening or join a planning session for future activities.

Feet

Some presenters have an unconscious habit of foot tapping or leg jiggling when sitting down. It usually betrays nervousness and while such movements may not ruin a presentation, they can be an irritating distraction.

★ Check for unconscious foot movements by regular performance feedback
★ For long presentations wear comfortable shoes
★ Unless they are properly broken in, avoid new shoes
★ Rather than standing for the whole presentation, rest your feet by sitting down

If your feet really hurt during a presentation what can you do? You could confide in the audience, saying something like 'hope nobody minds if I go back to nature' and remove your shoes. Or, if sitting down behind a table simply slip them off and hope that no one will notice or care. If participating in a video conference beware of being caught on camera in your bare feet.

Figures (see main body of text on page 31–3)

> *Torture the statistics long enough,*
> *and they'll confess to anything.*
> SEEN ON A T-SHIRT AND QUOTED BY C. MICHAEL ARMSTRONG,
> CEO OF HUGHES ELECTRONICS CORPORATION

Keep your business presentation simple with only the figures you absolutely must use to convey your message. Too often presenters include busy, figure-full tables with scores of numbers which no audience will absorb in the time available.

Inexperienced presenters like to include a mass of numbers to add 'weight' to their argument when the reality is that the most persuasive case is usually made with just a few well-chosen numbers powerfully presented.

Film (see also VIDEO)

Film and video can enliven your presentation if they are:

★ Relevant
★ Appropriate

★ Short – usually under a minute
★ Entertaining
★ Professional-looking
★ Firmly linked to the message

Film sequences can rapidly detract from a presentation, rather than enhance it. Only use material which makes you look better and helps you achieve something quickly that would otherwise take a long time.

Lengthy sequences risk turning your presentation into a film show and distance you from your audience. While the clip should be entertaining, it can also prove too powerful. For example, the audience may become so absorbed that it returns to your presentation with a twinge of regret.

★ Practise making the clip start and finish exactly where you want it to.

If your the audience is paying to watch your presentation you may need to obtain a licence to show a clip unless the sequence is under about thirty seconds. Check that you are in the clear.

Finish (see END)

> *Never think that you've seen the last of anything.*
> EUDORA WELTY, *THE OPTIMIST'S DAUGHTER*, 1968

Flip charts (see main body of text on pages 103–4)

Flow (see main body of text on page 30)

Business presentations usually flow logically from one point to the next. Achieving this is more an art than a science since strictly logical sequences can prove boring and predictable.

You can achieve a flow in the overall structure of your presentation by having a clear beginning, middle and an end. Within these distinct parts continually test the material against the question:

★ Does this follow on from what I have just said?

Another way to achieve a satisfactory flow is to adopt a theme which unfolds naturally as you explore it. Thematic flows are like stories in which you link each portion of the presentation with the next, using some common idea that holds it all together.

Fonts (see also VISUALS in main body of text on pages 40–48)

So you have access to 250 fonts. This does not mean you need more than a couple in your visuals.

★ A single consistent font throughout an entire presentation is usually enough, with minor variations using bold, italic, quotations and colours
★ Choose a font easily readable from the back of the room
  Sans serif fonts are crisp, unfussy and usually easy to read. This is sans serif.
  Serif fonts look fancy but are usually harder to read. This is a serif font.

Food

> *If you give them food, they'll come.*
>
> JEFF BERKOVITZ

A heavy meal just before an important performance can cause

★ Stomach pain
★ Burping
★ Food stuck to teeth or clothing
★ Sleepiness

If you are invited to a meal with your audience before an important pitch – more likely in certain countries than others – eat lightly and avoid alcohol. Use the time further to probe the audience about what they want to hear at the presentation, what is going on in the organisation, the gossip and who is important.

★ Your presentation starts the moment you are with your audience

Foreign audiences

Business presentations to foreign audiences require extra care during the preparations stage:

★ Assume that people will understand only about 40% of what you say
★ Send your material in advance to the interpreters so they have time to do the translation
★ Go over the material with the interpreters when you arrive at the venue

During the delivery stage,

★ Enunciate well, without talking down to people

★ Avoid reading written material aloud in English while the people read it in their own language. Instead, ask a volunteer to read in the local language

★ Avoid idioms, stale metaphors and streetwise language, which can be confusing or fail altogether. However, some use of such words introduced with 'as we say in English . . . ' can also flatter an audience

★ Beware idiomatic verbs that natural English speakers take for granted like 'sales took off', or 'we got the go-ahead'

★ Sarcasm rarely works in translation

★ Holding members of the audience with direct eye contact may be counter to their culture

★ People from other cultures may show little reaction so do not be put off if you are received in total silence

★ In certain cultures respect for authority and fear of looking stupid may inhibit people posing questions. Instead, get people talking in small groups and as you circulate informally the questions will almost certainly start coming

★ Be yourself: your sincerity and passion will have as much impact as the content of your presentation

★ Choose words with an international meaning, rather than popular ones that might be used in the tabloids. Words with a classical ring such as those with a Latin origin can be particularly useful as audiences can often deduce the meaning themselves

★ Facial expressions and strong body language work well

Questions and answers

During the question-and-answer sessions you may find that your intentions have not come across to everyone. Don't blame the interpreters or assume the person raising the issue is dim.

Instead, treat questioners with extra respect, accepting responsibility for failing to get the message across. Do your homework with the people locally to discover what questions you might be asked and discuss with them the sort of answers that might satisfy.

Forget (see main body of text on page 58)

> *I have a memory like an elephant.*
> *In fact, elephants often consult me.*

NOËL COWARD

The more material you try to remember the more likely it is you'll forget something during the actual presentation. Rather than trying to remember every word of your presentation, focus on memorising only the ideas you are using. These can usually be added to a small prompt such as a palm-sized card.

If you forget what to say,

★ Stop, breathe and look at the audience

If you do forget something don't mention it unless you must. Where it's obvious you have forgotten to include material or bring an object apologise and either find it or move on swiftly.

Frameworks (see also FRAMEWORKS in main body of text on page 23)

A framework is the scaffolding on which you erect the structure of your presentation.

Frameworks must suit an audience's particular needs; there is no single structure that works everywhere. For example, a selling message requires a different framework where the emphasis is mainly on further action from a telling message where you are mainly conveying ideas and information.

In simple information-giving presentations you identify the core message and put it in some familiar context. For instance, if you intend to explain why the need to stay late and come in early must change, you may first have to outline why such arrangements are so important.

In developing a framework for your presentation it may be necessary to include facts, examples and sub-issues. Where do these go? Your framework provides the structure on which you progressively build the presentation, bit by bit. A useful way of creating such a framework is to consider the issues you need to answer on behalf of the audience:

★ Listen to me because . . .
★ Here's what's happening . . .
★ What we must do is . . .
★ This is how we'll do it . . .
★ It'll cost us . . .
★ The benefits will be . . .
★ You'll know if we get these benefits because . . .
★ Here's what could go wrong . . .
★ This is what I want you to do . . .
★ I want you to do that because . . .

★ If you don't do it this is what will happen . . .
★ What I want you to do right now is . . .

Freeze (see Nerves in main body of text on pages 71-73)

No passion so effectually robs the mind of all its powers of acting and reasoning as fear.

EDMUND BURKE, 1756

Fun (see also Play)

People learn and absorb more if they are being entertained and having fun rather than being lectured. Even the most serious business presentation can benefit from introducing elements of fun, without necessarily descending into frivolity.

Look for opportunities in which the audience 'play' together. This could mean conducting an experiment, asking people to imagine a situation and act it out, solve a puzzle, answer a quiz, literally play with some objects, make a series of competitive guesses and so on.

In major pitches, for example, bidders may introduce many ways for an audience to enjoy themselves while absorbing the core messages. This might include a night on the town, a meal at a top restaurant, a visit to a theatre and so on.

Funny (see Humour in body of text)

Anyone who is considered funny will tell you, sometimes without even your asking, that deep inside they are very serious neurotic, introspective people.

WENDY WASSTERTON, *JEAN HARLOW'S WEDDING NIGHT*

G

Gabble

Presenters who gabble soon lose their audience. While you don't need to speak like an elocution teacher, it's important that you do speak clearly. Ask for regular feedback from colleagues on whether you are articulating your words well and not swallowing them.

To avoid gabbling,

★ Open your mouth fully when you speak; tight lips obstruct clarity
★ During rehearsals speak artificially slowly at first
★ Allow special rehearsal time for difficult or unusual words
★ Keep sentences short so you avoid rambling or getting lost

Gaffe (see EMBARRASSMENT)

Gag (see also HUMOUR in main body of text)

Because most business presentations tend to be quite serious affairs, there is usually scope for including some humour without the risk of appearing to be flippant. Whether you can include jokes depends on both the situation and your particular personality.

Most audiences welcome some light relief in a formal presentation. If you are a naturally humorous person you can probably get away with more gags and jokes than someone who has to wind themselves up to tell a funny story.

Use gags with care, they need to fit in with your core message, rather than be artificially inserted just to get laughs.

Gargle (see also VOICE)

If you are making a long and important presentation, have an antiseptic gargle available. You can even gargle as part of your warming up just before going on-stage.

If gargling immediately before performing, be sure to protect your clothing from any liquid.

Gender (see also POLITICAL CORRECTNESS)

Gender issues can play havoc with an otherwise perfectly effective business presentation.

★ Avoid sexist remarks that might unnecessarily offend your audience
★ Some computer programmes will highlight sexist words in preparatory presentation text

Consider the gender balance of the audience when devising your presentation. Gender represents a hidden force that can influence how people react. For example, if you are presenting to a group in which there are several women it is hardly tactful to keep using analogies that refer to mainly male sports such as soccer or baseball.

Gestures (see BODY LANGUAGE in main text on pages 97–100, and also EXPRESSION)

Give-aways (see also HANDOUTS)

Audiences love give-aways, the free items to support your

presentation. While these won't rescue a bad presentation, they can be an effective way to engage the audience during it or on closing. Give-aways include items with your presentation message on small plastic cards, pens, cut-outs, folding cards, photos, books, pamphlets and so on.

To prevent your give-away taking the focus from your message choose a time for distribution when the audience no longer needs to concentrate on you or what you are saying.

Even if you never intend using a give-away imagine creating one. It's a way of reducing your presentation message to its bare essentials. What would be your basic presentation message if it had to be on a T-shirt, or a retractable pen?

Glasses

When an audience cannot see a presenter's eyes it suggests someone rather sinister or untrustworthy. Use contact lenses if possible; avoid wearing tinted glasses when presenting.

If presenting on TV or video do so without glasses if possible, since these may reflect powerful lights and prevent your eyes from being seen.

Glasses, though, can sometimes be a useful device in meetings, as you slowly remove them looking thoughtful, or carefully polish them while you buy precious moments to consider what you want to say next.

Goals (see also PURPOSE)

> *If you don't know where you're going,*
> *you'll end up somewhere else.*
>
> YOGI BERRA

What is your presentation goal? Get clear on this and most other aspects will quickly fall into place.

Graphics (see VISUALS in main body of text)

Graphs (see also VISUALS in main body of text)

The best presentation graphs are simple and easy to read. Avoid ones with complicated names on the two axes that people have to struggle to read. Likewise keep the number of variables plotted to just one or two and certainly no more than three.

Each graph needs to convey a clear message through a trend, a shape or a sudden change. Give your graphs a title that communicates what the message is, for example,

* ★ Money supply rises over the quarter
* ★ Increase in new product launches
* ★ Investment downturn levels off
* ★ Decline in rate of rejects

Gratuity

If you receive special care and attention from the technical staff, consider giving them a small token of your appreciation. After all, you may need their help again some time in the future. It need not be money, though 'have a drink on me' accompanied by a couple of notes will certainly be appreciated.

Meticulously well-prepared presenters have also been known to tip catering staff to keep a low profile while they are performing, to avoid distractions such as cups and saucers being laid out next door.

Graveyard Shift (see also LUNCH)

> *One cannot think well, love well, sleep well,*
> *if one has not dined well.*
> VIRGINIA WOOLF, *A ROOM OF ONE'S OWN* (1929)

This is when your presentation can die a slow death. Post-mealtime is a notoriously bad slot to be allocated, so most presenters try to get it changed. Yet after lunch is also when people feel most relaxed and at one with the world. It could be a great time to present if you can

* ★ Get people up and doing, rather than just sitting
* ★ Keep the presentation really short
* ★ Focus on a simple message requiring minimal audience thinking effort

Gravitas (see also PRESENCE in main body of text)

There's no one so transparent as the person who thinks he's devlish deep. W. Somerset Maugham, Lady Frederick (1907)

Grooming (see also Image in main body of text)

> *From the cradle to the coffin underwear comes first.*
> BERTOLT BRECHT, *THE THREEPENNY OPERA* (1928)

First impressions count and for most business presentations you need to be well-groomed and appropriately dressed. Good

grooming means taking care of yourself so that you look clean and well turned-out. Often it's the small details that count, such as tie knotted neatly in place, clean nails, hair not awry and so on.

Being well-groomed doesn't mean you compromise your personality and appear unduly conformist. But if you're giving a presentation you will be under intense scrutiny and even the tiniest details can send a signal to an audience about your attitude and attention to detail.

Gut (see also NERVES in main body of text)

Sometimes your best ally in preparing a presentation is sheer gut instinct. Your intuition tells you that something is wrong, you feel it as an itch in your mind, a nagging 'gut feeling'.

Go for what you think works, learn to 'listen' to gut instinct; it will often guide you away from disasters and towards success.

H

Hair (see also IMAGE in main body of text on pages 88-96)

People get comfortable with their features. Nobody gets comfortable with their hair. Hair trauma. It's the universal thing.
JAMIE LEE CURTIS, US ACTRESS

★ Wispy hair covering bald patches is a give-away and an audience distraction
★ Hair falling over eyes looks like you have something to hide
★ Over-elaborate hair can do you a disservice
★ Beware the lank or unwashed look
★ Frequently tossing excess hair out of the way can be an audience distraction

If you're bald and working under bright lights, your most prominent feature may become the gleaming top of your head. Take the shine off with some powder – talc will do fine, or borrow some from a female colleague.

Handicap (see DISABILITY)

Handouts

Few things are more annoying than realising that your audience's attention is on the handout rather than on you. Handing out your speech in advance is nearly always a mistake. Providing copies of slides and visuals in advance is usually sensible.

If you are speaking at a conference you may be asked to supply the text of your presentation in advance. The assumption is that you have it written out as a script. Since this is seldom good presentation practice the answer to conference organisers is that while you know the broad territory you intend to cover you will not be talking to detailed notes. That reply forces them either to tape the presentation or leave you to provide something in outline form only.

So resist handing out your speech in advance, except to interpreters who have to translate your presentation into another language.

Occasionally a condition of speaking at an important conference is that you supply your presentation in written format, well in advance. In this situation,

★ Ask the organisers for a written confirmation that they won't distribute your presentation ahead of time, including to those who leave early

★ Offer to supply the copies that you will distribute at the end

If everyone has your material as you speak, why do they need you there?

Audiences certainly find it helpful to have in their possession charts and other visual material while you present. This makes it easier for those with poor eyesight to see the material properly and allows everyone to take notes as they listen. A useful technique is to place three visuals on one side of the page, leaving the rest for notes. This saves the audience acquiring huge files of materials that they will probably never refer to again.

★ Individual information sheets disrupt the flow of your presentation if distributed during it. Choose a moment when it won't detract from your message
★ Check all handouts for spelling and other errors; have a second person check them too
★ Handouts should be neat, self-explanatory and laid out attractively
★ Copies of overheads or slides without accompanying explanations seldom work well
★ Mark any copyright material clearly
★ For foreign audiences send handouts in advance for translation

★ If addressing a non-English-speaking audience avoid reading handout materials in English. Instead, ask a volunteer to read in the audience's language
★ Ensure there are sufficient copies for everyone
★ If there aren't enough handouts and it's too late to get more:
     Don't distribute them all. Instead put the ones you do have at the exit doors and invite people to take them on leaving. With luck not everyone will
     Conduct an exercise in which they have to talk to each other about the contents
     Don't mention you are short of handouts
★ If you drop your handouts stay calm, ask someone for help in picking them up and once they've begun doing so, continue with your presentation; thank them afterwards

Hands (see also BODY LANGUAGE in main text on pages 97–100, and also EXPRESSION and IMAGE)

★ Sounds obvious, but make sure your hands and nails are impeccably clean
★ Avoid elaborate rings that could distract your audience
★ While hands and fingers are great for ticking off points as you complete them, use this technique sparingly

Handshakes (see also IMAGE in main body of text on pages 88-96)

A firm hearty handshake gives a good first impression and you'll never be forgiven if you don't live up to it.
P. J. O'ROURKE, *MODERN MANNERS* (1988)

At the start of many business presentations there is an opportunity to meet everyone and shake their hands. Take advantage of this way of making physical contact with your audience; it is a powerful method of starting to build relationships in the room.

Listen carefully to what the other person says when shaking hands. If they introduce themselves by their name and title, look interested and maybe make a short comment. This will prolong the handshake and increase the intimacy.

Hangover (see ALCOHOL)

Nobody ever stops drinking until the cost of drinking becomes higher than the cost of not drinking.
ISABELLE HOLLAND, *THE LONG SEARCH* (1990)

Hardware (see also EQUIPMENT)

Avoid the hardware dominating your presentation. Once the equipment becomes more powerful than you are it's no longer really your performance. You can't hand the job to hardware, no matter how sophisticated it becomes. If you could, why be there in the first place?

Each piece of hardware makes its own demands on a presenter. Mastering it, knowing its strength and weaknesses, is therefore an important aspect of intensive preparation.

How reliant are you on the hardware? What would you do if it ground to a halt? Being ready for every technical eventuality is probably not possible, but you can prepare for the main disasters.

Choosing the right hardware is always tricky, since what works in one place may prove troublesome in another. Even when you have a whole technical back-up team equipment can still cause trouble. Stick mainly to presentation hardware you know is reliable and with which you feel comfortable.

Headline (see also CLARITY)

Reduce the main point of your presentation to a single headline. From that clear starting point you're ready to excel.

Heat (see TEMPERATURE)

Hecklers (see also INTERRUPTIONS in main body of text on pages 101–2)

Even the boardroom can suffer hecklers. Such people are usually insecure, enjoy making trouble and are argumentative. Since they're attention seekers, almost anything you do to tackle them merely feeds their habit.

★ Be wary of using smart one-line put-downs; hecklers often do it better. Also it merely turns you into the baddy

In a boardroom presentation call a break and tackle the heckler personally. Ask what the problem is and indicate that you'd really appreciate his or her points coming at the end with questions. Rather than raising a significant point in an inappropriate way, the heckler may just be making jokes, perhaps at your expense. If, due to time pressure, you cannot call a break, try something along the lines of

★ 'I love your jokes, but could we keep them till I get to the end? Thanks'
★ 'There's quite a lot at stake here; I think it would help if we stayed focused'

Hecklers in the boardroom, important meetings and pitches can be turned to your advantage:

★ If they raise issues that you want to deal with anyway, you just explain that you are going to do it on your own terms
★ The audience wants you to sort out the heckler, however senior

When the heckler is the most senior person present you need all your diplomacy skills. Put-downs or ignoring the person's points will probably backfire. Instead, be more direct:

★ Stop and explain that obviously your current approach to the presentation does not seem wanted
★ Suggest a change of format, for example, to one of questions and answers. Look directly at the chief heckler when you say this. This may shame them into backing down, even apologising and letting you get on with your performance as planned

In large business conferences most heckling is usually fairly polite, rather than vicious. Either ignore the hecklers or invite them to make their points during question time.

Action you can take includes:

★ Research the audience to learn who might be disruptive
★ Develop strategies for handling each person, whatever their status
★ Whenever possible use peer pressure to deal with the person
★ Refuse to get upset or angry, retain a sense of humour
★ In a large audience ask hecklers to identify themselves by name and role – they usually prefer anonymity
★ Give hecklers enough rope to hang themselves; your audience will soon make its views felt
★ Take hecklers seriously, answering their points with respect even if only briefly
★ Try walking over to troublemakers and standing beside them; this can be enough to silence them and regain the initiative
★ Wait for the heckler to make a mistake on facts and then ask the audience for a correction
★ If you're prepared to laugh at yourself, good heckling can

even help your performance, by showing you retain your sense of humour

When dealing with hecklers first make direct eye contact, treating them with respect. However, let your eyes gently slide away from them as you answer so that you end up speaking to someone else. This avoids giving them 'permission' to carry on talking at you. Absolutely refuse to deal with a heckler who won't look you in the eye. Insist they do, by asking for their attention if necessary.

Serious verbal comebacks to deal with the situation might include:

★ 'I think we're going over old ground. Why not meet with me afterwards and I'll be glad to explore this more with you'
★ 'I'd love to continue with this but I'd like to move on'
★ Ask 'What do other people feel? Should I continue or do you want to spend some more time on this issue?'

A humorous approach to hecklers might include:

★ 'Let's call it a draw'
★ 'I really wish I'd said that, but I will'
★ 'Could you repeat that please.' Heckler remarks usually sound silly the second time around. If the person says nothing, insist they repeat it so the rest of the audience can hear it. The person will probably soon be thoroughly uncomfortable
★ 'I'll do a deal, you agree not to interrupt me and I'll promise not to have hysterics'
★ 'Good point, let's discuss it over a drink afterwards.'
★ 'Thanks, I need all the help I can get'
★ 'Listen, the rule is only one person at a time can make a fool of themselves and right now it's my turn'

Help

You can obtain more help in presenting by

★ Attending a public course on learning to present
★ Obtaining one-to-one coaching
★ Reading more about the subject
★ Seeking continual feedback from friends, colleagues and your audiences

Hiccups

A bad case of hiccups just before an important performance is a

presenter's nightmare. Even worse is developing one during it. The world is full of infallible cures for the hiccups, from a sudden shock to doing vigorous exercise. One of the most reliable is:

★ Sit down with a glass of water filled to the brim
★ Take as tiny a sip as you can
★ Keep taking tiny sips in steady, but not rapid succession

This cure usually works because repetitive swallowing ends most people's hiccups within a minute or less.

It's rare to suffer hiccups while actually presenting. If it happens to you,

★ Call a break and do the above
★ Shorten the presentation and explain why
★ Carry on regardless and milk it for laughs
★ Involve the audience, ask them for their favourite cure

Highway code (see also Nerves in main body of text on pages 71-73, and Relaxation)

The presenter's highway code is:

★ Breathe
★ Stop
★ Look
★ Listen

Do this just before starting your actual performance. Take your time doing it, spending a few moments prior to saying your first words.

These simple steps are never a waste of time. It will enhance your presence, give you time to 'arrive', allowing your audience to settle down and ready themselves for what you have to say.

Hits

Marketeers swear by the 'five hits' rule. This says that people only buy or do important things you want them to do when they receive your message at least five different ways at five different times. What number hit is your presentation? Other hits could be a letter, a phone call, an e-mail, a brochure and so on.

If your presentation is to lead to another one, be sure to set it up speedily and tell all the people involved when they need to attend.

Hoodwink (see BLUFF)

We are never so easily deceived as when we imagine we are deceiving others.

LA ROCHEFOUCAULD, *MAXIMS* (1665)

Hook (see OPENERS in main body of text on pages 75–7)

Hostility (see also ANGER)

Winning over a hostile audience is the ultimate presentation triumph. You are dealing with people's feelings, which are never entirely rational, so the sooner you can return to firmer ground with some hard facts the better.

Steps to handle hostility include:

★ Discover the source of the anger
★ Be willing to 'hear' people recounting their view of the situation
★ In some cases list on a flip pad issues arousing hostility
★ Acknowledge the hostility, without attacking people for feeling that way
★ Show empathy for people's feelings
★ Where you have limited powers to affect the source of their anger explain this clearly to people
★ Ask if people are prepared to consider some facts
★ Present facts that can be well substantiated with additional evidence
★ Deal systematically with issues raised and obtain agreement to move on

Leave your own hostility at home when you come to give your presentation.

Humour (see HUMOUR in main body of text on pages 83-86)

Humour is richly rewarding to the person who employs it. It has some value in gaining and holding attention. But it has no persuasive value at all.

J. K. GALBRAITH

I

Ideas (see also AUDIENCE, RESEARCH, SUBJECT)

If you are possessed by an idea, you can find it expressed everywhere, you can even smell it.

THOMAS MANN, *DEATH IN VENICE*

If you're planning a business presentation you probably already have a clear picture of what it's about. If in doubt, choose a topic by talking to some of your potential audience. Ask what issues currently concern people; what worries them right now, what problems do they want fixed? Among their responses will almost certainly be a germ of an idea that you can develop and elaborate into a proper presentation.

Injecting ideas into your performance

★ Link the topic with a current or recent event

★ Find a connection between your topic and somebody famous

★ Choose something totally irrelevant to your subject and see what new connections – no matter how crazy – you can make between it and your subject

★ Write down all the words you can think of associated with your topic. Use this list to begin expanding your thinking around the topic

★ Draw a mind map of the connections between your central topic and associated themes; explore the linkages

★ Regardless of how embryonic it may be, say your presentation aloud. Hearing it may stimulate you with ideas

★ Choose a physical object. Explore the connections between this object and your topic; what ideas does this forced association generate?

★ Use your audience to generate the entire presentation. Having announced your topic, ask them what aspects they would like you to cover; list the ideas on a flip chart and you will soon have more than enough material with which to work

★ Explain your topic to a young child of ten or twelve and use the resulting questions to expand your thinking

New ideas are one of the most overrated concepts of our time. Most of the important ideas that we live with aren't new at all

ANDREW A. ROONEY IN PREFACE, *PIECES OF MY MIND* (1984)

If you're trying to sell an idea, people need to understand its benefits. Explain how it relates to the old way and describe how it will work differently.

Will your idea affect people adversely, or make them seem old-fashioned or stupid? How you present it may matter just as much as the idea itself.

Idioms (see also CLICHÉ, and INTERPRETERS)

If you say things like

★ 'Pull a face'
★ 'Kill it stone dead'
★ 'In a manner of speaking'
★ 'For crying out loud'
★ 'Dummy run'

you're using an English idiom. Like clichés, idioms are popular and have established their meaning over time. Someone unfamiliar with English, though, may find your idioms hard to understand, since the phrases mean rather more than the actual words themselves.

★ Avoid idioms, particularly if talking to an audience whose first language is not English

If you're wondering whether a phrase is perhaps really an idiom you can consult one of the standard reference sources such as *The Oxford Dictionary of English Idioms*, by A. P. Cowie et al (1997, ISBN 0-19-43128-79).

Illness (see also AUDIENCE, and PAIN)

I'm not ill, it's just that I'm made of second-rate materials.
SPEAKER EXPLAINING A HEAVY COLD TO AN AUDIENCE

If you're genuinely ill, cancel. For important pitches this is hard to do, since you may not get another chance to present your case again to that particular audience. But if you're constantly coughing and sneezing or clearly suffering in some way, you won't do yourself justice or endear yourself to the audience.
For important engagements take along a small medical kit to handle headaches, stomach problems and other possibilities, such as eye infections.

If you feel unwell during a presentation invite the audience to do some task such as talking in pairs about an issue, while you leave the platform to take an aspirin, stomach settler, or other medicine.

If a member of the audience is ill, stop and deal with this. Indicate to the organisers that someone is clearly in distress and needs help. Your audience will appreciate your solicitude and be grateful that you have done something on their behalf. If the person has to leave early because of illness, wish them well on their departure and promise to send them your material. If they are taken away to hospital, try to discover some news to give the audience before the end of your presentation.

If one person is constantly coughing or sneezing call a break and during it ask if they need help. Suggest that they sit at the back to cause less distraction for others. If everyone is doing it, either there's an epidemic or there's something wrong with your presentation so switch tactics:

★ Use new material
★ Get people talking in groups
★ End the presentation early

Image (see IMAGE in main body of text on pages 88–96)

> *I don't change my style of dress when*
> *I go to lunch with my bankers.*
>
> RICHARD BRANSON

Imagery (see also SIMILE)

Most people in your audience will hardly remember what you said a week later, let alone detailed contents. Strong mental or visual images can make your ideas memorable, cementing them in place.

Imagery can literally be a picture of some kind, or simply a powerful figure of speech that creates a picture in people's minds.

★ Find a single image, picture or event that encapsulates your entire presentation message

For example, an insurance expert presenting to a board of directors was advising on employee benefits. He drew a picture of a bath to represent the present scheme and explained that company contributions going in were controlled by the tap much as water flow is controlled into an ordinary bath tub. The tap was the actuary advising on when to increase the inward flow of company contributions.

You might show a picture of a herd of fleeing antelope to suggest that the competition facing your company is on the run. Or you might talk of a problem being 'a maze' to convey the idea that solving it is likely to be difficult. People are more likely to remember an image than any verbal message.

Specific imagery can enable you to raise important issues in an acceptable manner. For example, you might use a picture of a flock of sheep to signify complacency or failure to think about direction. The sheep and what they stand for become your real message.

You could use a physical object to bring to life the image you want to put over. For instance, you could hold up a boxing glove to convey your concern about excessive conflict. The glove is likely to stay in people's minds long after you have ended your presentation.

Verbal imagery is equally effective: 'More black holes spotted in the public finances than in outer space recently' was the imagery used to describe the UK government's view of the financial legacy from the previous administration.

Metaphors, similes and analogies can all create vivid imagery that underpins the basic message.

Try to invent your own imagery, rather than using well-worn examples that hardly stir the blood. For instance, this is tired imagery heard too often:

★ 'The project fell at the first hurdle'
★ 'The report leaves the door ajar'
★ 'We've hit a roadblock on the way'
★ 'The heat's off'
★ 'An iron-clad argument'
★ 'A shadow cast over the future'
★ 'We should pull the plug on this project'
★ 'Get them on board'

Imagination (see also Spontaneity)

Audiences love the unexpected, wanting to be surprised and delighted. So many business presentations follow a highly predictable path that those on the receiving end often yearn for something different.

Give yourself permission to go for the outrageous image, the challenging idea, the dramatic high point. Let your imagination run wild when devising your presentation. You could begin by exploring

★ What would a totally different presentation look like?
★ What might people least expect?
★ How could I delight these people?

★ What would shock them?
★ What single image sums up my message?
★ How would my message be presented by a famous pop star, politician, Disney character, or other personality?
★ If I sang the presentation in three minutes, what would the words and tune be?

Even if you never use these in the final performance, wondering how you might use them can stimulate you to devise a more exciting presentation.

Using your imagination is also important during the actual presentation situation. If you stay fully alert and allow yourself the freedom to adapt and improvise, you may spot important ways to enliven your performance.

Impact (see PASSION in main body of text on pages 77–80)

His speech was rather like being savaged by a dead sheep.
DENIS HEALEY ON THE THEN UK CHANCELLOR OF THE EXCHEQUER

Impress

Impressive presentations are an art, not a science. One of the best ways is to build a memorable performance is to follow the five Ps of presentation:

★ Preparation
★ Purpose
★ Presence
★ Passion
★ Personality

Work on each of these and you certainly have the basis for a powerful and memorable performance. Read more of the five Ps in *The Perfect Presentation* by Andrew Leigh and Michael Maynard (Arrow Books).

Impromptu (see IMPROVISE and SPONTANEITY)

Improve

The best presenters know there is always another level to reach. They spend time analysing their last performance for clues about what worked and what didn't. Large-scale bidders persistently seek ways to improve because of the amount of resources it takes to mount a serious, large-scale bid. Improvement comes through

persistence, with lots of small changes eventually creating major enhancements to the presentation performance.

Improving is not merely about practice, it's also based on

★ Regular feedback, from the audience, colleagues and via video
★ Obtaining professional help
★ Tracking each performance and analysing it systematically
★ Remaining open to new ideas and ways of communicating
★ Continuous experimentation

Improvise (see also SPONTANEITY)

It usually takes me more than three weeks to prepare a good impromptu speech.

MARK TWAIN

'Improvisation is the essence of good talk,' argued Max Beerbohm and the best presentations are usually the ones where there is plenty of room for spontaneity.

Yet improvising is not always quite what it seems. According to a report in Newsweek, during his political career, Ronald Reagan squirrelled away bits of misinformation and, sometimes years later, would casually drop them into his public speeches, 'like gum balls in a quiche'.

Oscar Wilde and Mark Twain, both masters of the bon mot, demonstrated that the best impromptu remarks are carefully planned. To be ready for that moment when someone asks you to give a presentation without prior warning,

★ Carry a memory jogger to remind you of jokes, stories or one-liners
★ Get a friend to fire miscellaneous topics at you and practise talking for five minutes on each
★ Draft a possible speech – just in case. The sort of situations where you might be asked to improvise in public might include:

a welcome to someone visiting
thanks to somebody for their efforts
explain failures or problems
call for help
congratulations
make an announcement
your presentation ends too early
question time

Ways to prepare for improvisation include collecting materials you might use and adopting a reliable structure for handling short-notice presentations.

Material

Experienced presenters prepare at least twice as much material as they intend to use. Keep appropriate material ready to hand on compact memo cards in case you are asked to speak without warning, or to extend a speech longer than originally planned.

If asked to give an impromptu performance ask for a few moments and a quiet room in which to collect your thoughts. Jot down some ideas and preferably a structure for your presentation. Think of a story, a quote or an image to grab people's attention.

Structure

A well-tried structure you can use for impromptu presentations is:

★ Situation – you describe something
★ Complication – you elaborate on it in some interesting way
★ Question – you raise an important question
★ Resolution – you resolve the question with a viewpoint, a story, an appeal

Inadequate (see also N<small>ERVES</small> in main body of text on pages 71–73)

> *Remember no one can make you feel inferior*
> *without your consent.*
> ELEANOR ROOSEVELT, *CATHOLIC DIGEST* (1960)

It happens to the best of us. Asked to give a business presentation we wonder, 'Can I really do it well?' Yet people ask you to present because they think you

★ Have something to say
★ Can do it

A major cause of feeling inadequate to the task is lack of clarity about purpose. For example, a summons to present to the board of directors may be based on a poor brief or insufficient information about what is required.

Another source of inadequacy is insufficient preparation. This could be poor research, lack of rehearsal practice, or uncertainty about the strength of your arguments.

If after several different challenging presentations you still feel inadequate it's time to seek professional help. Obtain some private coaching or attend a presentation course.

Inaudible

> *The inability to hear is a nuisance.*
> *The inability to communicate is the tragedy.*
> LOU ANN WALKER, *A LOSS FOR WORDS* (1986)

No matter how brilliant your presentation, if the audience can't hear properly it's wasted. With a small amount of professional help, anyone with a quiet voice can soon learn how to project without shouting or straining.

One of the silliest questions inexperienced speakers sometimes ask is: 'Can everyone hear me at the back?' Obviously those who cannot hear would not receive the question in the first place. Instead, prior to starting your presentation, ask one or two people to sit at the back and during it to signal by raising their hands if they cannot hear you properly.

Many people believe that they are speaking loudly when in fact they are not. Asked to speak louder, they feel that they are almost shouting when they are really a long way from that level. Only independent feedback will clarify whether your presentation speaking voice is coming across strongly enough.

The secret of good voice projection is breathing. Just try this simple exercise:

★ Hum as loudly as you can while letting most of your breath out
★ Now inhale a big breath, without raising your shoulders. Again hum as loudly as possible

Your second attempt should be much louder than the first and certainly easier. Plenty of air in your lungs allows your larynx to vibrate and enables you to expel sounds with considerable force without yelling.

Other ways to improve your projection include:

★ Stay away from smoke or smokers
★ Avoid straining your voice by pitching it too high or too low
★ Speak slowly
★ Give your voice a rest by having refreshment breaks
★ Avoid iced water, drink something warm or just cool
★ Clear your throat gently, without a rasping sound

★ Do a pre-presentation warm-up by loosening your vocal chords and exercising your mouth and tongue with some practice phrases or tongue twisters

While a microphone makes being heard easier, experienced presenters still practise voice projection. Consequently, they are not disconcerted if the sound system fails.

Inductive (see REASONING in main body of text on pages 30–1)

Influence (see PERSUASION in main body of text on pages 26–39)

I should always prefer influence to power.
KINGSLEY MARTIN (1897–1969), *FATHER FIGURES*

Innuendo (see also SEXISM)

The only way graceful way to accept an insult is to ignore it; if you can't ignore it, top it; if you can't top it, laugh at it; if you can't laugh at it, it's probably deserved.
RUSSELL LYNES

In most business presentations people expect to hear about what you want to do, or how you see a situation. Disparaging remarks seldom help your case. It's a sign of weakness to knock competitors by name, or indirectly criticise a specific colleague whose actions you disapprove of.

Sometimes in a pitch situation you may be asked what you think of your competitors, or be told about what a competitor has said, done or promised. Despite the temptation, avoid innuendoes that may leave a nasty taste in the mouth.

If during your presentation you receive an insulting remark don't rise to it. Either take it at face value and deal with it in factual terms, or smile calmly and move straight on without responding.

Insight (see also PRESENCE in main body of text on page 73)

One learns people through the heart,
not the eyes or the intellect.
MARK TWAIN

Knowing what an audience wants comes from

★ Careful audience research
★ Solid preparation
★ Being totally present during the event

★ Listening to your intuition

Good insights are only worth having if you follow them, taking action based on what you have realised. In a presentation, that can mean scrapping the whole thing or radically altering the contents. For example, after a few minutes' presenting you may become aware that the audience is not listening with much interest and it makes no sense simply to plough on regardless.

Inspiration (See also IDEAS and SPONTANEITY)

You can't direct it and it refuses to come. It's as tiring as constipation. It might start tomorrow.

LAWRENCE DURRELL
ON WRITING POETRY, INTERVIEW IN THE *GUARDIAN* (1985)

To inspire your audience first inspire yourself. Look for events, stories, situations, people that uplift you and make you feel good. Use these to shape your presentation material and your delivery.

People have created business presentations using everything from pantomime to science fiction, from cartoon characters to popular songs. Sources for inspiration are endless:

★ How a favourite admired person might deliver the presentation
★ Poems
★ Paintings
★ Films
★ Literature
★ Famous speeches
★ Images, metaphors or analogies
★ Events that have inspired you
★ Nature
★ Biographies, stories of outstanding human beings

Internet (see Web Sites)

Interpreters (see also main body of text on page 44)

If you're talking to people whose first language is not English you may be working with interpreters. They need as much help as possible, so

★ Speak slowly
★ Supply an advance a copy of your presentation

Speaking slowly helps both the interpreters with the job of

translating your meaning and the audience who may take time to realise it. However, it also changes how you present. If possible, go through the text with the interpreters to discover any words they don't know, to clarify any metaphors, concepts or references.

Getting the interpreters on your side can be enormously helpful. Take particular care to thank them in advance and afterwards for their support. Check on where they sit. Can they see you? Are they in a stuffy box with lack of air-conditioning? If so, you can win friends by offering a break after, say, thirty minutes, to give them time to get out and stretch their legs.

If you can see the interpreters at work, arrange an agreed signal with them so they can warn you if they are getting behind you or are confused. Also, if you decide to depart from your script, give them a signal such as using a phrase like: 'Something I'd like to mention that is not in my prepared speech . . .'

Building a relationship with an audience through interpreters requires extra preparation and increased sensitivity to audience needs.

Preparation

★ Research the culture and expectations of your non-English-speaking audience

★ Discover what technical words can be readily translated and which may need special handling

★ Be careful of using too much humour, which may not work well in translation

★ Reduce your material by half – people listening in a foreign language soon lose concentration. You also need to say everything important in several different ways

Interruptions (see main body of text on pages 101–2)

Have you noticed life consists mostly of interruptions, with occasional spells of rush work in between?'

BUWEI YANG CHAO IN YUENREN CHAO,
AUTOBIOGRAPHY OF A CHINESE WOMAN (1947)

Interviews

★ Prepare for your interview like any other type of presentation

★ Decide in advance what are the key points you want to convey

★ Research the organisation and those likely to do the interview

★ Give particular attention to physical appearance and clothing

★ Hold a vision in your mind of the interview going outstandingly well
★ Have at least a couple of questions you could ask if you get the chance

Interviews are merely another form of business presentation. Instead of giving a straight talk, you have a personal message to communicate. During it, you are offering yourself for scrutiny and must perform at your best. Like any form of business presentation it pays to prepare well and you can often anticipate the important issues that will arise.

'Tell me about yourself' is a question usually asked at some point. It's deliberately open ended so that you can expound at length. You may think you could talk endlessly about yourself and indeed you probably can. The trouble is the time is limited. What is the main point you want to get across? Can you sum up in a single headline your main message? For example,

★ 'I'm really reliable'
★ 'I make things happen'
★ 'I'm a real self-starter'
★ 'I know how to get things done in an organisation like yours'
★ 'I am hard-working and dedicated'
★ 'I get on well with most people'

The opening question may well set the tone for the rest of the interview. A job interview is like a sales presentation and that means not hiding your light under a bushel. Now is the time to tell them how good you are, to show them how you could add value, to explain why you are worth hiring. False modesty at this point is a waste of everyone's time.

Find out about the company you expect to hire you. Don't go in blind and hope to wing it. It's always impressive if you can say things like:

★ 'I visited your web site and have a good feel for what sort of company you are'
★ 'I know your main products and am impressed with the range and quality'
★ 'You're known as a company that cares about developing people and that's why I want to come here'
★ 'Your investment in research and development shows you are committed to the long term'

Get hold of the company's available publications and find some

important points to recount in the interview. The sort of publications to track down include:

★ The annual report
★ Employee newsletters
★ Recent news profiles of the company
★ Special publications such as product catalogues
★ Information published on the company's web site

You are competing with maybe dozens, even hundreds of other candidates. Your interviewers soon get punch-drunk with seeing people one after the other.

★ Find a way to stand out from the crowd

Introduction

To be introduced properly before your presentation give the chairperson or the organisers a written note about yourself. Keep it short, factual and easy to read.

★ Check whether the person giving the introduction is using the one you provided
★ Take a spare copy of your introduction in case it hasn't reached the chairperson
★ Ask the person introducing you if they would mind having a small rehearsal, even if that risks you sounding like you're on an ego trip. That way you'll discover if they are intending to add any strange bits of their own

Supposing the introduction is truly awful, what can you do? Rather than scowl at the other person and show any anger, merely thank them politely and start right into your presentation, or offer a short introduction in your own words.

Involvement (see PARTICIPATION in main body of text on pages 106–9)

> *It is better to wear out than rust out.*
> RICHARD CUMBERLAND (1730–1802)

Irony (see SATIRE)

J

Jaded

Life is one long process of getting tired.
SAMUEL BUTLER, WRITER, 'LORD WHAT IS A MAN?' IN *NOTEBOOKS* (1912)

Even the best presenters can weary of performing. If you think you're burning out, take a break. Let someone else have the limelight for a while.

You may become jaded if you start treating regular presentations as mere routine, requiring no emotional commitment or involvement. For example, if you are regularly presenting a standard sales message to potential customers it can be difficult to see each new presentation in a fresh way.

Ways to avoid becoming jaded include:

★ Use a visual reminder that this is the first time people have heard your message
★ Take more risks
★ Inject more creativity
★ Look for new angles to challenge you – for example, present the entire message using three pictures, doing it from among the audience, making it all interactive
★ Keep changing how you present: use of phrases, whether you stand or sit, your visual aids and so on
★ Experiment with new equipment and other support materials
★ Alter the balance between speaking and asking the audience to do things

Jargon (see also JARGON in main body of text on page 35)

She calls a spade a delving instrument.
RITA MAE BROWN, *SOUTHERN DISCOMFORT* (1982)

Are you a jargon junky, perhaps without even knowing it? If you're deeply immersed in a specialist profession jargon can seem part of everyday language. Yet it's excluding, even when your audience understands it. The simpler your communication the better.

★ Avoid jargon as a way of trying to impress people
★ Ask a colleague to do a jargon check on your presentation
★ Explain any jargon that you use for those in the audience who don't know it

Jitters (see Nerves in main body of text on pages 71-73)

I feel so agitated all the time,
like a hamster in search of a wheel.

CARRIE FISHER, *POSTCARDS FROM THE EDGE* (1987)

Jokes (see Humour in main body of text on pages 83-86)

Jokes have little to do with spontaneous humour. The teller has
the same relationship to them that he or she might have to a
Hertz Rent-a-car. A joke is a hired object, with many previous
users, and very often with other people's cigarettes, and its gears
are worn and slipping, because other people have driven this
joke very badly before you got behind the wheel.

JONATHAN MILLER, BRITISH DOCTOR, HUMORIST AND DIRECTOR,
'AMONGST CHICKENS' IN *GRANTA* (1988)

K

Keynote (see also Celebrity Speaking)

Occasionally you may be asked to give a keynote address at a conference or company meeting. This is an important role – you set the tone for the rest of the day and perhaps for much longer.

Keynote speakers usually have something to say, they don't just follow a prescribed topic. To be a keynote speaker you need to be someone willing to step out and raise challenging issues for the audience to consider.

People are relying on you if you to accept this role so it's important both to prepare and to arrive.

You will probably have plenty of notice that you are a keynote speaker so will have time to do your research and ensure that your presentation really does hit the mark and create the right atmosphere.

One issue you may need to consider is, as a keynote speaker whom do you represent? If you work for a company, for example, are you speaking as a representative of that organisation or merely someone in your own right? It may be important to clarify this early on for your audience.

Keystoning (see also Overheads)

Keystoning is when the image from a projector looks wider at the top than the bottom. It happens because the distance to the top of the image from the projector is greater than to the bottom. Projectors close to the screen are more likely to create this effect than those placed in the middle of the room.

★ Reduce distortion by tilting the screen from the top, outwards towards the audience

Keywords (see also MEMORY)

Relying on using the exact words of the script is a recipe for trouble. A script is best used only as a starting point to

★ Order your thoughts
★ Structure your message
★ Rehearse and become familiar with the material
★ Memorise material
★ Identify keywords and phrases

Kids (see CHILDREN)

Know-how

Presentation know-how is cumulative. It is important in big organisations regularly doing large-scale bids and presentations systematically to capture and record information about what works and what doesn't.

Ernst and Young, for example, have developed the Hive, an intranet site, accessible to all its presenters around the globe. The Hive contains a vast amount of data concerned with preparing and making large-scale bids and presentations. Anyone can tap into this know-how.

On a personal level, presenting know-how stems mainly from having plenty of practice and always pushing to reach another level of performance. Sources of know-how for individuals include:

★ Other presenters
★ Newsletters on presenting
★ Books, magazines and web sites
★ Technical people selling or operating equipment
★ Presentation coaches
★ Courses on presenting

L

Label

Clearly label your notes, slides and overheads to show

★ Their order
★ Which way up they should be
★ Which way round they should be

You'll only realise how glad you are you did this when you drop them just before your performance or right in the middle of it.

Laminates

★ Laminate large-scale charts or pictures used repeatedly, to keep them clean and unbent
★ Heavily laminated charts on a flip-chart stand may not fold back easily. Use large clips to hold them in place
★ Lamination sheets reflect the light and may prevent some people viewing them. Test prior to the presentation for the best place to locate them
★ More than four or five large laminates are heavy and can be awkward to carry on long journeys

Language (see also INTERPRETERS)

If you're presenting to audiences whose first language is different from yours and in a culture not your own,

★ Speak slowly; allow plenty of pauses and don't be worried about silences
★ Your full personality will carry you a long way. If you're thoroughly yourself, your natural sincerity and wish to communicate can overcome formidable language obstacles
★ English is a highly efficient language and it's hard for translators to keep up. They're usually at least ten words behind you
★ Check with the translator that any jokes will work both verbally and culturally
★ Research your audience's cultural expectations
★ Learn some of the foreign language to introduce or end your presentation
★ Issue your translated presentation in written form afterwards
★ Avoid phrases, words, images, metaphors and analogies that have special meaning in your language but not necessarily in

the other

★ Irony and sarcasm don't translate well. In Fiji, for example, audiences won't understand irony and will take what is said literally

★ In some cultures, particularly Asia, direct eye contact makes people feel uncomfortable

★ Translate all words on charts and visuals

★ Don't read materials aloud in your own language while the audiences read in theirs; instead, use a volunteer to read in the audience's own language

★ Don't be surprised or upset if your audience shows little reaction; in some cultures lack of reaction is a sign of politeness

★ Watch the audience carefully, particularly eyes and expression. If people look even slightly confused stop and ask if you said it wrong or are not being clear. People will appreciate your concern and it sets the right mood

★ If you're confident enough to present using a second language, your audience will usually be delighted and fairly forgiving of weak grammar and accent. However, it's better to rely on simultaneous translation if you're talking at length, unless you are really proficient in the other language

Handling questions needs special care when presenting to a foreign audience

★ In some cultures people are taught not to question authority so asking questions just doesn't happen

★ People may be afraid of losing face and appearing stupid in front of colleagues

★ The audience may not wish to embarrass you so avoids questions

★ If you are asked the same question twice it may be that some people did not understand your presentation

For audiences reluctant to speak up, ask people to form small groups to discuss your presentation and to identify questions they would like to ask you. Circulate among the groups and offer them a safe way of communicating or get the group to write their questions down.

Laptops (see also EQUIPMENT)

If using a laptop connected to an overhead projector, practise until you are thoroughly at home and can cope if the technology

fails. Take a spare set of printed overheads so that you can resort to these if necessary.

You'll probably be cursed with all sorts of trailing leads and other appendages. Just as you start, you or the person introducing you may well trip over the wires and kill the technology. Use a roll of wide plastic tape to stick the wires to the floor out of harm's way.

If your audience is also using laptops to keep notes of your presentation as you speak, you face several dilemmas:

★ People are typing and distracting other members of the audience
★ They are not paying attention to you
★ You cannot contact these people or see their reactions

By having copies of your presentation to hand out afterwards you can legitimately request people with laptops to refrain from using them and disturbing others.

Last

If you're speaking at a business conference, discover from the organisers who precedes you. Check whether their material will in any way clash with yours.

The advantage of being the last speaker is that your words are the ones the audience is most likely to remember. If you know you're the last speaker,

★ Keep your presentation short
★ Find ways to inject fresh energy into the room both at the start of your performance and right to the end
★ Find a particularly memorable way of closing your presentation
★ Acknowledge the previous presentations

Late (see INTERRUPTIONS in main body of text on pages 101–2, and TIME)

> *Punctuality comes high on my list of unforgivable sins.*
> DOROTHY CANNEL, *THE THIN WOMAN* (1984)

For large formal presentations,

★ Arrive several hours before you are due to speak
★ Don't take the last train or flight to a venue
★ Assume you'll hit serious hold-ups if you drive there

If you arrive late, take it seriously – while a joke may diffuse tension, don't let your audience think you are treating lateness lightly. Also apologise but don't refer to it again and certainly avoid lengthy or multiple excuses.

Latecomers

An important business presentation can be seriously affected if some of the key people don't arrive on time. If the audience is coming to your premises and there is a great deal at stake it may be better to send transport to pick everyone up. That way at least you can put pressure on people to be ready and you needn't start till everyone arrives.

At conferences there's little you can do to prevent latecomers, although you could try asking the organisers not to let latecomers in until you are finished.

Avoid punishing latecomers with jokes at their expense such as:

★ 'Where on earth have you been?'
★ 'So you finally got here'
★ 'Did the alarm clock fail?'

They may have had serious difficulties arriving at all. Be sympathetic, welcome them and, if appropriate, direct them to the nearest empty seat.

To minimise the chance of late returnees from a break,

★ Set a clear time for returning
★ Explain politely that you expect to start on time
★ Give people early warning that they are expected back shortly
★ Appoint someone to round up everyone
★ Use a whistle, music or other sound to signal when you want people to return

Have something ready for people to discuss or look at while waiting for the stragglers. If people are late coming back from breaks it could mean they are:

★ Excited to talk about the issues you are raising
★ Too bored to bother returning promptly
★ Forgetful and need rounding up

Laugh (see Humour in main body of text on pages 83-87)

The most wasted of all days is that on which
one has not laughed.
NICOLAS CHAMFORT (1741-94), FRENCH WRITER

Lavatory (see Toilets)

Layout (see Venue in main body of text on pages 63, 120–21)

LCD Panels (see also Equipment)

LCD or Liquid Crystal Displays are making big inroads into presentations around the world. The two types currently available are:

★ Panels that fit on Overhcad projectors
★ Self-contained LCD projectors

These systems project powerful images and are controlled by a portable computer, usually managed by the presenter. The panels project on to the screen anything appearing on the computer screen. You can show video, animation and graphics, all in the same presentation.

It's not nearly as daunting as it sounds, although you do need to practise to feel comfortable with the technology.

LCD panels work like an electronic slide. There are two types, active and passive. The former have better contrast and faster electronics, giving you the ability to show animation and video. Passive panels are cheaper with less good colour. Both offer high-resolution images.

Pros	Cons
Portable	Needs a strong OHP projector
Easy to set up	Pixelation intrusive in large
Simple to use	projections
Audience involvement possible	Top models cost as much as self-contained CRT
Fast updating	projectors
Highly suitable for computer data	Not ideal for video images
	Relatively expensive

Once the panel is plugged in, it can usually be operated by remote control, from the panel itself, or via the nearby computer.

You may not even need a computer as some panels have their own built-in hard drive, so you can arrive at your presentation carrying only one piece of equipment. Alternatively, you could have a specialist portable computer, which has as its screen an LCD panel that detaches for placing on an OHP.

Tips on using an LCD panel:

★ Use a proper projection screen designed to give optimum performance
★ Use the best quality OHP you can manage with a minimum 400-watt bulb and good-quality optics
★ Use a high-grade colour panel for displaying colour photographs, graduated tones or video images
★ Use an electronic laser pointer from a distance, rather than standing by the screen gesturing at images
★ Keep the computer screen turned away from the audience
★ Rehearse more than usual

LCD Projectors (see also EQUIPMENT)

Liquid Crystal Displays began in small pocket computers and have expanded to large-screen formats. At one end of the market there are the highly portable, increasingly compact and easy-to-use systems for screens up to about ten feet across. At the other end there are the super projectors with extremely bright images for screens up to thirty feet across. The larger machines are usually already installed in conference halls.

LCD Projectors are more convenient than panels and advancing portability means that presenters can increasingly take a machine with them to a site.

Pros	Cons
Fast and easy to set up	Image pixelation at high magnification
Very bright	
Portable	Keystone adjustment only on some models
Easy to use	
Low running costs	Audio systems not always adequate
Low maintenance	
	Cost, especially at hi-tech end

Tips on using LCD projectors:

★ Get the best system you can afford with video quality
★ Keep spare lamps on hand
★ Check the links with video and computers, colour-coding them for ease of connection
★ Always see the system operating, don't just buy from catalogues

★ Check the audio, particularly for large rooms; you may need a separate amplification system
★ Don't touch the projection lens
★ Practise until it's second nature

Lectern (see also PODIUM and STAIRS)

You put your notes on a lectern and stand on a podium. Many people confuse these two when talking to conference organisers. Be tactful in asking for what you want: nobody wants to be reminded that they are not clear about the meaning of a word.

If you are a short person ask whether the lectern can be adjusted and if so, arrive early to ensure that it meets your needs. Some lecterns also incorporate lighting, sound and audio-visual technology. If you are expected to operate these, allow time to practise.

As you rise to go to the lectern, your adrenalin will probably be pumping wildly. Now is the time to draw a deep breath and take the walk slowly. If you trip on the way it shows you are human, shrug it off and continue on your way. The audience will like you better if you can laugh at yourself and your clumsiness.

Lecture
Don't.

Length
Keep it short! Even if invited to speak at length, stick to the simple rule:

★ Leave them wanting more

Few presenters can hold their listeners much beyond thirty minutes without audience fatigue. The best presentation is usually the shortest. In preparing material, have twice as much as you need, kept in reserve.

Time your presentation and cut the material in half. Once you allow for audience reaction and your own delivery foibles you will almost certainly overrun.

If you run out of things to say, involve the audience in discussing your views rather than speaking longer.

Lettering (see also VISUALS in main body of text on pages 40-48)

Nowadays, everyone can create professional-looking lettering for charts and handouts. Designing your own lettering is seldom justified for a business presentation and best left to specialists.

Basic lettering can be created on computer and quickly transferred to overheads using a suitable printer, such as a laser or ink jet system.

★ Hand lettering makes the presentation seem less formal but if untidy can also make you appear unprofessional

Lights

★ Go to the middle of the room where you are presenting and check what people will see when you are speaking
★ Establish whether you'll be able to see the audience or not because of the lighting
★ Determine whether you'll be clearly visible
★ Check whether you can control the lighting from your speaker's position
★ Discover whether you can turn off lights or remove bulbs that shine in the audience's eyes

If performing to a really large audience you need to be well lit. The best lighting is with the house lights off but this prevents you from seeing either the audience or the edge of the stage. There is no reason you should suffer this. You are entitled to see the people you are addressing and there's nothing wrong with asking the technical team to turn up the house lights so that you can see whom you're taking to. Some presenters refuse to start until they can see their audience's eyes.

If you can't see the audience because of the lighting,

★ Focus on an imaginary person at the back or in the middle of the room
★ Keep addressing different parts of the audience

Listen

> *The opposite of talking isn't listening.*
> *The opposite of talking is waiting.*
> FRAN LEBOWITZ, *SOCIAL STUDIES* (1977)

When you are about to start your presentation, STOP! Look around you, breathe and take in your surroundings. Listen carefully to the sounds your audience can hear. In this moment of waiting you build your presence and begin really to get in touch with your listeners.

Some speakers can tell immediately how effective they are being by simply listening to the sounds the audience make. Warning signs include:

★ Papers rustling
★ Feet shuffling
★ Coughing
★ Talking
★ Throat clearing
★ Shifting in seats

★ Breathing sounds
★ Writing
★ Keyboard tapping
★ Cases opening and shutting
★ Snoring
★ Yawning

If you invite a question from the audience, show that you really have been listening by summarising it back to each person, who confirms you have understood it correctly.

Probing also shows you have been paying attention. Do it in a neutral way by encouraging the person to be more specific. For example,

★ 'In what ways are pressures on the company increasing?'
★ 'Can you give me an example?'
★ 'How might I do what you're suggesting?'
★ 'Would you like to explain how best I can help?'

Non-verbal messages that show that you are listening include: nodding, eyebrow raising, interested looks, leaning forward and smiling. Verbal signals include short words or phrases such as 'mm', 'uh huh', 'I see', 'really', 'sure'. These are not 'tricks' and need to be incorporated into your normal style through practice.

Feelings:
The time really to show you're listening is when your presentation stirs up people to express anger or dissatisfaction. Hear what people are feeling, not just what they are saying. Listen for emotive words that tell you the situation. You can convey a listening message if you

★ Reflect back feeling: 'Seems to me you're really angry', 'Looks like I've upset you'
★ Paraphrase: use your own words to describe what they have said
★ Summarise: condense the information into brief points or themes

Location (see VENUE in main body of text on page 63)

Long before you leave for the presentation check that you have

★ Understood the location – the correct town, state or even country
★ A clear, correct map of the location
★ Adequate time to reach the destination
★ Clarified the best means of travel: for example, which of two airports is the best, is it quicker to go by train or road?
★ Information on alternative train or plane times if you miss a connection
★ The phone number of the place to which you are travelling

Logic (see REASONING in main body of text on pages 30–1)

> *Logic must take care of itself.*
> LUDWIG WITTGENSTEIN

Logo (see also THEMES in main body of text)

Try converting your presentation message into a single picture, drawing or symbol. This could act as your logo throughout the presentation, constantly re-enforcing your message.
A message logo can appear on all charts, in a corner, as bullets, or as a faint watermark. You might even hand to your audience a small plastic card or some other gift, with the logo on it as a reminder of what you said.

Long-winded (see main body of text on page 35)

> *Good things, when short, are twice as good.*
> BALTASAR GRACIÀN (1601–58), SPANISH WRITER

Loud (see main body of text on page 00)

Inexperienced presenters often have no sense of how loudly they are speaking. Too quiet is as bad as too loud. Using a mike can make it even harder to judge one's volume.
Prior to starting your presentation in a large venue, test for excessive volume. If, during the presentation, someone yells 'We can't hear you' acknowledge their contribution, then

★ Stop and wait for the technical people to take action
★ Start a discussion exercise while the problem is sorted
★ Ask people at the back to come forward to fill empty seats
★ Move out and walk among the audience
★ Offer a place nearer the front, if necessary asking someone to swap seats

Luck

> *I am a great believer in luck, and I find the harder*
> *I work the more I have of it.*
> STEPHEN LEACOCK (1869–1944),
> ENGLISH-BORN CANADIAN ECONOMIST AND HUMORIST

Experienced presenters don't rely on luck to be outstanding. They prepare meticulously, maximising the chances of success. Having covered all the angles, they are absolutely ready to take advantage of luck whenever it occurs.

Lunch (see also GRAVEYARD SHIFT)

> *Never drink black coffee at lunch; it will keep you*
> *awake in the afternoon.*
> JILLY COOPER, *HOW TO SURVIVE FROM NINE TO FIVE* (1970)

Blood sugar peaks around ninety minutes after a meal and probably the worst time to present is just after lunch – the graveyard shift. If you are presenting to a large audience,

★ Try to renegotiate to speak either later or in the morning
★ Adjust your material to include some audience participation so people stay awake
★ Cut your material and talk for half the planned time
★ Discuss whether it can be a low-fat, relatively light meal
★ Change the dynamics so people have to pay attention and are stimulated. For example,
   Why not start your presentation at the back of the room so that people have to turn around?
   Get people standing up and doing some stretching and breathing exercises 'so we can all stay awake'
   Take the entire audience on a quick lap around the building
   Get everyone to change places every five minutes

M

Magic

You don't need to be Houdini or David Copperfield to use magic to good effect in business presentations. A good conjuring trick can break the ice, win a laugh, punch home a point and make the presentation memorable.

For example, the directors of Maynard Leigh Associates sometimes introduce their company by explaining that they are in the business of adding sparkle to people and helping to transform them. While making this point, one of the partners lights a large red candle and on the word 'transforms', the candle vanishes, becoming a large red silk scarf.

Most over-the-counter magic tricks are easy to learn and can be used to liven up your presentation. Here are the secrets of doing it well:

★ Learn the trick so thoroughly that you don't look at your hands or the equipment
★ Choose a trick relevant to your message
★ Show that you are really enjoying yourself

Make-up (see also IMAGE in main body of text on pages 88–96, and COSMETICS)

Wearing make-up is an apology for our actual faces.

CYNTHIA HEIMEL,
GET YOUR TONGUE OUT OF MY MOUTH, I'M KISSING YOU GOODBYE! (1993)

Manager

Few managers reach the top without mastering the basics of good presentations. If you feel you don't do yourself justice, consider having some training in presentation skills.

When presenting to other managers, particularly those that really matter for your career, stick to the three rules of good presentations: rehearse, rehearse, rehearse.

Managers are inevitably a tough audience. Because they usually sit through plenty of presentations they naturally become blasé about yet another. Further, if the presentation is by a colleague with whom they feel in competition they can be intolerant of any mistake.

What the average manager asks when watching a presentation is, 'What's in it for me?' This is only partly selfish. It is also an attempt to relate the material to the practical day to day, or their sphere of activity. 'How will this affect me?' is therefore a sensible question and one that your presentation needs to anticipate.

Mannerisms (see also IMAGE in main body of text on pages 88–96)

A well-known actor was playing a Shakespearean part, dressed

in a toga and sandals. Afterwards he asked a friend what he thought of an important speech he had made. 'I can't really say,' said his friend. 'You see, right through it your left big toe kept twitching up and down, up and down. I became so engrossed with watching it that I completely forgot to pay attention to what you were saying.'

If left uncontrolled, ticks, strange body movements and other quirks can undermine any presentation. For example, if you keep playing with your hair, or scratching your head, people will be drawn to watching these distractions.

Ask a friend to monitor your performance or use video playback to discover if you have annoying mannerisms. We often have such traits without even realising it. Distracting mannerisms include:

★ biting or chewing lips; scowling or frowning; jerky actions; leg-shaking while sitting; foot-tapping; hand-wringing; finger-massaging; sniffing; fiddling with clothes, hair or furniture; scratching or rubbing parts of face or body; playing with loose change in pockets; doodling

Distracting mannerisms mainly occur because you are unconsciously using up nervous energy. So it's important to practise relaxation and breathing as part of your development as a powerful presenter.

Material (see main body of text on pages 20–1)

A sentence is not emotional, a paragraph is.
GERTRUDE STEIN, 'SENTENCES AND PARAGRAPHS', *HOW TO WRITE* (1931)

Media (see EQUIPMENT and MULTIMEDIA)

The medium is the message.
MARSHALL MCLUHAN (1911–80)

Meetings

Even if you never give stand-up business presentations, you'll almost certainly attend meetings. In these, too, you need to become an effective presenter, able to hold your audience and get your message across. Meetings are mainly a more informal setting for a business presentation.

There are usually opportunities in informal situations such as meetings to build a relationship more quickly with the audience. Because there are fewer people, you can give each person more

attention, whether it's eye contact, or responding to their particular information needs.

To enhance your presentation impact in meetings:

★ Aim for eye contact with everyone attending
★ Build on what previous speakers have said rather than just making your point
★ Be a dedicated listener so you can decide when best to claim the limelight
★ Leave space for others by keeping your own contribution short
★ Adopt an unhurried pace that allows people to absorb your message
★ If you know important people are attending, prepare carefully for the meeting and bring relevant support documents
★ If asked to a meeting for the first time, check the protocol. For instance, how do you add items to the agenda, how long are people expected to stay, what are their expectations about supporting material, the kind of visual aids required and so on

Memory (see also NAMES)

> *A retentive memory may be a good thing, but the ability to forget is the true token of greatness.*
> ELBERT HUBBARD, *THE NOTE BOOK* (1927)

Brilliant business speakers don't rely on remembering an entire script; instead, they depend on three simple principles:

★ Rehearse endlessly, commit half an hour for every minute of presentation
★ Know the essence of the message rather than trying to remember lines
★ Use keyword notes or a few drawings rather than full notes

Even experienced presenters occasionally forget what they are supposed to say. Yet when they deal with temporary memory lapses you may hardly realise these have occurred because they

★ Ask the audience to do something collectively while they get back on track
★ Have a couple of quotation cards ready on the subject which they use to buy time
★ Initiate a quick question-and-answer session
★ Restate the last point just presented to the audience
★ Summarise

★ Use humour:

'It may look as if I haven't the faintest idea what I am supposed to say next, but don't let that fool you'

'My notes are a little confusing, it seems I am about to read you my shopping list'

'The next point is incredibly important. It's just a pity that I've completely forgotten what it is'

Message (see main body of text on pages 34–5)

Each presentation will have a message and a series of sub-messages. These need to be backed up with

★ Facts
★ Examples
★ Stories
★ Demonstrations
★ Arguments

The more complicated the message you choose, the harder it will be to get it across to your audience, so aim to simplify it down to a single, easy to remember line.

Metaphor (see SIMILE and IMAGERY)

Metaphors are much more tenacious than facts.

PAUL DE MAN (1919–83), US LITERARY CRITIC

Microphone

Most business presentations don't involve public address systems. The exceptions are conferences and addressing large numbers of people in organisations, such as a 'town hall'-type meeting. If there are more than 100 you'll almost certainly need a mike and it's essential with over 500 people.

Most experienced speakers have been sabotaged by acoustics. Mics in particular possess an amazing repertoire of tricks:

★ Crackles
★ Cut-outs
★ Feedback
★ Picking up short-wave transmissions from the police
★ Howls
★ Short leads
★ Wrong height and unalterable
★ Unstable stands

Do a check before going live with an audience. Discover all the likely pitfalls and minimise the chances of them occurring. If the mike isn't working before you start, don't continue until it's fixed. If there are technical people on site they will appreciate your thoroughness. For example, ask for a spare mike to be set up and ready to grab if yours dies.

Too often people plough on, hoping that they will be heard and they aren't. Even if you have excellent voice projection you won't make much of an impression if you have to shout to be heard. If you have to perform without a mike at a conference, insist that the organisers first explain the situation to the audience and that you have agreed to continue.

If the sound fails as you are talking don't blame anyone, just launch an audience participation exercise while the technology is repaired.

Given the frequency with which mics behave badly, some presenters keep a small arsenal of quips or comments ready such as:

★ 'I love feedback but that's ridiculous'
★ 'Is somebody trying to tell me something?'
★ 'Was it something I said?'
★ Staring hard at the microphone: 'You realise this means war'

If the mic fails in mid-presentation, you could

★ Hurl it to the floor in mock disgust
★ Regard it sadly and mutter, 'Rest in Peace'
★ Dangle it from the lead, saying, 'You might well hang your head in shame'
★ Hold it with disdain, saying, 'That's the last time I get my equipment at a bring-and-buy sale'

Mind map

This versatile device can help with both preparing and delivering your presentation. It visually represents connections between ideas, instead of a linear list.

A mind map starts with a simple word or idea, usually in the centre of a blank page, and additional words are added to create a network. Some people also call these spider diagrams because they are rather like webs. Here's the start of a mind map about presentations:

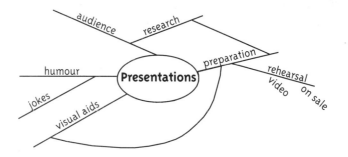

Mind maps are also excellent for stimulating you to think about your presentation. They encourage you to identify the issues or points that you'll be dealing with and how they relate to one another. They tend, also, to highlight areas where you don't have enough information and where further research is needed.

The mind map is also a different way of keeping your notes for a presentation. Instead of a series of lines on a card or a complete script, the mind map sums up your material and just a glance at it tells you where the issue you are dealing with fits in the overall presentation.

Mirror

Experienced presenters have mixed views about how useful mirrors are for checking on their presentation performance. Some argue that practising in front of a mirror is essential and that a full-length one is required so you can watch how you are moving.

Others claim that because a mirror shows you reversed – that is you see your left side as right and right as left – it only confuses. If a mirror helps, use it but you may find video more revealing.

Misquote

If using quotes as part of your presentation be sure to get them right. It's mortifying to have a member of the audience correct you. Check sources thoroughly and, if unsure, use the quote without attributing it to anyone.

If you do misquote in some way, take it seriously. Explain that you'll take immediate steps to discover the source or the correct words and thank whoever has put you on the spot.

If someone challenges you about the authenticity of a quote, thank them publicly and say you'll call them in a couple of weeks to confirm the correct information.

Mistake (see also MISQUOTE)

If I had to live my life again I'd make all the same mistakes
– only sooner.

TALLULAH BANKHEAD IN JOHN ROBERT COLOMBO,
POPCORN IN PARADISE (1979)

We all make mistakes when presenting. What counts is how we recover from them. Typical mistakes you might make are:

★ Start your presentation too early
★ Call someone by the wrong name or title
★ Give the wrong information
★ Drop all your notes
★ Trip over the microphone lead
★ Knock over a glass
★ Forget your speech in mid-flow
★ Put up the wrong slide or foil
★ Show a visual upside down
★ Overrun or finish too soon
★ Mix up your facts
★ Answer a question wrongly
★ Present incorrect information

Even though you know you have made a mistake your audience may not. Before rushing to draw attention to the error, give a moment to consider whether it's necessary.

If you need to make a correction apologise, put it right and move on. An audience is usually forgiving when a presenter is humble and acknowledges an error. If you try to bluster your way out of the situation you merely antagonise people.

Mockery (see SATIRE)

Mockery is often the result of a poverty of wit.

LA BRUYÈRE, *CHARACTERS* (1688)

Mouth

When you articulate clearly your mouth has to work quite hard. So if you're about to start a presentation take time to warm up by practising some tongue twisters or some easily remembered rhymes.

The more you open your mouth fully when speaking the less you will swallow your words. It is also the natural way of projecting your voice more fully.

Multi site (see also VIDEO CONFERENCES)

There is a growing trend towards presentations made to audiences in several sites at once. These include video and telephone conferences where there may be six or seven locations participating, with a score or more people watching and listening.

In these situations, try to determine who are the critical people, the key influencers who can block, approve or delay matters. Analysing these people, rather than absolutely everyone watching, makes preparing the presentation somewhat easier.

Having identified these key infuencers, prepare your presentation by further analysing:

★ What's in it for that person to agree or disagree, to support or oppose

★ How the person might be affected by what you present or propose

★ Whether the person previously supported or opposed anything similar and the outcomes

★ The likely response of this person to negative or positive reactions from others

★ Whether this person might be upset that you didn't consult or allow them to put forward the ideas you are presenting

★ The specific information this person might require, such as budgets, risk analysis, projections of market share, feasibility assessments, human implications and so on

Finally, some key influencers may not be at the site. How will these people react to what you are presenting?

Multimedia (see also EQUIPMENT and TECHNOLOGY)

Nowadays just about everything electronic is casually branded 'multimedia'. True multimedia is a combination of technologies that helps present your message. The choice of media is constantly growing and subject to rapid obsolescence. Only a few years ago an LCD plate set on an overhead projector and powered by a computer was becoming standard. Increasingly, computer-linked projectors are taking over. Similarly, while static or two-dimensional images are still popular, animation and 3-D graphics are increasingly used.

★ If the information in your presentation is time sensitive, pick a medium that allows for updating material easily and quickly

★ Select a medium to enhance your message, not because it is flashy or technically sophisticated

★ If you have to mix different media such as video, slides and overheads give the graphics a consistent design and ensure they are of similar quality

★ Choose a medium appropriate to the audience size. For instance, overhead projectors seldom work well with an audience of more than about thirty. Similarly, video for an audience of more than about twenty requires a really large screen

★ Choose non-linear interactive electronic methods when you want to present varying information as and when you need it, rather than in a set sequence such as a slide carousel

Some presentations can be made interactive by adopting multimedia. That is, the audience participates in the presentation by using the technology. An example is a group of people who use a hand-held device for voting on issues with the results instantly shown on the screen.

To create interactive programmes that involve your audience is extremely time-consuming and probably best contracted out to a specialist. For example, there are an increasing number of methods of recording the interactive material, including CD-ROM, CD-I and PhotoCD.

The technology can tend to blind one to the need to stick to the basics of good presentations in which you take centre stage.

★ You are the presentation, not the media

Pros and cons of using multimedia

Pros	Cons
A quick way of collecting audience information	A confusing range of technologies available
Allows tailoring of presentations to an audience	Some systems are expensive
Can be readily updated	Considerable resources of time, money and effort required

If you regularly present, try to keep abreast of what is happening in this field. It's changing so fast that what seems costly, complex, or time-consuming now, may soon not be. It isn't much fun if your carefully crafted and rehearsed presentation follows someone who delivers a stunning one using multimedia.

Mumbling (see Mouth)

Murphy's Law (see also PREPARATION)

The best-known application of this law of perversity is that

★   If something can go wrong, it will

Murphy was probably an optimist. Your presentation planning will be sound if you assume that you'll face disaster in some form. You can't anticipate all contingencies, so it's best to focus on the main ones that could cause serious trouble.

Ask yourself:

★   'What's the worst possible thing that could happen?'
★   'How would I handle it?'

Music

Music during a presentation gives it an added dimension and professionalism. However, it can also be pretentious if you are trying to create an informal atmosphere.

During coffee breaks, music can create a mood and tap into people's emotions. If you choose music that is too attractive the audience may want more than you are willing to give, leaving them feeling slightly frustrated.

You may need to pay a royalty for music not in the public domain, even if you are doing your presentation in-house within an organisation. The fees for using copyright music are modest and if you give many presentations during the year, rather than pay per session you can buy an annual licence covering any music you may play no matter how often.

To discover the royalties you must pay you should contact the performing rights organisation in your respective area. For example:

Country	Organisation	Telephone
AUSTRALIA	SALAIC	0054 1 371 2883
CANADA	CMRRA	001 416 926 1966
USA	AMRA	001 813 488 9695
USA	MRL	001 212 586 3450
USA	ASCAP	0171 439 0909
UK	PRS	0171 580 5544
FRANCE	SDRM	00 331 4 715 4715
GERMANY	GEMA	00 49 89 480 03 495
DENMARK	NCB	00 453 312 8700

★   Keep the music excerpts short
★   Select music that doesn't swamp the presentation

★ Choose music relevant to your message
★ Check that the audio system can reproduce music well, otherwise it may undermine your impact
★ Practise cueing the precise start of the music so that it happens smoothly and finishes at the right spot. If technical people are handling this aspect be sure to have several run-throughs with them, particularly where lights and music must be synchronised

Mystery (see also MAGIC)

Adding a touch of mystery to your presentation can give it added audience interest, though you need to think through the exact purpose of creating a mystery. It could be to

★ Intrigue
★ Raise awareness
★ Challenge
★ Puzzle
★ Distract
★ Amuse
★ Involve

For example, you might

★ Flourish a strange object and invite people to guess what it is
★ Put something on show without revealing it fully until later
★ Suggest there is a famous member of the audience without saying who
★ Pose a question and indicate you will answer it later
★ Take some unexplained action, the significance of which only becomes apparent later

Be sure that your mystery enhances your presentation and doesn't simply confuse people.

N

Names

> *Listen to how they say your name.*
> *If they can't say that right, there's no way they're*
> *going to know how to treat you properly, neither.*
> RITA DOVE, *THROUGH THE IVORY GATE* (1992)

Mention someone's name during a presentation and they feel recognised and included. With a small audience you can mention

just about everyone at some point. Find an opportune moment, otherwise it can appear contrived. Done well, it personalises your message and enrols your audience.

With an audience of more than around twenty people it's hard to use many names without seeming unfairly to favour certain individuals.

Remembering names: Do you have trouble remembering people's names? Most of us do, yet it's not as difficult as it might seem. For example, in a small group of, say, twenty people, draw the shape of the seating layout and mark the location of each person by name. Use this map whenever you need to refer to specific individuals.

In a meeting or small group, ask people to write their names large on a stand-up name card and place it where you can see it. After a while you will begin to put names to faces and won't need the cards.

A particularly useful method is to ask each person to introduce themselves and share one unusual thing about themselves. Not only is this entertaining for everyone, it makes it easier for you to associate that person with the strange fact.

A widely used memory device for recalling names is deliberately to associate the person and their name with some strong or absurd image that you dream up – the weirder the better. Since the image remains in your head it can be as outrageous as you wish, so long as it helps fix the person's name. For example,

★ John has reddish hair. So you imagine him with his hair on fire and the smoke curling upwards to make the letters J-O-H-N
★ Carol has nothing memorable about her appearance so you imagine her leading 1000 naked Carol singers all dancing around a chocolate Christmas tree
★ John Piper has slightly staring eyes, so you think of him as the Pied Piper of Hamlin in brown rags, followed by thousands of rats all with little labels around their neck saying 'John'
★ Brian wears a particularly expensive-looking suit, so you envisage him behind an enormous desk filling an entire room and on it there's a nameplate with moving coloured lights flashing his name

If you are introduced to people just before your presentation it can be especially hard to remember their names because you are hyped up for your performance. A good method is to repeat them back immediately and then use them in a sentence again within a few moments. You can also use the association device explained previously to cement their name into place.

National Speakers Association

The National Speakers Association is an international organisation of more than 3800 members dedicated to advancing the art and value of experts who speak professionally. You can contact the Association through its web site at: http://www.nsaspeaker.org/

Natural (see main body of text on pages 69–70)

> *Nothing prevents us from being natural*
> *so much as the desire to appear so.*
> LA ROCHEFOUCAULD (1613–80), *MAXIMS*

Negotiation (see also main body of text on pages 129–31)

> *It's a well-known proposition that you know who is going*
> *to win a negotiation. It's he who pauses the longest.*
> ROBERT HOLMES À COURT (1937–90), AUSTRALIAN BUSINESS EXECUTIVE

Bids and pitches that turn into negotiation sessions are best avoided. Keep the two tasks of presenting and negotiating separate.

Nerves (see main body of text on pages 71–73)

> *Without anxiety life would have very little savour.*
> MAY SARTON, *THE HOUSE BY THE SEA: A JOURNAL* (1977)

New (see also SUBJECT and PERSONALITY)

> *'What's new?' is an interesting and broadening eternal question,*
> *but one which, if pursued exclusively, results only in an endless*
> *parade of trivia and fashion, the silt of tomorrow.*
> ROBERT PERSIG, *ZEN AND THE ART OF MOTORCYCLE MAINTENANCE* (1974)

Even if there is nothing really new under the sun, as a presenter you are expected to bring something fresh and different to each performance. What could that possibly be, in a world saturated with media messages and information?

What is always new is your personality, how you use it and what aspect of yourself you bring into the room with you. Your playfulness, your seriousness, your commitment, your excitement, your optimism, your humour, all can bring a 'newness' that the audience comes to appreciate.

There is always some way you can enliven and differentiate what you say from what others have said before you. If all the audience really wants is information, then hand them a report. The essential question is: 'How can I be different from other presenters?' The answer is that there is bound to be some new angle that your creativity can discover, a fresh thought, an original approach to your subject. It just takes some ingenuity.

The more you delve into your topic, researching and making connections, the greater the number of opportunities you will find for introducing something different and unexpected.

Nicotine (see SMOKING)

> *It is now proved beyond doubt that smoking is one of the leading causes of statistics.*
>
> FLETCHER KNEBEL, *READER'S DIGEST* (1961)

Noise (see INTERRUPTIONS in main body of text on pages 101–2)

> *Noise has one advantage. It drowns out words.*
>
> MILAN KUNDERA, *THE UNBEARABLE LIGHTNESS OF BEING* (1984)

Nose (see also DISTRACTIONS)

> *I loved Kirk so much, I would have skied down Mount Everest in the nude with a carnation up my nose.*
>
> EVIDENCE GIVEN AT EPSOM MAGISTRATES COURT, 6 DECEMBER 1977,
> *THE TIMES* (7 DECEMBER 1977)

Touching or scratching your nose can be a serious audience distraction. If it itches violently during a presentation it's almost certainly a sign of nerves. If you ignore it and pay more attention to your audience the itching will fade away.

If the feelings persist, rather than constantly scratching, try pinching your nose hard, while ostentatiously looking down at your notes. If that doesn't work, give the audience some task to do, take a break and go to the nearest toilet and bathe your nose gently with cold water.

Notes (see PROMPTS in main body of text on pages 57–62)

> *The Room was hushed,*
> *The speaker mute,*
> *He'd left his speech*
> *In his other suit.*
>
> KENNETH MCFARLAND, *ELOQUENCE IN PUBLIC SPEAKING*

Novelty (see also New and Subject)

> *The New is not a fashion, it is a value.*
> ROLAND BARTHES, FRENCH SEMIOLOGIST,
> *THE PLEASURE OF THE TEXT* (1975)

Numbers (see Numbers in main body of text on pages 31–3)

> *Round numbers are always false.*
> SAMUEL JOHNSON (1709–84)

O

Objections (see Main Challenges and Questions in body of text)

The best way of handling objections comes from having anticipated them. If you have analysed what difficulties people might raise in response to your presentation it is far easier to deal with them when they surface.

This means being ruthlessly honest about

★ What are the tough questions people might pose?
★ Are there any personal or political reasons for raising objections?
★ Who would have a motive for in creating objections?
★ When are the objections likely to arise?
★ How will the objections be dealt with at the time?

It can be disconcerting when people start seemingly to pick holes in your presentation. Having invested considerable energy and time in your performance it can be hard to stay calm and deal with the objections systematically. Yet it's essential not to become angry or impatient, since the difficulties raised may be silently held by everyone else listening to you.

In a sales pitch or a major bid situation it can be tempting to try to minimise objections. This is nearly always a mistake. Instead, acknowledge the importance of the objection and treat it as another opportunity to re-enforce your main message.

Objective (see also Purpose in main body of text on pages 4–8)

★ What is the reason for the presentation?
★ What specifically are you trying to achieve?
★ What would you like people to do immediately afterwards?

Answer these essential questions and you will be a long way towards being able to devise an effective presentation.

Obscure (see Clarity in main body of text on page 34)

> *What is conceived well is expressed clearly.*
> *And the words to say it with arrive with ease.*
> NICOLAS BOILEAU, *THE SPIRIT OF LIBERTY* (1959)

Observer (see also Feedback)

If you are making an important pitch or conference presentation, consider having an independent observer on site to analyse the performance. Choose someone who can really stand back from the situation and see it objectively. What you want to know from the observer are ways you could improve and what went well.

The observer is also useful during pitches to watch people's body language and facial expressions. These might provide important clues about what they are thinking, what they may need in the way of additional information or reassurance.

Offence

During your presentation, references to issues, people, or even places may have unexpected connotations. Sexual, racist, ageist or political remarks can undermine an otherwise sound performance. Good preparation and rehearsal can reduce the chances of an ill-chosen phrase or reference.

Be particularly alert during question time when, in the heat of the moment, you may be less vigilant about these issues. Sometimes, though, offensive remarks or references stem not from you but a member of the audience. To handle these calmly and with professionalism you could:

★ Choose to go deaf and ignore the person
★ Look puzzled and ask the person to repeat their remark – most will be too embarrassed to do so
★ Refer the remark or question to the person chairing the meeting
★ Respond that you don't agree with their sentiments but respect their right to have an opinion and move on swiftly
★ Use humour to defuse the situation without either attacking the person or making light of their offensive remarks

Omission

Like a painting by Matisse in which the empty spaces are as vital as the coloured bits, so in a presentation what you leave out is as important as what you include.

Tips on what to omit:

★ Material you can consign to handouts or appendices
★ Large amounts of numbers, tables of figures
★ Unsubstantiated evidence
★ Complex concepts
★ Elaborate or convoluted jokes
★ Lengthy diversions from the main message
★ Material that is 'nice' to know, rather than 'must' know
★ Obscure references to people or places
★ Untranslated quotations in another language
★ Attacks on the integrity of others present
★ Criticism of named competitors
★ Racist, sexist or ageist remarks
★ Information the audience knows already
★ Material that is neither urgent nor important

If you inadvertently omit some part of your presentation this may not be obvious to the audience immediately. Since people don't know what you had intended in the first place an omission may not really matter.

If it is obvious, however, that something important is missing, draw attention to it only if it's unavoidable. For example, if you spot a figure is missing on a chart only comment if the omission makes the material incomprehensible, or if it undermines your case.

If you do need to apologise for something missing, offer to supply the information later if it is not immediately available.

One-liners (see also Hecklers and Interruptions in main body of text on pages 213, 101–2)

One-liners are choice phrases used to

★ Open or close a presentation with impact
★ Make a particularly powerful point
★ Get you out of trouble
★ Win laughs
★ Deal with a difficult member of the audience

One-liners are useful for various presentation disasters including:

★ Tripping over; equipment problems; lights fail; slides are wrong; fire alarm rings; a baby crying; you drop something; a failed joke; hecklers; you lose your thread

It may be worth developing some one-liners for your repertoire to cover various possible events. Choose ones that you really can make your own, reflecting your particular personality.

Powerful one-liners need time to land with the audience. Having delivered one, pause to give your audience time to appreciate it, before launching into the next part of your performance.

Openers (see main body of text on pages 75–7)

We are always afraid to start something that we want to make very good, true, and serious.

BRENDA UELAND, *ME* (1983)

Opinion (see PURPOSE in main body of text on pages 4–8)

Too bad all the people who know how to run the country are busy driving cabs and cutting hair.

GEORGE BURNS, US COMEDIAN

People want to hear your opinion when you present, no matter whether you are giving a factual report, or some high-powered analysis. An audience wants more than the facts; it wants feelings and opinions.

If you are a relatively junior member of an organisation and have to give a factual report is there really room for your opinion? It is a myth that anything is totally objective. In choosing what to say in your presentation you also decide what to omit and in doing so, by implication you express an opinion.

If all the audience wanted were the 'facts' then you might as well send a report. In a verbal presentation you are as important as the information you give people. What you think and your reactions to what you present should not be screened out as if they were irrelevant.

It is important to get the balance right between opinion and the rest of the presentation, which may be mainly factual. If your presentation is weighted down with opinion when people are hungry for hard facts then your views may not be well received. Similarly, if you stick just to facts and share no thoughts or feelings about what you present people may see you as lightweight having little to say for yourself.

Opportunities

Intentions often melt in the face of unexpected opportunity.

SHIRLEY TEMPLE BLACK, *CHILD STAR* (1988)

Some of the best moments in presentations stem from situations that you can turn to your advantage, but you'll only spot these if you're focused externally rather than on yourself.

For example, you might notice as you speak that many people are nodding in agreement, which you might use in several creative ways:

★ 'I see lots of people here seem to agree with what I'm saying. Hands up everyone here who strongly supports what I am saying'
★ 'Turn to your neighbour and share whether you agree with me or not'

When something goes wrong during a presentation you can either see it as a setback or yet another opportunity. For instance, suppose someone spots a mistake in your figures, rather than cringing with embarrassment you might thank the person for their astuteness and initiate a short discussion about what the true figure should be and why.

Some presentation problems allow you to use humour while the issue is resolved. For example, what would you do if the lights went out? You could be opportunistic and remark,

★ 'Hey, was it something I said?'
★ 'Don't panic, that's my job'
★ 'If any of you want the lights back on, please raise your right hand'

Opportunities often result from good research into the audience and the location. For instance, you may uncover stories about local characters, something special about the place in which you are presenting, a topical event and so on.

Right up to the closing moment in your presentation an unexpected opportunity may present itself. Watch for it; when you spot it – grab it!

Orator (see main body of text on pages 69–70)

> *Nothing is so unbelievable that oratory*
> *cannot make it acceptable.*
>
> CICERO, *PARADOXA STOICOM*, 46BC

You don't need to be a great orator to be an effective business presenter. Eloquence helps but plenty of good presenters are just straightforward speakers who rely on clarity and a clear purpose.

Order (see main body of text on pages 20–5)

Order and simplification are the first steps towards the mastery of a subject. The actual enemy is the unknown.

THOMAS MANN

Original

Utter originality is, of course, out of the question.

EZRA POUND, POET

Even when the message itself is not particularly new there's always a way to introduce something fresh and different. Every presentation is a challenge to your ingenuity and creativity. In what new ways can you present the information? Can you find an unusual metaphor, or image to emphasise your message? How can you hook people at the beginning or at the end?

Creativity techniques such as brainstorming are useful ways of producing unusual thinking around your subject. It may also be helpful to work with friends or colleagues who can stimulate you to look at the issue in a fresh way.

Creativity works through making strange or unusual connections. For example, try exploring what connections you can make between your next presentation and these unrelated items:

★ Oranges; the space programme; plastic rainwear; paint; aftershave; chess; juggling; music; hair; a grinding wheel; a unicorn; a vacuum cleaner; the galaxy; genetics

Which of these connections stimulate you to think of the subject in a new or unusual way? If none, try making a link with some issues of your own choice. When you make a connection between an unrelated topic and your presentation subject it may trigger all kinds of thoughts and ideas. Even if you never use this linkage, it can be a powerful force for expanding your thinking.

Outline (see FRAMEWORKS in main body of text on page 23)

Outrageous

There is no strong performance without a little fanaticism in the performer.

EMERSON, *JOURNALS* (1832)

Go on, let yourself go! What seems outrageous to you may turn out to be perfectly acceptable to your audience. You may be surprised at what you can get away with in a business presentation. The idea that you have to be utterly conventional just because it's a business audience is pure assumption.

Business audiences have often seen so many presentations that they give a collective sigh of relief when someone dares to do something different or extraordinary.

The bigger the risk you take the more likely the audience is to respond, so long as you do not use your outrageousness to detract attention from important issues.

You might be outrageous by

★ How you speak
★ How you look
★ What you say
★ What you do

For most business presentations, being outrageous simply means being willing to be thoroughly original. A dose of outrageousness in your presentation can be like adding spice to a meal. Unless it makes the whole concoction unpalatable it could improve the taste.

It is unacceptable, though, to cause gross offence just to make an impact. For example, swear words may seriously offend some of your audience, as could racist or sexist language. That kind of outrageousness is not only unprofessional, it's hurtful and shows lack of respect for the people listening to you.

Outside

Although not many business presentations occur in the open air, it does happen occasionally and is a real challenge, particularly if there's no public address system. If you're planning to speak outside, check on the acoustic arrangements.

Outside performances leave you vulnerable to a wide range of interruptions over which you have no control, such as planes, helicopters, traffic sirens, trains, building site noises, dogs barking and so on. In preparing your performance be ready with ideas on handling these distractions, including having some ready-made 'spontaneous' reactions:

★ Shouting at a passing noisy plane: 'I'll get you, Richard Branson, you just see'
★ At a police siren: 'I'm innocent I tell you, innocent'
★ At a dog loudly barking: 'Is that a question or an observation?'

★ At a helicopter whirring above: 'You're half an hour early, I'll call when I'm ready'

Overheads (see VISUALS in main body of text on pages 40–48)

IBM was once so committed to overheads that it even built projectors into its executives' desks. Nowadays, though, overheads (sometimes called foils) look increasingly unsophisticated against newer, more powerful devices. They are useful for small informal groups, are easy to create and control.

If your overheads are to support rather than undermine your business presentation there are some basics principles to follow:

★ Make sure the image you use is powerful; make each overhead count
★ Avoid small and hard to read lettering
★ Ensure the screen tilts to avoid picture distortion
★ Don't keep standing in front of the projector
★ Check the projector is at a comfortable height for you
★ Dust the lens
★ Arrange the electric lead so no one, including you, trips over it
★ Avoid finger marks showing by handling overheads at the edges or using card frames
★ Number transparencies in sequence
★ Have a back-up projector and bulb ready
★ No one should be further from the screen than six times the width of the image
★ Talk to the audience, not the screen; turn off the projector if you talk at length.
★ Use overheads sparingly
★ Make the technology subordinate to you, not the other way around
★ Rather than cover up the overhead and progressively reveal the next part, use a series of frames to build the complete picture progressively

Overrun

Finish on time. Assume that in no circumstances will you overrun. Even if it seems hard to fit everything into the agreed time, this is no excuse for exceeding your quota.

Good preparation can ensure your presentation fits the allotted time, but if you think you might overrun,

★ Discuss a change in the presentation brief

★ Simplify your message
★ Eliminate material not directly supporting your message
★ Alter the balance between speaking and the amount of audience activity
★ Consign more material to handouts or post-presentation texts
★ Use pictures or charts instead of words
★ Invite interested members of the audience to stay for a further session
★ Drop material in favour of waiting for audience questions

If you have planned a one-hour presentation and are told to deliver it in half the time, it's tempting to cram in everything you've already prepared. This seldom works. You either end up speaking much faster, or appear less coherent than you'd like. Instead, ruthlessly slice the material in half, leaving you plenty of time for a relaxed performance.

Stay constantly aware of how much time you have left. If necessary, remove your watch and place it where you can check on your progress. Or slide the face to the inside of your wrist so you can glimpse it in passing.

Organise regular reminders of how you are doing on timing. Such warnings could come from

★ Your own timing device – stop watch, vibrating pager-like device
★ Visible hand signals from a colleague or volunteer from the audience
★ A note from the chairperson

As you warm to your subject and the adrenalin flows, you may miss the warning signals. Ask the person helping with the timing to be persistent in their signalling until you acknowledge their message.

If you seem destined to overrun because previous speakers exceeded their quota, or there was a delayed start due to members of the audience arriving late:

★ Negotiate for extra time with the audience *before* overrunning
★ Avoid blaming anyone for the difficulties
★ Work to a tighter time schedule

P

Pace

For how much of your allocated time do you intend speaking? For most business presentation less is more. Allow time for people to discuss and debate. Also give yourself space to deliver a measured performance by varying

★ Loudness
★ Speed of talking
★ Pauses
★ Silence
★ Emphasis

Loudness

Anyone can shout a presentation but that seldom wins any converts. Sometimes, though, you can be deliberately loud so as to:

★ Wake people up
★ Grab attention
★ Make a point

At other times you can be deliberately soft, drawing in your audience, making your message more intimate.

Speed

Part of your presentation may best be delivered slowly, while another perhaps needs to be handled crisply, allowing little time for audience reaction. Some audiences need time to absorb a message while others may become bored if the pace is too slow.

Deliberately altering speed of delivery can produce particular effects such as:

★ Surprise; challenge; anticipation; laughter; anger; alertness, reassurance; curiosity; dissatisfaction; shock

For example, you might choose to slow down dramatically when announcing certain results, or adopt a rapid-fire delivery for punching home a series of powerful one-liners. Changing the pace stimulates an audience, preventing it from becoming bored or sleepy.

Pauses and silence

These can play an important role in varying pace and impact. For instance, a well-planned pause can

★ Draw attention to something important

★ Enhance your personal gravitas
★ Create a sense that 'this is worth hearing'

As you prepare your presentation keep a note where important pauses will be. Experiment in your next presentation with different length pauses to see what effect they achieve.

The difference between using silence and pauses is mainly one of length. While a pause tends to be only a few moments, planned silence lasts longer, perhaps thirty seconds, a minute or even more.

Strategically placed silence during a presentation can leave your audience with important think time and space to absorb your message. Nervous presenters, though, often find the pressure from silence too great to bear, filling the space with words and chatter.

Places for introducing an extended silence include:

★ At the start of the presentation
★ While showing visuals
★ Allowing people time to read handouts uninterrupted
★ A deliberate period of reflection or note taking
★ Immediately after a powerful audio-visual experience
★ After delivering a stunning fact or opinion
★ Just before the close of the presentation

Pagers (see Interruptions in main body of text on pages 101–2)

Bleeping phones and pagers can spoil an otherwise smooth presentation. Be assertive about getting the technology under control, no matter how senior and important your audience.

Model good behaviour by turning off your own pager or phone. If your pager is one that you can programme and that can vibrate without buzzing, use it as a timing device.

Ask your audience if anyone has pagers and mobile phones ready to go off. Usually people will own up and, albeit reluctantly, turn them off if requested.

If you're interrupted by someone's pager (or phone) ask again directly if they would switch it off, so that other people aren't disturbed. If it happens again, get the audience doing something like discussing a point you've made. Go over to the person and quietly ask if they need to be somewhere else right now as you're finding the noise a real distraction. Alternatively, suggest that they sit at the rear near an open door so they can escape quickly if it rings again. Be understanding rather than critical.

Avoid hostility or rudeness towards the techno terrorists, or

you'll risk turning the audience against you. Consider having some comebacks if the devices keep on buzzing:

★ 'That's probably for me, bring it here'
★ 'Must be tough to be so popular'
★ 'If it's my wife, tell her I'm busy'
★ 'That's probably your office calling to remind you to switch it off'
★ 'Thanks for the prompt, but I've only just got started'
★ 'Hey, I'm the supposed to be the one producing the buzz'

Pain (see also ILLNESS)

A wounded deer leaps highest, remarked author Emily Dickinson. Sometimes we perform at our best despite suffering. In many business presentation situations you simply cannot afford to cancel as there's too much at stake.

Although adrenalin from having to perform can often carry you through, if you're suffering from serious pain, cancel. You owe it to your audience to rearrange the event rather than continuing. You're not indispensable and people will be more angry if you persist and then don't perform well.

If you can't avoid the commitment, at least let your hosts know that you are in difficulty. Perhaps they can schedule your performance for later in the day. If you give many presentations keep a handy supply of ordinary pain-killers so you can handle indigestion, food poisoning, or unexpected headaches.

Panic (see NERVES in main body of text on pages 71–73)

Panic is not an effective long-term organising strategy.
STARHAWK, PREFACE TO 1988 EDITION, *DREAMING THE DARK* (1982)

When things go wrong in a business presentation it can produce a truly stomach-churning response. As realisation dawns that something is going seriously wrong, blind panic can sometimes set in. If your audience is panicky too, this is even worse. So what can you do in these situations?

The first step is to get your own emotions under control. Panic symptoms, which include panting, dry mouth, sweaty palms, palpitations and a feeling of tightness in the head or chest, are severe physical reactions that can stop you thinking straight. Deep breathing, sitting down for a few moments, counting to ten, progressive relaxation and so on can all help towards calming down.

If your audience is showing signs of serious anxiety it is up to you as the presenter to provide a lead. If it's necessary to leave the building, for example, either start giving clear instructions or hand over to someone else who can handle the situation.

Paralysis (see FREEZING in main body of text on pages 102–3)

Participation (see PARTICIPATION main body of text on pages 106–9)

Passion (see PASSION in main body of text on pages 77–80)

> *Passion is everything.*
> DAVID COPPERFIELD, US MAGICIAN

Pauses (see also PACE)

> *The right word may be effective, but no word was ever as effective as a rightly timed pause.*
> MARK TWAIN, INTRODUCTION, *SPEECHES* (1923)

A fifteen-second pause can seem a lifetime if you're focusing on how you are feeling. When you focus your attention on the audience, though, even a lengthy pause can feel perfectly comfortable.

Each pause needs a reason for being there. For example, it could be to alter the presentation pace, to signal a shift to a new issue, to review your notes, to draw attention to something and so on.

★ Make each pause count

Payment (see FEES)

Perform (see PRESENCE in main body of text on page 73)

> *Performance is an act of faith.*
> MARYA MANNES, *THE NEW YORK I KNOW* (1961)

Personality

> *Personality is the glitter that sends your little gleam across the footlights and the orchestra into that big black space where the audience is.*
> MAE WEST, US ACTRESS

Your unique personality is a major presentation weapon.

★ Value who you are, not just what you have to say

Think of a person you admire. What mainly sums up this individual? Is it humanity, directness, humour, kindness, astuteness, vision, enthusiasm, or what? These people don't waste time trying to be anyone else, unless they happen to be a stage impersonator.

What makes you special? Create a list of your most important qualities such as your thoroughness, intelligence, thoughtfulness, integrity and so on. Try summing up these characteristics as single words. Now ask several people you trust to describe you. Compare what they say with your list.

★ If a reporter were writing a short article about you, what would it say?

Use the information you're gathering about your personality directly to influence how you present. For example, if you conclude that one of your important aspects is your humour, allow this to pervade your presentation. Similarly, if you decide that one of your special characteristics is your down-to-earth focus on action, then make sure this comes across in your performance.

The more you dare to express your whole self during the presentation the more

★ Impact you'll make
★ Convincing you'll be
★ You'll feel you've done yourself justice

If you're a regular presenter, seek fresh insight into how you come across and what impact your personality makes. A professional coach offers an objective eye to suggest ways of enhancing what you do.

Persuasion (see main body of text on pages 26–39)

He who wants to persuade should put his trust not in the right argument, but the right word. The power of sound has always been greater than the power of sense.

JOSEPH CONRAD, *A PERSONAL RECORD* (1912)

Phone

Many business presentations now take place over the phone, often in a sales situation. A good phone presentation is always a two-way conversation in which you build the relationship.

Body language, eye contact or other visual techniques won't help when presenting over an ordinary audio phone. Instead, you will have to adopt different methods of communication. For example, on the phone you need to be acutely aware of how much air time you're claiming.

Business phone conferences are increasingly common and relatively easy to set up. Presenting to an invisible audience, though, is a real test of your communication skills. Presenting tips for phone conferences include:

★ Ensure the other person has time to talk
★ Seek regular responses
★ Analyse what isn't being said
★ Offer frequent opportunities for a response
★ Regularly request confirmation that you should continue
★ Each time you speak, keep the message short
★ Pay special attention to scheduling as conferences can be across different sites, time zones and countries
★ Pay special attention to clear pronunciation
★ Allow time for people to absorb your meaning
★ Make your voice calm and easy to listen to
★ The first time you speak, introduce yourself by name and state your role
★ Most times that you speak, restate your name: 'This is John here in London'
★ Avoid shouting
★ If someone interrupts, ask them to say their name, then before dealing with it summarise the previous person's point for the other listeners
★ Pause regularly, inviting people at remote sites to ask questions
★ Be assertive about saying your piece, silence makes you even more invisible
★ If you're facilitating a telephone conference, try to avoid also giving a presentation. Facilitation can take all your attention

Photographs

It can be disconcerting and distracting to have photographers snapping away while you perform. If you know photographers will be present,

★ Negotiate an acceptable time when they can move around freely
★ Arrange to restrict them to a single location most of the time
★ Apologise to the audience for any distractions

If photographers cause annoyance, stop the presentation and address the offenders directly. Offer to meet them afterwards if they want to create some action shots. Be direct, without being offensive, for example,

★ 'We'd all appreciate it if you could stay seated for the rest of this presentation'
★ 'I realise you've a job to do, but so have I. If you'd stay seated until I'm near the end I promise I'll let you know when that's coming'

If the photographers make special demands on you, turn it into a negotiation where you at least get something in return, such as asking for a written note from them, confirming they'll supply a complete set of the pictures free.

Pie diagrams (see Visuals in main body of text on pages 40–8, 102, 103–4)

Pitches (see Disasters in main body of text on pages 111–121)

Pitfalls

Which ones did you have in mind? There are countless reasons why your presentation could nosedive – most of them depend on you. For example, you could

★ Forget your words
★ Fail to get a laugh
★ Become sidetracked
★ Run out of time
★ Arrive late
★ Go to the wrong venue
★ Panic

★ Pass wind
★ Get heckled
★ Answer questions badly
★ Lose your temper
★ Mislay your visual aids
★ Trip over the microphone
★ Misread the audience mood

The only way of systematically avoiding these pitfalls is careful preparation and thorough rehearsals.

Pixels (see also Technology)

Pictures projected by an LCD system are usually high resolution defined in terms of how many pixels are used. Most LCD panels have a fairly low resolution of 640x480 pixels. The better LCD systems handle 1280x1024 pixels and if possible you should use these.

The technology and visual quality is changing so fast that it makes sense to check on maximum available resolution at the time of your presentation.

Plagiarism (see also Quotes)

The only 'ism Hollywood believes in is plagiarism.

DOROTHY PARKER, US WRITER

Everything is a legitimate source for a presentation so long as you're willing to acknowledge from whom you stole. You can get away with using material from just about anywhere, if it works. The most obvious form of plagiarism is stealing other people's jokes. Many presenters do this shamelessly and having one's jokes purloined is a form of flattery.

If you use someone else's material you need to do more than simply incorporate it into your presentation. Somehow you must personalise it to give it a special twist. Otherwise your delivery may sound derivative or false.

The danger of plagiarism is that you start to believe the materials or ideas are really your own. If you get caught – let's say a member of the audience realises what you have done – you could be in for some nasty moments of public exposure.

The best approach is to admit from where you are getting your ideas or quotes.

Plan (see Preparation in main body of text on pages 1–19)

By failing to prepare you are planning to fail.

BENJAMIN FRANKLIN

Platform (see Stage)

Platitude (see also Cliché)

Platitudes plague presenters and consist of

★ Trite remarks
★ Stating the obvious
★ Clichés

Avoiding platitudes does not mean always being stunningly original. It does mean not boring your audience with phrases and ideas that are worn out and tedious.

Podium (see also Lectern)

To be raised above the audience in a room without a full stage you need a podium, which you mount. Podiums are great places to trip over and make your first mistake. So when it's your turn to speak, take it slowly and carefully, rather than hurrying up the steps to stand in the limelight.

While the podium allows you to be seen it also distances you from your audience. A useful presentation technique is to step down from the podium and move among the audience. This creates greater intimacy, changes the pace and helps the audience to see you as approachable.

As part of your preparation use the podium for a rehearsal. Are there parts of it that creak or could trip you as you mount?

Pointers

Large sticks to point at overheads or slides are now outdated. Laser pointers do it more neatly and are more convenient. Be careful never to shine the laser towards your audience when picking out someone to speak or ask questions, since you could inflict eye damage.

Use the pointer sparingly as it can be distracting. Only highlight items which might otherwise not be spotted easily by your audience. If you have to use a pointer more than once or twice during your presentation it could mean that your material is not presented powerfully enough. A good visual doesn't need a pointer.

Polish

Like decorating a room or making a piece of furniture, it's the finish that counts. Adding the final touch to your presentation could be as simple as

★ Having that extra rehearsal
★ Refining the message
★ Improving the graphics
★ Adding local colour or context
★ Simplifying parts of the presentation
★ Getting a feel for the venue

Whatever it takes, add polish investing in that extra ingredient that makes the difference between a competent performance and an outstanding one. Only you can know what it takes.

Political Correctness

There are a lot more places where you can say 'spic' and 'bitch' than places where you can smoke a cigarette.
KATHERINE WHITEHORN, *OBSERVER* (1991)

Do you have to be politically correct during your presentation? Many words, ideas and phrases have become 'no-go areas' that govern how we think. Sometimes a good presentation will set out to challenge the present political correctness, particularly that established within an organisation.

There are two aspects of political correctness in a business presentation. The first is an organisation's particular culture and etiquette: how you address people or whether it is acceptable to refer to certain issues, situations or even people.

The second concerns the more general requirement to avoid offence because of remarks about current issues of correctness. References to sexual orientation, a particular nationality or racial grouping, or disability have all acquired their own political correctness requirements.

Failure to adhere to political correctness can antagonise an audience and undermine an otherwise sound presentation. If you are unsure what is politically incorrect, or are worried that you might unconsciously offend, ask several independent people to vet your presentation for possible pitfalls.

Posture

The way you stand, walk or sit conveys a message. If you sit slumped in your seat people conclude that you are tired, bored or uninterested. If you stand rigidly erect like a soldier on duty you may convey tension and anxiety.

Expert presenters nearly always prefer to stand because they feel more energised that way. Posture is one on those intangible presentation factors that make a difference without anyone really noticing. When you stand tall without straining, no matter what your height, you tend to exude alertness and confidence.

Correct posture only works if you feel relaxed and comfortable with it. Check your stance in a mirror when you rehearse, or get a colleague to offer some feedback on how you look and you'll find what might need changing. If necessary, try rehearsing with a book balanced on your head. You'll soon discover if you are slouching or bending.

If you're particularly concerned about posture invest in some professional help from a presentation coach. Alternatively, try a course of Alexander technique, which is all about posture.

Potential (see ABILITY in main body of text on pages 2–3)

The important thing is this: to be able at any moment to sacrifice what we are for what we could become.
CHARLES DU BOS (1882–1939) FRENCH WRITER, *APPROXIMATIONS*

PowerPoint (see Visuals in main body of text on pages 40–48)

For nervous presenters programmes like PowerPoint are an easy way of retreating into obscurity, hiding behind the graphics. It takes skill and practice to master PowerPoint as a live presenting tool. For example, so dominating is the impact of enlarged slides that even a blank coloured background can divert the audience's eyes away from you.

Death by PowerPoint comes from allowing the technology to substitute for your personality and presence.

★ Beware of spending more time on the technology, rather than on preparing yourself. Remember, you are the presentation

Practice (see Preparation in main body of text on pages 1–19)

Work on it until it's perfect. Then cut two minutes.
FRED ASTAIRE, DANCER

Prepare (see also Preparation in main body of text on pages 1–19)

I always knew I would turn a corner and run into this day,
but I ain't prepared for it nohow.
LOUISE MERIWEATHER, *DADDY WAS A NUMBERS RUNNER* (1970)

The amount of preparation you need to do can seem mind-numbingly dreary. Apart from endless rehearsals, time must be spent on issues such as how to stop a door creaking, preventing unexpected interruptions, practising with the technology and so on.

Virtually nothing else you do counts as much as careful preparation. The best presenters are obsessively concerned with it and don't rely on luck. They make their own, through being impeccably well prepared.

Presence (see main body of text on page 73)

To live exhilaratingly in and for the moment is deadly serious,
fun of the most exhausting sort.
BARBARA GRIZZUIT HARRISON, *OFF CENTRE* (1980)

Press conferences (see also Questions in main body of text on page 125–9)

I'll know my career's going bad when
they start quoting me correctly.
LEE MARVIN (1924–87)

Journalists have a different agenda from yours. Their job is to extract interesting facts and they are not interested in promoting either you or your organisation. They want controversy and catchy quotes.

Handling the media can be tricky and disillusioning. If necessary, obtain professional help from an experienced media coach. This may involve a rehearsal posing you with a barrage of tough questions to answer. Better that you stumble now than in the live press conference.

To make the best of the press conference, treat it as an opportunity to get your message across, rather than an ordeal to get through. Clarify what you want from it and don't be deflected from that goal, no matter how rough it gets. Tips for handling yourself with the press include:

★ Stay relaxed and be yourself
★ Be willing to smile
★ Avoid the cliché 'no comment'. Instead, explain why you have nothing to say
★ Be willing to admit that you don't know
★ Avoid sarcasm or rudeness
★ Don't attempt flattery or be obsequious
★ No journalist wants to hear you say 'I'm glad you asked that'. Try the more ambiguous 'Good question'
★ Expect and thoroughly plan for unpleasant questions
★ No matter how well-written your press releases, someone will enjoy testing you on completely unrelated issues. What might they be and how will you handle them?
★ Use examples and metaphors to illustrate your points

During press conferences, questioning can seem like an inquisition. Sometimes you need time to respond to various enquiries. Try some of the following:

★ Repeat the question by paraphrasing it, asking if that 'is what you meant'
★ Assert that before answering you must provide some background
★ Explain that the question needs an expert so you are referring it to a nearby colleague, which gives the other person time to compose their thoughts
★ Discuss and perhaps challenge the assumptions behind the question
★ Ask the person to rephrase or be more specific
★ Use your natural curiosity: answer with another question

Price (see CHARGE and FEES)

Pride

> *It is as proper to have pride in oneself*
> *as it is ridiculous to show it to others.*
>
> <div align="right">LA ROCHEFOUCAULD, <i>MAXIMS</i></div>

So many presenters end a presentation feeling that they could have done better. What will it take to feel proud of your next presentation? When you are proud of your performance you exit satisfied that you have done your absolute best to be outstanding.

Aiming to be truly proud of your presentation differs from false vanity. Pride comes with knowing that you gave it your best shot.

Projector (see also EQUIPMENT)

If the projector dominates then you won't. Since you are the presentation ensure that the projector serves your needs and not the other way around. For example, most projectors work best if the lights are dimmed and with the curtains closed. This puts a barrier between you and your audience.

If you do rely on an overhead projector,

★ Always test it several times before using it
★ Either bring or ensure there is a spare bulb nearby
★ Discover how to fit a new bulb
★ Prepare well enough to be able to continue without a hitch if the machinery fails. If it does, don't blame the equipment or those who provided it. Merely acknowledge the situation and rapidly move on

Prompts (see main body of text on pages 57–62)

Pronunciation (see also ACCENTS and VOICE)

People will forgive awkward or wrong pronunciation if you

★ Attempt a few words in an audience's own language
★ Acknowledge that you are having difficulty getting it right
★ Show good humour about your lack of accurate pronunciation
★ Seek help from the audience to say the words correctly

If you know that you have difficult words to say during a

presentation give your tongue and mouth practice, repeating the words until you feel you have mastered them. Practise and get right how you pronounce people's names. Mangling a person's name in public won't endear you to its owner.

Props

Props can enliven your business presentation and make you truly memorable. They can help you stand out from a crowd, since you can be sure that not many of your competitors will be using them.

Like metaphors, props convey a story. Use your creativity to think up ones that will support your performance and decide whether they will be integral props, act as running gags, or themes. You keep returning to them, lifting them up, pointing to them or moving them from one place to another while you make your point.

Choose the props with care, avoiding complicated ones that rely on elaborate mechanisms, which may go wrong. Too many props can distract both you and the audience, making you more like a conjuror constantly producing gadgets.

Tips on using props:

★ Ensure each one is relevant
★ Avoid breakable ones
★ Make sure they are easily transported safely
★ Check they'll be easily recognised from a distance
★ Decide how you'll introduce each item
★ Know where you will find every item as you reach for it and where to put it down
★ Practise using each prop so that you handle it with confidence
★ If you drop something, calmly pick it up and continue
★ Be human, drop something once in a while

Public speaking

Audiences for public speaking are looking mainly for entertainment. Business presentation audiences expect to be entertained, too, but the main focus is on action.

Public speakers also tend to be more dramatic than their business counterparts, though increasingly good presentations are tending to contain dramatic elements.

Purpose (see PURPOSE in main body of text on pages 4–8)

Punchline (see Jokes and Humour)

Remember it!

Q

Quantify (see Facts in main body of text on pages 26–9, 112)

The lure of quantity is the most dangerous of all.
SIMONE WEIL, *FIRST AND LAST NOTEBOOKS* (1970)

Questionnaires (see also Audience and Research)

Asking an audience to answer a questionnaire is a useful way to involve them. You could ask people to complete a simple form before or on arrival, or during the presentation.

★ Ask people to keep the answers short and clear
★ For fast analysis use multiple-choice questions where people tick boxes
★ Explain clearly how to return the questionnaire

Posing a simple and entertaining questionnaire to the audience can also be highly effective. You do not necessarily need to hand out forms to complete. You could, for example, use a slide or overhead to present three or four multiple-choice questions and ask people to jot down their answers. This approach gets people thinking and saves you speaking the whole time.

New technology now enables a large audience to 'vote' instantly in a live survey. Each person receives a small gadget that looks like a TV controller. By pressing various buttons people register a vote, which can be shown immediately on a screen. Clever though this technology may be, will it really enhance your performance, or merely get in the way?

Questions (see Questions in main body of text on pages 125–9)

The power to question is the basis of all human progress.
INDIRA GANDHI, *SPEECHES AND WRITINGS* (1975)

Quietness (see Pauses and the Highway Code)

He can keep silence well.
That man's silence is wonderful to listen to.
THOMAS HARDY (1840–1928), *UNDER THE GREENWOOD TREE*

Quiz (see also QUESTIONNAIRES)

An audience quiz is a useful way to

★ Warm up people prior to your presentation
★ Get people talking during your presentation
★ End a presentation
★ Extend your presentation
★ Avoid talking the whole time

Break large audiences into small groups and ask each to write a quiz for the others. Ask people to keep the questions simple, preferably multiple-choice ones where completion just involves ticking a box or a simple dual selection such as true/false, agree/disagree, yes/no.

Think carefully about the logistics. If you break an audience of fifty into ten groups of five, this is more complicated to manage than five groups of ten people. Similarly, use only a few questions as it will be time-consuming to analyse the results.

Quotations (see also WEB SITES)

I hate quotations. Tell me what you know.
RALPH WALDO EMERSON, (1803–82), *JOURNALS*, MAY 1849

People forget much of what you say by the end of a morning. Yet they will often remember and retell a quote that you use, sometimes years later. The quote may be terrific but not if it's by someone neither you nor the audience has heard of. President George Bush once told his speech writer, 'Don't give me any more quotations by that guy Thucydides.' In this case he could have said 'a wise Greek historian once said . . .'

A quote can drive a point home memorably, rekindle audience attention or shake up your listeners. But it needs to be

★ Relevant – appropriate to that particular part of the presentation
★ Sourced – you can state where it came from
★ Accurate – the words and meaning are correct

Adding an irrelevant quote is like putting an extra weight on a racehorse, it merely slows you down. Select quotes to enhance your message, rather than merely saying it in a different, more elegant way.

Two useful ways of bringing the quote to life are:

★ Show a picture of the person concerned with the words alongside the image

★ Play an audio or video tape of the person actually saying it

There are scores of published sources for useful quotations, including hundreds of Internet web sites. Several offer a subscription service aimed at business speakers, which includes a quotation data bank.

There are scores of books of quotes and they are mainly grouped in one of two ways: by author of quote and theme. Unless you specifically want to quote from a named individual, the most useful resource is to have the quotes organised by theme. Thematic quotation books are less common, yet growing in popularity. Some of the best ones are:

★ Andrews, Robert, *Cassell Dictionary of Quotations*, Cassell (1996, ISBN 0-304-34640-3)
★ *Bloomsbury Thematic Dictionary of Quotations*, Bloomsbury Publishing (1990, ISBN 0-7475-0735-X)
★ Cohen, M. J., *Penguin Thesaurus of Quotations*, Penguin Books (1998, ISBN 0-670-85884-6)
★ Ehrlich, E. and DeBruhl, M., (compilers), *The International Thesaurus of Quotations*, Harper Perennial (1996, ISBN 0-06-273373-7)
★ Maggio, Rosalie, *Quotations by Women*, Beacon Press (1996, ISBN 0-8070-6782-2)
★ Frank, L. R. *Quotationary*, Random House Webster's (1999, ISBN 0-679-44850-0)

Business quotations
There is a growing number of business quotation books. These have a limited range and are often quite dated. The speakers mentioned are seldom really well-known, even in their own countries. Sources worth investigating include:

★ *Book of Business Quotations*, Wiley (1998, ISBN 047-118207-9)
★ Eigen, Lewis D. and Siegel, Jonathan P., *The Manager's Book of Quotations*, by AMACOM edition (1991, ISBN 0-8144 5839-4)
★ *Forbes Book of Business Quotations: 14,366 Thoughts on the Business of Life Hardcover*, 1216 pages, Black Dog & Levanthal Publishers (1997, ISBN 1-884-82262-2)
★ *The Hutchison Dictionary of Business Quotes*, Helicon (1996, ISBN 1-85986-184-9)

R

Rapport (see Presence in main body of text on page 73, also Chemistry)

> *Well, sometimes you just don't like somebody.*
> HENRY FORD II, CEO OF THE FORD MOTOR COMPANY ANSWERING
> LEE IACOCCA WHO HAD DEMANDED TO KNOW WHY HE HAD BEEN FIRED

Reading (see Script)

> *Outside of a dog, a book is a man's best friend.*
> *Inside of a dog, it's too dark to read.*
> GROUCHO MARX (1890–1977)

Reasoning (see main body of text on pages 30–1)

> *We distrust our heart too much and our head not enough.*
> JOSEPH ROETHKE, *COLLECTED VERSES* (1961)

References (see also Books)

> *If God called my office looking for advertising, I'd check out his*
> *references. You can never be too sure in this business.*
> JERRY DELLAFEMINA, AMERICAN ADVERTISING EXECUTIVE

It can sometimes enhance your message if you can refer to a recently published book or sources. Such references give your message more weight, but doing it too often may end up irritating the audience and make you sound too academic.

★ Use references sparingly

Refreshments (see Lunch and Interruptions)

Rehearse (see main body of text on pages 49–56)

Relationship (see main body of text on pages 17–19)

> *There is no hope of joy except in human relations.*
> SAINT-EXUPÉRY, *WIND, SAND AND STARS* (1939)

Relaxing (see main body of text on pages 71–2, 74)

Relevance (see main body of text on pages 37)

Religion

> *Things have come to a pretty pass when religion is allowed to invade the sphere of private life.*
>
> VISCOUNT MELBOURNE (1779–1848)

Few business presentations touch on religion. However, members of your audience may have strong religious views and it is sensible to be careful with any references to religious matters. For example, references to the deity, jokes about certain issues, swearing or use of coarse words may cause upsct.

Repetition

> *What is so tedious as a twice-told tale?*
>
> HOMER, EIGHTH CENTURY BC, *ODYSSEY*

It's said that you need to say something three times to an audience before it finally lands with everyone. Powerful repetition uses words, phrases, images or stories to underline your message without necessarily repeating the exact words. Churchill's 'We will fight them on the beaches' speech adopted repetition to punch home the message of no surrender.

Simple repetition can be highly effective in underlining a message, for example, 'I'd like you to consider three essential facts:

Fact No. 1 is . . .
Fact No. 2 is . . .
Fact No. 3 is . . .'

As with running jokes, repetition can acquire a cumulative effect over the entire performance. Yet there's a fine line between powerful and boring repetition. The aim is to

★ Avoid the audience knowing exactly what is coming next

Repetition in visuals can soon lead to boredom, as when using a template to present slides that always repeats a logo or corporate identity. The sameness of these effects can seriously detract from the more important message of the visual itself.

Another form of damaging repetition is when previous speakers have used your material, such as a joke or some statistics. Suddenly you find yourself repeating what someone has already presented to the audience. The first you know about it is when people start glancing at one another. It is important to watch your audience closely for signs that you have hit a repetition mine.

If you suspect you have mistakenly started to repeat something,

★ Take the initiative, ask whether they have already heard the information
★ Turn it to your advantage: for example, ask people what they have concluded from such material
★ Don't knock previous speakers for using your material

Reports (see also Books)

You're the presentation not a report. *You* make a difference in the room, not a document or other written material.

A common challenge for business presenters is to give senior management or other colleagues, or a client, a status report. This is when you inform people how things are going, whether everything is going to plan, what's gone wrong, what needs to happen next and so on.

Status reports typically focus on

★ An overview
★ Significant changes to the expected situation
★ Solutions to current or expected problems

Although status reports are usually brief, you the presenter may have a lot at stake. Ways to make the most of this presenting opportunity are:

★ People want to hear what you have to say about the report, not just a description of its contents
★ If possible, circulate it in advance with a request that people read it. This gives them time to absorb it and identify questions to ask
★ By devoting only a small amount of your presenting time to the report's contents you create a chance to involve your audience in what the document is really about and its implications
★ Have spare copies for unexpected arrivals
★ When referring to specific contents repeat the page or paragraph reference several times to allow people to find it
★ Summarise in your own words your conclusions about the report
★ Be clear what you think should happen next and by when

Research (see Audience in main body of text on pages 4, 123)

Basic research is what I am doing when
I don't know what I am doing.

WERNHER VON BRAUN

Respect

Good presentations build a relationship with the audience. You achieve this through various ways such as involvement, establishing trust and showing respect. You demonstrate respect for your audience when you

★ Arrive on time
★ Show you are well prepared
★ Treat the audience as intelligent
★ Respond to their specific needs
★ Take time to look people in the eye
★ Speak sufficiently slowly and clearly
★ Use appropriate words and language
★ Listen
★ Finish on time

Rest room (see TOILET)

According to statistics, a man eats a prune every twenty seconds. I don't know who this fellow is, but I know where to find him.
MOREY AMSTERDAM, AMERICAN HUMORIST

Retention

Five minutes after you've finished speaking, few of your listeners will recall more than a fraction of what you said. Most will leave only with an overall impression, a feeling about you and your message.

★ What three things do you want your audience to remember?

It is worth deciding what are the three main points you want to convey and, better still, to reduce them to a single, easy to remember headline statement.
Evidence from research suggests that

★ People only remember around five to seven points from a twenty-minute verbal presentation
★ It takes several repetitions of a statement before people fully register it

The implications of this for presenters are that it makes little sense to pack your communication with endless facts and figures, since this won't advance your cause. Also, that it's advisable to repeat your core message at the beginning, the middle and the end of the presentation.

Reviewing

The way to a better business presentation is through repeatedly reviewing what you do, knowing that you can always improve. Committed presenters constantly reassess how they come across, trying to decide what worked and what didn't.

★ The more systematically you monitor personal performance, the more information becomes available for improving performance

Examine completed presentations to probe for weak spots and capitalise on successes. You can acquire feedback in several ways:

★ Directly from the audience through questionnaires or talking with people
★ Comments from colleagues whom you have asked to assess your performance
★ Through studying a video or audio record of your presentation
★ By keeping your own presentation log over a succession of performances

What is important is that you do review regularly and welcome frank and even critical feedback.

★ Act on the new information
★ Seek help from experts if necessary

Rhetorical Questions (see also QUESTIONS in main body of text on page 125–9)

A common presentation technique is to ask the audience rhetorical questions, that is ones that you don't expect people to answer. For instance, you might say: 'Have you any idea of the effect this had on profits?'

Having posed the query, rather than wait for a reply you proceed to answer it yourself. The rhetorical question is a powerful way of interesting your audience, pointing up an issue and setting the scene for a well-prepared answer.

Constantly posing questions to which you don't really expect much of a reply, can soon irritate people and make them feel vulnerable. They begin to wonder whether they might be next in line for a difficult or challenging question. So use this device sparingly.

Ridicule (see SATIRE)

Ridicule may be a shield, but it is not a weapon.

DOROTHY PARKER, 1937

Risk (see also SUCCESS)

What you risk reveals what you value.
JEANETTE WINTERSON, *WRITTEN ON THE BODY* (1992)

Lady Godiva, as W. C. Fields explained, put everything she had on a horse. A risky presentation means that you put everything into it, no holds barred. A risky presentation isn't the same as a reckless one. Risky ones stretch you and for audiences tend to be memorable. Reckless presentations threaten your reputation or that of your company because you are attempting unreasonable things with too high a cost attached.

For example, it is reckless to go to a major pitch with valued customers without some preparation. Similarly, it is reckless to launch into an important presentation using complex equipment without mastering it.

Risky presentations that capture an audience's heart happen when you

★ Do something that makes you vulnerable
★ Show the depth of your feelings
★ Reveal some personal aspect of your life
★ Do something relevant yet outrageous
★ Act unexpectedly
★ Place your reputation on the line
★ Throw away your notes
★ Improvise
★ Do something that could obviously go wrong (but doesn't)

Risky presentations test you to the limit, forcing you to raise your game. For experienced presenters who must keep repeating the same sales message, being risky is a way of injecting new energy into the performance.

Introducing a new element of risk to your business presentation through being more creative, testing out a new approach, trying something entirely different is a way of adding sparkle to your performance.

Finally, as Neil Simon the playwright argued, if no one ever took risks, Michelangelo would have painted the Sistine floor.

Rivals

If you know that your rivals are good presenters you need to work even harder to perform at your best. This is when it may really pay to employ a professional to help you be outstanding.

For example, in one of the world's largest consultancies people regularly apply for senior posts and face fierce internal competition. Some of the smarter contenders obtain one-to-one professional coaching from an outside expert so as to maximise their presentation impact.

Similarly, in business pitches where the stakes may run into millions it's often a sound investment to use outside help to ensure that the presentation exceeds anything that a rival may deliver.

Doing something risky or unusual are ways of distancing yourself from rivals. For instance, a company pitching for new business from a transport utility invited the potential client to meet in a carefully selected venue. When the clients arrived they were kept waiting, left in a cold, grimy room and given no coffee or refreshments. Just as they rose to leave in a fury, the CEO of the company pitching for their business entered and explained: 'You've just experienced what it's like being one of your customers. That's what we're here to help change.' They got the work.

Avoid knocking rivals during a presentation; it seldom goes down well. Instead, talk about 'what our competitors do or don't do'.

You have at least one advantage over a rival. You are unique, there is no one quite like you. Capitalise on who you are and what you stand for. That way you will be sure that you differentiate your presentation from that of your rivals.

Road map

Good presentations take an audience on a journey. Some people, however, cannot really join you on that journey unless you provide a clear route map explaining where you are intending to take them. Since this is how they make sense of messages it is unwise to ignore their needs.

Road maps can take several forms such as

★ A verbal summary of the presentation
★ A visual showing the order of the presentation
★ Notes circulated before the event
★ A symbol encapsulating the core message
★ An explanation of where the presentation is leading

If an audience knows where you are taking it, people can begin to order their thoughts in response. So you might announce at the start of the presentation:

★ 'We need to continue investing in developing this project and that's what I want to persuade you to do today'

★ 'We've had serious problems with the network and after I've given you more information I'd like us to agree action to stop it happening again'

★ 'Based on our research about your company, we believe that we can increase both your productivity and competitiveness. We're going to present you with a new approach to monitoring the supply chain'

★ 'We need to raise sales by 50% and I'm going to suggest changes so that this can happen'

Rules

There are no presentation rules.

S

Sarcasm (see also SATIRE)

Sarcasm I now see to be, in general, the language of the devil.
THOMAS CARLYLE (1795–1881), SCOTTISH HISTORIAN

Sarcasm leaves a nasty taste in the mouth and, while audiences may laugh, it won't enhance your reputation as a skilled presenter.

Satire (see HUMOUR in main body of text on pages 83–86)

*Satirists gain the applause of others through fear,
not through love.*
WILLIAM HAZLITT, *CHARACTERISTICS* (1823)

In business presentations there is sometimes scope for gentle mockery, subtle irony and ridicule, so long as it's clear you're not being vicious or plain nasty. Satire which includes mockery and sarcasm can be hard to spot and easy to use by mistake. To get away with them so they enhance your presentation may take careful thought.

Using satire often rebounds on the satirist, rather than the victim. For example, if you impugn a competitor's integrity or mock a colleague's good intentions it may do you more harm than good.

Audiences, particularly non-English-speaking ones, seldom recognise satire in its many forms. So avoid it when speaking to foreign audiences and when working with an interpreter.

Scan (see also EYES)

Scanning is simply making a visual sweep across the audience. This is different from making eye contact and won't necessarily enhance your performance. It may even convey the message that you're not interested in building a relationship with the audience.

True eye contact is 'seeing' who is there, what they are doing and searching for signs of how people are reacting. When you scan by sweeping across the audience, taking in the clock, the door, or some other distraction, people will tend to follow your gaze.

★ If you want people's attention, obtain it by focusing directly on them

Scratch (see NOSE)

> One bliss for which
> There is no match
> Is when you itch
> To up and scratch.
>
> OGDEN NASH, 'TABOO TO BOOT', *VERSES FROM 1929 ON*

Screen (see also PROJECTOR)

The best position for a screen is usually in the corner and high enough for everyone to see without having to move.

To avoid the keystone effect in which the image is unduly distorted, the projector needs to be at nintey degrees to the screen, which may have to be tilted. It's better to tilt the screen than the projector as the overheads tend to slide off.

The giant screen: Some venues use a giant screen for projecting a huge live picture of the presenter. This can be a disconcerting experience so ask for a rehearsal beforehand. Every facial, hand or body gesture acquires enormous significance on the giant screen and you may need to modify your presenting style to reflect this reality.

The blank screen: Another sort of screen that can cause problems is the blank between each slide or the next overhead. For overheads you can switch off the machine. With slides it's usually better to insert a blanked-out picture, so the screen shows black, rather than a coloured blank than can prove a distraction.

Script (see main body of text on pages 59–60)

Self-doubt (see Nerves in main body of text on pages 71–73)

> *Doubt remains a luxury I won't do without.*
> ELEANOR CLARK, *EYES, ETC.* (1977)

Self-Esteem (see Nerves in main body of text on pages 71–73)

> *Self-esteem isn't everything; it's just that there's nothing else without it.*
> GLORIA STEINEM, *REVOLUTION FROM WITHIN* (1993)

Selling (see Disasters in main body of text on pages 115–21)

> *Everyone lives by selling something.*
> ROBERT LOUIS STEVENSON (1850–94), *ACROSS THE PLAINS.*

Seminars (see main body of text on pages 136–8)

Sensation (see Shock)

> *The ear tends to be lazy, craves the familiar, and is shocked by the unexpected; the eye on the other hand, tends to be impatient, craves the novel, and is bored by repetition.*
> W. H. AUDEN, 'HIC ET ILLE', *THE DYER'S HAND* (1962)

Sentences

Keep sentences short and simple, particularly when addressing an audience whose first language is not English. Convoluted phrasing with sub-clauses quickly turns an attentive audience into a bored one. So-called rules such as:

★ Never use 'and' to start a sentence
★ Don't split infinitives
★ Avoid ending on a preposition

seldom matter in a verbal performance. Use whatever sentence structure seems comfortable. From the experience of Master presenters, four useful guidelines are:

★ Put your strongest sentence at the start of a paragraph, rather than at the end
★ Find the keyword in a sentence and build the structure around it
★ Include only one major idea in each sentence

★ Make each sentence follow on logically from the previous one

There's no standard length for a sentence in a verbal presentation. A good presenter can sometimes get away with an extremely long one if there are plenty of well-placed pauses.

Generally aim for sentences of around fifteen to twenty words. This is an average, not a rule. You can often make considerable impact with one or two word sentences such as 'Why?', 'Next', 'I disagree', 'Who agrees?'.

The entertainment media have trained us to expect short, punchy soundbites. To attack a lengthy or convoluted sentence:

★ Split the sentence into two or more separate ones
★ Create two sentences joined by connecting words, like 'however', 'but', 'yet', 'also'
★ Instead, present a list as an overhead, slide or flip chart
★ Cut verbiage
★ Dump the entire sentence and start again

Sexism (see also STEREOTYPES)

Watch out for it! You can be sexist with the wrong choice of words, innuendoes or use of stereotypes. Choose phrasing that avoids giving offence to either sex, particularly by assuming that all 'people' are men. For example, 'choosing the best man for the job' may work for the Pope but in most cases 'the best person for the job' works better.

To avoid accusations of sexism

★ Choose male/female-related words with care – women may be preferable to ladies
★ Avoid references drawn from sports mainly favoured by one particular sex
★ Try using the plural, for example rather than 'him' or 'her' you could use 'them'
★ Avoid words that make unwarranted assumptions about the sex of an interest group. For example, do you mean house-wives or consumers, mothers or parents, businessmen or business people?
★ Convert sexist words to neutral ones:
    Businessmen become business people
    Firemen become fire fighters
    Fishermen become fishers
    Man becomes person, individual, you
    Man-hours become working hours

Man-made becomes manufactured, artificial
Salesman becomes sales agent, representative
Workman becomes worker

The first problem for all of us, men and woman,
is not to learn, but to unlearn.

GLORIA STEINEM, *NEW YORK TIMES* (1971)

Shake (see NERVES, in main body of text on pages 71-73)

The man who has ceased to fear has ceased to care.

F. H. BRADLEY, ENGLISH PHILOSOPHER, *APHORISMS* (1930)

Shock

Many people who imagine they are live wires are only shocking.

MARY PETTIBONE POOLE, *A GLASS EYE AT A KEYHOLE* (1938)

Shock tactics can be highly effective in the right hands. Be wary of doing it solely for effect; people usually resent being toyed with. In a business setting, shocking the audience can punch home a point with devastating effect. Years ago a CEO used to call his staff together and set fire to a desk. It was his way of announcing someone had been sacked and the word 'fired' entered the vernacular.

When can a shock really enhance your presentation? It could be used to

★ Start with an impact
★ Punch home your core message
★ Wake people up
★ Get people thinking
★ Create controversy
★ Gain or regain attention
★ Highlight an issue
★ Amuse
★ Close with a bang

Shocking does not necessarily mean offending or seriously upsetting your listeners, though that might be your intention. Anything to wake up a sleepy audience is possible; the main crime is allowing people to get bored. To shock you might

★ Show a disturbing picture
★ Present a challenging fact
★ Burst into song
★ Play a confronting video or audio piece

★ Make sudden noises
★ Shout
★ Break something
★ Throw something to the floor
★ Use slang or taboo words
★ Make an unexpected announcement
★ Do something that is counter culture
★ Say what people least want to hear

The only limitations are your imagination and knowledge of your audience.

Shock tactics cease to have an impact if overused. They also tend to increase expectations – you have to beat your last shock. Repeated shocks may lead people to think you are excessively provocative.

Shoes (see Feet)

If high heels were so wonderful, men would be wearing them.
SUE GRAFTON, *'I' IS FOR INNOCENCE* (1992)

Short (see Simplify)

Showcase (see main body of text on pages 137–8)

Sick (see Illness)

Most of the time we think we're sick, it's all in the mind.
THOMAS WOLFE (1900–38), US NOVELIST

Sidetracked (see also Distractions and Questions in main body of text on page 00)

Even the Master presenters occasionally lose the thread and find themselves sidetracked. It happens, for example, when someone interrupts to make a statement or pose questions, diverting you from the route map you're trying to follow.

To avoid being sidetracked,

★ Know your core message and main staging posts in the presentation, rather than learning every word
★ Thoroughly rehearse
★ Decide in advance how you'll handle irrelevant questions
★ Treat the person asking the irrelevant question with respect but spend little time answering it. Link it back to the presentation theme

★ If you lose the plot, don't be afraid to own up. Perhaps ask the audience where you've reached. They'll be quick to tell you and consequently feel more involved

Silences (see *Pauses*)

Who . . . tells the finer tale than any of us? Silence does.
ISAK DINESEN, 'THE BLANK PAGE', *LAST TALES* (1957)

Simile (see also METAPHOR)

Kenneth Clarke, the former UK Chancellor of the Exchequer, dismissed a call for a referendum saying that 'Britain was becoming like Switzerland without the cowbells' (*Independent*, 2 July 1997).

A simile is a figure of speech making a comparison of one thing with another. For example,

★ 'Like a bolt of lightening', 'like a bat from hell', 'similar to a boat going downriver'

Similes and analogies are powerful ways used to make comparisons between things so as to punch home a message. These verbal devices

★ Usually have a visual or emotional content
★ Appeal to an audience by bringing the message to life
★ Cut through dry facts to produce a powerful picture in the listener's mind
★ Are useful when communicating a difficult or complex message
★ Should be used sparingly
★ Grab an audience's attention

To create a simile or analogy:

Step 1:
Start with the idea or concept you want to communicate – a new product, a piece of news, a fact.

Step 2:
What particular message about it are you trying to convey – e.g., this is exciting, this is trouble, it's important, it's useless, it happened so fast and so on.

Step 3:
Start looking for similarities elsewhere that capture what this message is about. You can look just about anywhere – the world

of sport, television, politics, literature and so on.

Step 4:
Choose one that seems to work well with your original idea or concept.

Step 5:
Hone the similarity to your purpose.

Example

★ You are giving a talk on writing proposals to clients
★ You want to stress the importance of getting the basics right
★ Before writing it, seek something similar that conveys the same message, such as build a house from the foundations up; pack a parachute carefully before jumping; write a play by devising the plot first
★ Finally choose one analogy or simile, for instance, writing a play
★ Hone this to your use, to convey your point about how to write a proposal. Plays, and by implication proposals, usually need a denouement, well-constructed ones have an opener, a story line and a closer, experienced playwrights fully devise the plot before starting on the detail – the dialogue

Simplify

Less is More.

ROBERT BROWNING, POET

Great presentations are invariably simple ones. The more you can simplify the messages, structure, contents, sentences, visuals and so on the more impact you are likely to achieve.

Complexity seldom impresses a business audience, which is frequently looking for quick answers and manageable solutions. One of the best simplifications you can adopt is

★ Keep the presentation short

This forces you to reduce everything to a tight framework where the priorities are clear and the message is stripped of all irrelevancies. Likewise, if you aim for great simplicity in your visuals you will increase your persuasiveness because people can rapidly absorb the key issue.

A classic way to simplify a written presentation script is to try to eliminate every other word. It is surprising how much of the original sense remains.

Slander

People are more slanderous from vanity than from malice.

LA ROCHEFOUCAULD, *MAXIMS* (1665)

Slander or defamation is saying something during a presentation that ends up in court. Even if you finally win, it could still cost you a fortune.

Slander is hard to prove, though, and the rules vary widely across nations. For example, when on a US talk show Oprah Winfrey made adverse remarks about meat she ended up in court, though she ultimately won her case. In the UK, slander cases are traditionally hard to pursue and provide a bonanza for lawyers.

In presentations, avoid remarks which refer to people, organisations or even places in disparaging terms that could be demonstrably damaging.

★ If in doubt, leave it out

Slang (see also JARGON)

Slang is the language that rolls up its sleeves,
spits on its hands and goes to work.

CARL SANDBURG (1878–1967), AMERICAN POET

Like metaphors, slang can sometimes produce useful effects, such as make your performance seem more impromptu and relaxed. Acceptable slang to one audience may be anathema to another so check what yours will know or tolerate

★ Excessive slang can reduce your impact by making you seem too casual
★ Phrases that work in conversation may not quite work in a formal presentation
★ The larger the audience the greater the chance of unwittingly upsetting somebody with slang
★ Slang travels badly. If addressing an audience whose first language is not English avoid it. If your speech is being simultaneously translated, work with the interpreters to ensure that any slang expressions are explained in the local language

Sleep (see also AUDIENCE and RELAXING)

The amount of sleep required by the average person
is about five minutes more.

MAX KAUFFMAN (ATTRIB.)

Get plenty of sleep before a major presentation so that you're full of energy for the performance. While it may be tempting to join in a party, steel yourself, explaining that 'I have to perform tomorrow and want to stay fresh'. People will respect your professionalism.

If excitement prevents you sleeping practise progressive relaxation where you tense each part of your body in turn for fifteen seconds and then let go. Work your way right round your entire body, including face muscles, neck muscles, chest, abdomen, legs, calves and so on.

If you're a heavy sleeper or fearful that you will be late, back up your alarm clock by asking someone to give you a morning call. That way you can sleep secure in the knowledge that you'll be woken on time.

Slides (see POWERPOINT)

Slips – of the tongue (see FAUX PAS)

Let us retire and seek a nosy cook.
LILLIE LANGTRY TO A STAGE LOVER, 1907

Smile (see main body of text on page 92)

She smiled quickly, brightly, all manners and no meaning.
DOROTHY M. JOHNSON, BEULAH BUNNY TELLS ALL (1942)

Smoking (see also NERVES in main body of text on pages 71–73, and VOICE)

Smoking just before a presentation is asking for trouble. It may trigger a cough or further ravage your throat. Even if you're addressing a tribe of tobacconists it's disrespectful to your audience to smoke during your presentation. Worse still, it sends a clear message that you're nervous.

Lighting up during a presentation will cause at least some audience offence, so why risk it for the sake of a drag and looking slovenly? It sends a signal that you're more worried about performing than satisfying the audience.

★ Avoid stubbing out a cigarette before stepping into the limelight
★ Deep breathing and relaxation are better ways to control nerves and anxiety
★ Stay away from other smokers and their smoke just before the presentation

If some of your audience are smoking, act positively on behalf of those who aren't and who may be too embarrassed to object. If it's a long presentation explain that you'll be breaking at regular intervals to allow smokers to indulge.

Best of all, arrange with the organisers to place prominent notices saying that smoking is not permitted. If someone starts smoking you can then politely point to the notice by explaining that the organisers have asked you draw attention to it.

Snore (see also AUDIENCE)

Laugh and the world laughs with you, snore and you sleep alone.
MRS PATRICK CAMPBELL, ACTRESS, 1912

What do you do if someone in your audience is snoring? It happens even in business presentations – sometimes because the offender has just arrived after a long tiring flight.

Your snorer and the rest of the audience will almost certainly be as embarrassed as you are. Take it in good fun, but realise that a loud snorer can also be disturbing to the audience and you have a duty to do something to do about it.

Making a sudden noise or talking loudly may jolt the person awake but is hardly reliable. Instead,

★ Treat snoring as a sign that somehow you're failing to get through
★ Find a way to put the audience on its feet so people can stretch their limbs
★ Get people talking in groups and quietly visit the offending snorer and ask if you could send them a copy of your presentation so they need not stay any longer
★ Deal with a stuffy room by altering the air-conditioning or opening windows

Speakers' Organisations (see WEB SITES)

Speech (see also AUDIENCE and FRAMEWORKS)

*I dreamt that I was making a speech in the House.
I woke up, and by Jove I was!'*
DUKE OF DEVONSHIRE (1833–1908), CONSERVATIVE POLITICIAN

Business people have numerous opportunities to give speeches, of which business presentations are only a part. Whether it's an after-dinner situation, an award ceremony, a goodbye to a long-serving employee, or a conference, you may be called on to deliver some formal words to match the occasion.

In a presentation you are probably making a case for some kind of action a speech, though, is usually more wide-ranging. A good speech demands much the same discipline as a good presentation.

In seeking inspiration for your own speech you may like to explore speeches by leading executives and you can get access to these and over 6000 others via the Internet at http://www.idea-bank.com/, for a subscription fee. You can even try the service free first.

Speech writers

Having a presentation written for you may cost rather less than you think. There are many professionals who can rapidly produce good business presentations at an economic price.

How good the presentation you receive from a professional writer is depends as much on the quality of the brief as the talent of the individual. A good brief will guide the person on the sort of research you may not have time for.

To obtain the best from a speech writer,

★ Choose someone who understands your business culture
★ Really get to know the person so you understand each other as people
★ Be specific about what help you want – a list of ideas, amusing stories, a tight structure, a detailed script and so on
★ Clarify the deadline and enquire about progress regularly
★ Explain the context of the presentation, where it will take place, timing and facilities, and so on
★ Discuss what you are prepared to do and not to do; for example, run an interactive session for most of the time

There are plenty of business speech writers ready to write for a fee. You can even have your speech e-mailed to you without ever having met the writer. Pre-prepared speeches can be sent within twenty-four hours and personalised speeches within two to five days, depending on length.

You can contact web-based business speech writers at
http://speeches.com/open.asp
http://www.speech-writers.com/

An automated speech writer, which asks a series of questions and produces an instant speech, exists on some sites, but don't expect much originality.

Spontaneity (see Improvise)

> *Through spontaneity we are re-formed into ourselves.*
> VIOLA SPOLIN, US THEATRE DIRECTOR,
> *IMPROVISATION FOR THE THEATRE* (1963)

Speed (see Pace)

> *. . . speed helps people think they are keeping up.*
> GAIL SHEEHY, *SPEED IS OF THE ESSENCE* (1971)

Stage (see also Eye Contact and Podium)

Are you presenting on a raised stage? While it allows you to see your audience and be seen, a disadvantage is that you are cut off from people and it prevents you from moving around among them. If you have a choice, try to avoid a stage, unless the audience consists of at least seventy-five or more people.

If you're going to be on stage, arrive sufficiently early to explore getting on and off it without stumbling. Now is also your chance to gain a feel for what it's like to be up there. You might even say a few paragraphs of your presentation to hear what the acoustics are like.

Try sitting where your audience will be, to gain a feel for what it would be like to look at someone on the stage. What will they see? What is the backdrop like, does the lighting need adjusting, will you need a different arrangement of the furniture?

Stage fright (see Nerves in main body of text on pages 71–73)

> *Stagefright is the sweat of perfection.*
> EDWARD R. MURROW (1908–1965), BROADCAST JOURNALIST

Staging

How you look on stage can have a big impact on how you come across. For example, if you are dwarfed by a huge multicoloured screen you may struggle to hold the attention on you, rather than the picture.

Similarly, the backdrop and equipment can either support or undermine your presentation. Take care to get the effect that helps build a relationship with your audience. For example, if you dress up the stage to enhance your message select colours and a design that complement your role. Avoid clutter or over-busy images that may deter an audience from giving you full attention.

If you know that there will be a professionally created stage set, try to discover well in advance what this will be. You may be able to build in some interesting effects to take advantage of the arrangements. Ask about the colours of the staging so you can dress in suitable clothes with non-clashing colours.

Stairs (see TRIP)

Careful grooming may take twenty years off a woman's age, but you can't fool a long flight of stairs'

MARLENE DIETRICH

Stammer

The greatest orator of ancient Greece was a man named Demosthenes who achieved great speaking skills in spite of having been born with a severe stammer. To cure it he stuffed his mouth with pebbles and practised speaking with them slowly. He learned to overcome audience noise by going to the seashore and speaking above the roar of the waves. He mastered breath control by reciting poetry as he ran uphill. His fame as a speaker is still synonymous with extraordinary speaking ability.

Some of our best business leaders either cannot pronounce their 'r's properly or, like Jack Welch of General Electric, suffer from a slight stammer. For business presentations it may not matter if you are not totally fluent. Hesitancy can be turned to good account by allowing you to appear vulnerable and therefore more real as a person.

Standing

Standing up to present raises your energy level and this translates into your performance. It also gives you more freedom to move around. If you discover that you are expected to stay tied to one place, challenge that requirement, for instance, by demanding a roving mic.

It isn't essential to stand for your presentation, even on many formal occasions. If you choose to sit down there isn't a lot the organisers can do about it, though you may spoil the acoustic arrangements.

It's important that you feel comfortable when you stand, so be sure to wear shoes and clothes that add to your confidence. While no single stance is right or wrong it's generally best to adopt a balanced position in which you plant your feet slightly apart and firmly on the ground.

Start (see main body of text on pages 75–7)

'Where shall I begin, please your Majesty?' he asked.
'Begin at the beginning,' the King said gravely, 'and go on till
you come to the end: then stop.'

LEWIS CARROLL, ALICE IN WONDERLAND

Statistics (see NUMBERS and also CHARTS)

It was popularly supposed that figures couldn't lie, but they did;
they lied like the dickens.

MARY STEWART CUTTING, TITLE STORY, THE SUBURBAN WHIRL (1907)

No nation ranks higher in its collective passion for statistics than Japan. They are the subject of holidays, local and national conventions, award ceremonies and nationwide statistical collection and graph-drawing contests. If you're presenting in Japan, don't let up on the numbers.

Statistics not only show the hard truths; they also reveal the future. In business presentations people usually expect some figures yet like anyone else the audience is swayed by emotional factors too.

Learn to make numbers talk. If you do present statistics, keep them simple and ensure that the message is unmissable. It's better to present a few statistics of high quality than a mass of data that may look impressive yet leave the audience numb.

Steps (see FRAMEWORKS in main body of text on page 23)

Stereotypes (see SEXISM)

If a man does something silly, people say, 'Isn't he silly?' If a
woman does something silly, people say, 'Aren't women silly.'

DORIS DAY, NATIONAL ENQUIRER (1988)

Stomach (see NERVES in main body of text on pages 71-73)

Oh the nerves, the nerves; the mysteries of this machine called
man! Of the little that unhinges it, poor creatures that we are!

CHARLES DICKENS, 1844

Many presenters suffer from stomach cramps and other pre-performance ailments, mainly due to nerves. These only really matter if they start getting in the way, for example, by keeping you awake when you'd like to sleep before an important event.

Otherwise pre-performance tension may even sharpen your awareness of last-minute improvements to your presentation.

A hot milky drink may help settle your stomach. The dangers of even mild sedatives are that they may continue affecting your system just when you need to perform, when you want a bit of tension to prevail. Generally avoid sedatives either the night before or on the day of the performance.

Strange stomach noises have been know to embarrass a presenter, usually by being picked up by an ultra-sensitive mike. If that happens, either move the mike or just shrug and get on with the presentation.

Stop (see also CLOSE)

Most business presenters go on too long. Two signs to watch for are when the audience is

★ Fully alert and ready to applaud

★ Sending signals that you should end

If you're really alert to your audience you'll quickly sense when you have reached the peak of their attention. This is the time to stop, no matter how much precious material you have waiting in the wings.

★ 'Say what you need to say, then "full stop"'

Story

The Master presenters tell terrific stories. Choose ones that you care about, that are relevant and that affect you in some way. An audience quickly picks up the feelings and you create a powerful impact. By telling stories that matter to you, you'll tend to stop worrying about what to do with your hands, or forgetting your lines.

Think of your presentation as one big story you want to tell. What's the story about, how does it start, what's the denouement? You can even go further and identify a hero and a villain. For instance, is your story a tragedy, a comedy, a farce, a soap opera and so on? Even if you never use these ideas during the actual presentation, just thinking this way can firm up your approach to the performance.

Storyboard (see main body of text on page 22)

Stress (see NERVES in main body of text on pages 71–73)

Structure (see FRAMEWORKS also main body of text on page 23)

Stuck (see also FREEZING and QUESTIONS in main body of text on pages 102–3, 125–9)

Don't know what to say? Troubled about building your presentation? Start with the one place you can be sure will help: the audience. Dig down deep into the audience and you'll find what to say.

Stutter (see STAMMER)

Style (see also PERSONALITY)

Your presentation style is a combination of your personality and the way you prepare and deliver your message. There is no one best way, no 'correct' style to adopt. It is more important to be yourself.

Presentation styles vary enormously and if they didn't audiences would soon get extremely bored. Treasure what makes you special; think of ways to inject into your presentation aspects of yourself that can bring the performance alive. For example, if you have a good sense of humour then be sure this is fully used in your presentation. If you are someone who is thoughtful or studious then allow this to show through in what you say and do.

Although style is personal to you, it may need to be adapted to suit the situation or audience. So if you tend to be someone who hardly ever prepares and the occasion is an important one, then relying totally on improvisation may be inappropriate.

Subject (see also IDEA)

'We'd like you to give us a presentation, choose any subject you want.' That kind of invitation is some people's dream request or a nightmare. Like a painter facing a blank canvas, choosing a presentation subject can be stressful, particularly if you have only a short time to create a high-quality result.

Professional presenters keep their previous presentations carefully filed under subject, so if necessary they can adapt them for a new purpose. Others go even further, retaining cutting files full of possible items that could trigger a suitable presentation.

If you are stuck for a subject, start with what you know. You already possess a huge amount of knowledge; it's just a case of narrowing down the possibilities to those that challenge your creativity.

Choose a topic about which you have some strong feelings. Delve deep enough into practically any topic and you'll soon hit ideas, opinions or facts that create a personal reaction. This is the starting point. Once you feel involved, it's simpler to begin converting the topic into an outline presentation.

Another basis for choosing your presentation subject is your knowledge of the audience. The more you know about your listeners the greater will be your confidence about your chosen subject. Possible criteria for choosing topics include:

★ Topicality
★ Direct relevance to audience
★ Personal experience
★ Available research and other source material
★ Your own strong feelings about an issue

If you can't find a subject to engage your enthusiasm it's time for some extended audience research. Talk to or meet some of your potential audience. Conduct a mini-research project on what concerns them. By the time you finish you'll have plenty of ideas on which to base your performance.

Finally, use organisations such as professional institutes, expert colleagues and others to guide you in identifying possible subjects for your presentation.

Sub-text (see also PURPOSE in main body of text on pages 4–8)

Watch for hidden meanings within your presentation. Actors call these sub-text and they can be almost as important as what you actually say. Audiences often read between the lines even when there's no planned hidden message.

Sub-text can be either deliberate or there by mistake. When it's a mistake you are saying one thing but your audience hears something different.

You identify sub-text by asking questions such as:

★ 'What is the speaker really saying?'
★ 'What is the speaker not saying?'
★ 'What does the speaker mean by that?'
★ 'What are the implications of what the speaker is saying?'

Sometimes it helps to have one or more other colleagues listening to you rehearse your presentation specifically to check out the sub-text.

Success (see also RISK and UNEXPECTED)

To win without risk is to triumph without glory.

CORNEILLE, *LE CID* (1636)

A winning presentation is one that leaves
★ Your audience wanting more
★ You feeling you have done yourself justice

It is only too easy to settle for a merely competent presentation, rather than an outstanding one. Go for outstanding every time, even though you may not always achieve it.

Support

Even the greatest actors and performers need encouragement and support from those with whom they work. Support isn't just to make you feel better, it's to stimulate you to do even better.

Find someone with whom you can team up to support you with each presentation. It should be a person or group who really want you to succeed and are willing to be frank.

Often you get the support that you deserve. If you don't bother to ask for it you probably won't receive it.

Sweating (see main body of text on page 71)

If you know that you tend to sweat a lot choose white clothing rather than, say, dark blue, which will show stains. Arm yourself with plenty of tissues to mop up. A sweating presenter is not necessarily a bad presenter and audiences will forgive practically anything except boredom.

Symbols (see VISUALS in main body of text on pages 40–48)

Symbolism is a powerful way of conveying your presentation message. Anything visual can act as a symbol and so, too, can actions. For instance, when you start by announcing that your presentation will finish on time this is a symbolic way of saying that you respect people's time.

Visual symbols can be used throughout your presentation to convey ideas. For example, suppose your core message is that the situation is 'on a knife edge', you might produce a large real knife, or have a picture of a knife on all your visual aids. This symbol would convey everything you needed to say without having to re-emphasise it.

Symbols tend to be highly memorable, acquiring a life of their own. When one presenter used Humpty Dumpty to convey the dangers facing his organisation, for years afterwards people talked about 'the Humpty Dumpty effect'. Choose your symbols carefully; they can have a profound effect and if misunderstood can undermine rather than support your message.

★ Symbols are also an excellent way to refine your presentation
★ What single symbol would sum up your core message?

T

Tables (see also Visuals in main body of text on pages 40–48)

If you present from behind a table, it's an unnecessary barrier between you and your audience. Master presenters usually reject such an artificial restriction to making contact with their audience.

If you can't move the table, try walking around to the front to address people. At conferences, the organisers may not encourage this change but it can improve your rapport with the audience.

Taboos

What can't you say or do in a presentation? For some audiences, any mention of certain subjects may be unacceptable and even a positive insult. Early research should identify what might offend your audience. For example, in the top management team of a pharmaceutical company, any discussion about the purpose of the team was strongly resisted by the CEO.

Rules, however, are made to be broken and even taboo subjects can sometimes be raised. If you know a subject is taboo and intend raising it, consider telling people in advance about your intentions. Say that you will fully understand if some people don't want to stay and listen, but remember that this is also inviting people to leave and may backfire.

Humour is an effective way of tackling taboo topics, though again you need to handle this with care and people may not take kindly to you being witty around something sensitive.

Unless you are keen to shock your audience, it may be best to avoid taboo issues for your presentation.

Talent (see main body of text on page 2)

Everyone has talent. What is rare is the courage to follow the talent to the dark places where it leads.

ERICA JONG, 'THE ARTIST AS HOUSEWIFE,
THE HOUSEWIFE AS ARTIST', *MS* (1972)

Talks (see also FRAMEWORKS)

Talking's just a nervous habit.

MARTHA GRIMES, *THE DEER LEAP* (1985)

Teams (see main body of text on pages 51–6)

Technicians (See also TECHNOLOGY)

There are three roads to ruin; women, gambling and technicians. The most pleasant is with women, the quickest is with gambling, but the surest way is with technicians.

GEORGES POMPIDOU, *SUNDAY TIMES* (1968)

In many business presentations the technicians hold sway. They control machines that deliver sound, vision, lighting, temperature and many other aspects of a presenting environment. It pays to make friends with the technical team, meeting them personally and finding out how you can help each other.

Some Master presenters know that their whole delivery can be ruined by technicians' withdrawal of co-operation. So they go to considerable lengths to ensure that they enrol these experts in what they are attempting to achieve. For example, some will resort to near bribery by handing over money 'to buy yourself a drink' the day after a technical rehearsal and before the live presentation.

Be direct with these people, explaining exactly what you want: 'Here's how I think you could help me come across well.' While most technicians are keen to show how they can support a presenter, they often have a tendency to expect the presenter to fit in with their technology rather than the other way around. You may need to be assertive to get what you want, pushing to ask, 'Why can't it be done differently, as that's what I need?'

Technology (see also EQUIPMENT)

Any sufficiently advanced technology is indistinguishable from magic.

ARTHUR C. CLARKE, *THE LOST WORLDS OF 2001*

Will you be a master or a prisoner of presentation technology? It's easy to push buttons or worry about some gadget, rather than focusing on the audience. Keep your presentation technology simple and only use something elaborate if you have plenty of practice time available.

Presentation technology available includes:

★ Overhead projectors
★ Slides
★ LCD panels and projectors
★ CRT projectors
★ Multimedia and interactive machines
★ Video and CD-ROM
★ Desktop presentations
★ Portable presentations

It takes considerable practice to make computer-based slide systems subordinate to the speaker, rather than the other way around. A particular disadvantage of some projection technology is the tendency to take up the centre of the room, pushing the audience to the back, causing yet more distancing from the presenter.

Despite the drawbacks, well-suited technology can transform a presentation into an exciting, stimulating experience. The electronics company Sharp produce a useful *Guide to Audio Visual and Video Presentations.*

Telephone (see PHONE)

> *All phone calls are obscene.*
> KAREN ELIZABETH GORDON, *THE WELL TEMPERED SENTENCE* (1983)

Teleprompt (see TELEPROMPT in main body of text on pages 60–1)

> *The text is never important. One has to say it, play it of course. What is vital is what's in-between the words – behind them.*
> JEAN-LOUIS TRINTIGNANT, *FILMS ILLUSTRATED* (1979)

Television (see also QUESTIONS in main body of text on pages 125–9, and VIDEO NEWS RELEASE)

Television creates a whole set of its own pressures on presenters. For example, there is considerable expectation that the presenter will get it right which, combined with the often tense atmosphere, bright lights, heat and perhaps a persistent interviewer, can be a challenging experience for even the most experienced performer.

If you expect to appear on television presenting your company or with a personal message of some kind, seek professional help. This can take the form of

★ Coaching in handling the media
★ Familiarisation with studio practice

Some of the methods that work in ordinary presenting are unsuitable for television, such as getting up suddenly and walking around, or making large gestures that may be outside camera range. Similarly, you have no one to look in the eye, only an inanimate lens, unless you are being interviewed, in which case look only at the interviewer.

Ten TV tips

★ When looking at the lens, speak as if to someone you know on the other end
★ Keep it simple
★ Whatever the context, stress the advantages for the average person of what you are saying
★ When possible, use examples to deal with complicated questions
★ If giving technical answers, use analogies or stories to illustrate your point
★ Don't knock competitors, TV lives off controversy and will always try to generate it
★ Keep your body language open, even when you think you're off camera
★ Keep hands, glasses, pens and other items away from your mouth
★ Reframe questions, putting them on your terms: 'Yes, some people do think that, but another way of looking at it is . . .'
★ If you're constantly interrupted, get tough – 'If you'll just let me finish I'll answer your question.'

All you have to do on television is to be yourself, provided, that is, that you have a self to be.
CLIVE JAMES, *OBSERVER* (1981)

Temper (see ANGER)

Nothing is so aggravating as calmness. There is something positively brutal about the good temper of most modern men. I wonder we women stand for it as well as we do.
MRS ALLONBY IN OSCAR WILDE'S *A WOMAN OF NO IMPORTANCE* (1893)

Temperature (see Venue in main body of text on page 63)

Tension (see Nerves in main body of text on pages 71–73)

When you suffer an attack of nerves you're being attacked by the nervous system. What chance has a man got against a system.
RUSSELL HOBAN, BRITISH AUTHOR

Terror (see Nerves in main body of text on pages 71-73)

Don't hesitate: get some professional presentation help.

Thanks

Gratitude is the most exquisite form of courtesy.
JACQUES MARITAIN (1882–1973), FRENCH PHILOSOPHER

'Thanks' is such a little word, yet it makes people feel so good to be on the receiving end. You have many opportunities for using it as a presenter so be generous with it. You can thank

★ Your audience for listening to you. Don't be effusive, just politely grateful for a good hearing
★ People who ask questions, no matter how difficult these may be
★ Volunteers who help you
★ Technical staff who manage equipment, such as sound and A-V systems
★ Those who asked you to present in the first place. Their efforts are often taken for granted, it costs nothing to express thanks for their hard work

Theft (see also Plagiarism)

If you steal from one author it's plagiarism;
if you steal from many, it's research.
DOROTHY PARKER

The first step in creativity is theft – we all build on what we know, which is often based on what others have said, done or discovered before us. Having a totally original presentation idea is rare, so when you see or hear something good, use it.

It's important somehow to make what you use from other people into your own, giving it a special angle that reflects your personality. For example, you can steal another person's jokes, yet this won't necessarily make you as funny or produce the same reaction.

The Masters of presentation are always stealing from each other, seizing on an idea and altering it to suit themselves and their particular personality or situation.

Be sure to acknowledge your sources where you are taking someone's ideas and using them virtually unaltered.

Themes (see THEMES in main body of text on pages 21–2)

Thinking on your feet (see IMPROVISE in main body of text on page 85)

Throat (See VOICE, BREATHING and NERVES)

Time

Cuba's long-serving President Fidel Castro used to harangue his audience for six hours or more. His audiences apparently loved it, or didn't dare say otherwise. Your audiences are unlikely to be so compliant. So how long should your presentation last?

Audiences have a short attention span. Regardless of your brilliance as a presenter, people mentally begin drifting away after about fifteen minutes. Even the most outstanding presenter can have problems holding an audience beyond half an hour. The general rule is rehearse, time it and then cut the presentation in half.

Some of the best potential business presenters suffer from a dreadful disease – they simply don't know when to stop. Instead of leaving the audience yearning for more, they drone on and ruin whatever excellent impact they had originally achieved.

★ Few people ever complain about a *short* business presentation

★ Find out for how long the audience expects you to talk

★ If you stick to a maximum of twenty minutes you will probably not outstay your welcome

Ten Time Tips

★ Leave your audience wanting more

★ Try to speak for ten minutes or less, then give the audience a chance to comment, ask questions or work on some aspect of your presentation. You can then continue talking for another ten minutes, having given everyone a break from your voice

★ If it's a team presentation such as pitching for new business, speak for only about five minutes and let another member of the team have a say. This adds variety, changes pace and keeps the audience alert

★ Always start on time
★ Keep a clock in visible range to stay aware of the time limits
★ Finish on time – if you overrun, especially in business presentations, people may conclude that you can't plan
★ If speaking for a prolonged period, say over half an hour, offer your audience regular breaks for coffee, a chance to smoke or use the toilets
★ If you expect to overrun, renegotiate the extra time with the audience – some people might have to catch trains or attend other meetings
★ Have a volunteer act as your timer, giving a signal when you are halfway through your presentation and nearing the final ten minutes. Because one can easily get carried away when presenting, train the timer to keep signalling you until you acknowledge the message with a nod

Timeliness (see TOPICALITY)

Title (see VISUALS in main body of text on pages 40–48)

A good title for your presentation can get you off to a good start with your audience, so it's worth the effort to create an intriguing one. The best titles are

★ Provocative
★ Descriptive
★ Short
★ Relevant
★ Topical

Exercise your creative muscles to find the right title. Start with a simple *working title* for everyday purposes. Keep it short, merely a brief statement of what the presentation is about. Use this working title for a while, without trying to devise a more permanent one. When you become clearer about what you intend to talk about, shorten the working title into two or three words. As you research your subject and audience, you may encounter facts or situations that stimulate you to adapt the working title to have more relevance to your audience.

Try your proposed final title on objective colleagues who can tell you whether it seems compelling.

Tips for creating titles

★ Ask a question, e.g.: Will the Internet survive? Who cares about the Euro?

★ Select some puzzling or evocative words, e.g.: Indiscretions; Market Madness

★ Devise a statement with an active verb, e.g.: Renationalising the Railways

★ Use alliteration, e.g.: Making the Millennium Manageable

★ Issue a challenging claim, e.g.: The Coming Crash

★ Include a relevant name in the title, e.g.: BP and the Next Oil crisis

★ Look for contemporary themes in society and incorporate them into the title. For example, when the film Armageddon was hitting the news, one speaker who was talking about the possibility of global recession called his presentation: 'Will the Market Avoid Armageddon?'

Toastmasters

Toastmasters is an international organisation that helps its members to learn to speak in public by giving them plenty of practise, working with others in a supportive environment. A typical Toastmasters club consists of up to thirty people who meet weekly for about an hour. These gatherings give everyone an opportunity to practise: conduct meetings; give impromptu speeches and present prepared speeches.

There are clubs in more than sixty countries worldwide. To find a local one visit the Toastmaster web site at: http://www.toastmasters.org/

Tobacco (See Smoking)

> *As ye smoke, so shall ye reek.*
>
> ANON, *READER'S DIGEST* (1949)

Toilet (see also Water)

> *France is a country where the money falls apart in your hands and you can't tear the toilet paper.*
>
> BILLY WILDER, AMERICAN SCREEN DIRECTOR

Always use the toilet just before heading for the limelight. Otherwise, with your nerves already taut you may find you need to leave in the middle of the presentation.

If nature calls, create a break or put people into discussion groups while you sort out the problem. Don't call attention to your urgent need, just go.

Tools (see also TECHNOLOGY)

There is a huge variety of presentation tools from which to choose:

★ Slides, LCD panels, projectors, laptops, video, multimedia, sound, laser pointers, lapel microphones, overheads, photo-quality printers, electronic whiteboards and so on.
★ The best tools of all are you and your *personality*
★ The more sophisticated the technology the more the audience becomes bemused by what is happening, rather than focusing on contents or meaning

Topic (see IDEA and SUBJECT)

Topicality (see also Subject)

The more topical you make your presentation the easier it will be for audiences to identify with what you are saying.

Topicality tips
★ Don't distort your basic message just to be topical
★ Limited research will nearly always produce a name, an issue or something topical for a particular audience
★ Ask the conference or event organiser about people or situations that are of concern to the target audience
★ Meet some of your potential audience and frankly explain that you are giving a presentation and would like to inject some topicality into it. Most people are happy to offer suggestions
★ Obtain local papers, watch local TV stations, listen to local radio for more clues about issues that might be linked with your presentation. If you really keep your eyes and ears open you will soon discover ammunition for your performance

Toupee (see WIG)

Training (see also COACHING)

You can always reach another level in presenting and most people can benefit from professional help. Apart from plenty of practice, the main ways of improving are:

★ Attendance on a presentation course
★ Individual coaching

Courses vary considerably in quality and it can be difficult

initially to decide what separates a good one from a bad one. In some countries there are independent assessment organisations who help make sense of what is available. For example, in the UK the OMTRAC organisation nominates top courses.

Courses last from around one or two days to up to four, along with follow-up sessions. Generally, though, a two-day programme is enough to make a real difference to your confidence and widen your repertoire of tools and techniques. When choosing a presentation course look for:

★ A training supplier with a demonstrable record of success
★ Course leaders who are successful presenters in their own right
★ Courses where most of the time is mainly spent practising, rather than being lectured at
★ A small number of participants – usually around eight to ten
★ A focus on the individual, rather than teaching 'rules'

You can see details of one of the UK's top presentation courses, 'Performing with Presence', at the People Development Site: www.maynardleigh.co.uk

Translators (see INTERPRETERS)

Travel (see also AUDIENCE, INTERPRETERS and ILLNESS)

When you travel your first discovery is that you don't exist.
ELIZABETH HARDWICK, *SLEEPLESS NIGHTS* (1980)

The longer your journey to the presentation the more you may need to

★ Research the local situation and the particular audience
★ Recover and recharge your batteries
★ Check out the venue and its facilities
★ Keep your overall timetable flexible to allow for missed connections and altered plans

Trip (see also LECTERN and PODIUM)

As you head towards the limelight you may first have to navigate difficult stairs or thread your way around tables. It is obviously not a good start if along the way you trip or stumble but if you do, show a sense of humour.

Comments you might offer as you pick yourself up include:

★ 'You can tell I qualified in deportment'

★ 'I come from a long line of circus performers'
★ 'Bet you're wondering what I'll do for an encore'
★ 'I might never make it back'
★ 'Which one of you planned that?'
★ 'You can immediately see I'm a professional'
★ 'Imagine what the rest of it's going to be like'

Having arrived at your destination you might smile wanly and comment, 'Safe at last! Maybe I should quit now while I'm winning.'

Tuning in

A business presentation is not just about talking. It's concerned with tuning in, finding out what your audience is thinking and feeling.

★ Are you broadcasting when you should be tuning in?

A good example of failing to tune in occurred when a team gave a presentation to a major airline. Within the first ten minutes the team realised the audience were not really concentrating. Yet instead of stopping the show and asking what was happening, the team ploughed on regardless. Later they realised that the audience were still distracted from the previous presentation.

Type size (see FONTS)

U

Uncertain (see NERVES in main body of text on pages 71–73, also VISUALISATION)

Doubt and mistrust are the mere panic of timid imagination, which the steadfast heart will conquer, and the large mind transcend.
HELEN KELLER, *OPTIMISM* (1903)

Understate (see also EMOTION)

Don't be so humble – you're not that great.
GOLDA MEIR IN MARY SHENKER (ED.), *AS GOOD AS GOLDA* (1970)

Almost by definition, business presentations are a chance to show off. You are the presentation and false modesty does not ring true. In many situations people expect you, in effect, to

boast. For example, a showcase presentation is all about putting you and your company on display.

The British in particular can be masters of the understatement, offering a hidden language that others around the world either don't understand or mock mercilessly. Yet in many presenting situations it pays to downplay how wonderful you or your company are. It may be far more important to concentrate on showing off what you can do and how you do it.

In important pitch situations you are seldom allowed through the door unless you are competent in the first place. To spend much of the time extolling your own virtues could simply be a waste of time, a missed opportunity really to build relationships with the solutions you offer.

What is certainly not worth understating is your core message. Either this is important or it shouldn't be the centre of your presentation. There is no case for hiding this communication with false modesty, which your audience may interpret not as understatement but lack of clarity.

Unexpected (see Surprise and Openers in main body of text on pages 116 and 75–7)

> *Truly nothing is to be expected but the unexpected!*
> ALICE JAMES, *MOON OVER MINNEAPOLIS* (1991)

If a train you're travelling on arrived somewhere you never intended to go you would not necessarily be pleased. Likewise, delivering the unexpected in a presentation is not about totally disconcerting or disappointing your audience. It's about finding new ways to surprise and delight people.

The Master presenters never cease worrying away at this issue, constantly seeking to deliver the unexpected that an audience can relish. You can surprise your audience in so many ways, it is simply a matter of using your creativity. Once a presentation becomes predictable it also becomes boring.

Delivering the unexpected inevitably means taking risks, experimenting with new ways of communicating. On a personal level you could do the presentation in a risky way that really challenges you. For example, what would be the effect if you delivered the entire presentation in rhyme, or you flew in a team of world experts whom the audience knew of only by reputation?

Groucho Marx once wisecracked: 'This report is so simple a child could understand it. So go out and bring me back a child.' Imagine the reaction of an audience that was told during your presentation that your machinery was so simple a child could operate it and you brought in a child to demonstrate. It would certainly be surprising.

Doing the unexpected just for the sake of it, is not what it's about. Distorting the entire presentation just to be different won't necessarily help. You need to do it because it will

★ Enliven the performance
★ Focus attention
★ Clarify a point
★ Wake up the audience
★ Delight or inspire people
★ Ram home a point
★ Precipitate action

Unique (see PERSONALITY)

Since you are not like any other being ever created since the beginning of Time, you are incomparable.
BRENDA URLAND, *IF YOU WANT TO WRITE* (1938)

Unlucky (see LUCK)

Luck is always to blame
JEAN DE LA FONTAINE (1621–95), FRENCH POET

Unprepared (see PREPARATION in main body of text on pages 1–19)

Unreceptive (see AUDIENCE in main body of text on pages 4, 123)

Unsure (see NERVES in main body of text on pages 71–73)

If you think you can, you can.
And if you think you can't, you're right.
MARY KAY ASH, *NEW YORK TIMES BOOK REVIEW* (1985)

Unwell (see also ILLNESS, AUDIENCE, and PAIN)

You don't get ulcers from what you eat. You get them from what's eating you.
FELICIA LAMPORT, 'LINES ON AN ACHING BROW', *SCRAP IRONY* (1961)

Upstage (see also INTERRUPTIONS in main body of text on pages 101–2)

It's every actor's nightmare to be upstaged during an important

performance. It happens when someone or something steals the limelight, leaving you in a minor role, with little or no audience attention.

You could be upstaged by

★ Previous speakers
★ The chairman of the session
★ Well-informed members of the audience
★ Unexpected interruptions, such as a bomb scare or fire alarm test
★ Someone talking or crying
★ A well-known personality in the audience
★ A fellow presenting team member

Solid preparation and an ability to think on your feet will often carry you through even the trickiest moments. Depending on your ego, a determination not to be pushed out of the limelight also helps.

Ten ways to avoid being upstaged

★ Be alert to what is happening in the moment (see Presence in main body of text on page 73)
★ Know that you can regain the initiative
★ Use the acoustics and the technology to dominate the situation
★ Continue speaking and holding the stage
★ Break into the other person's flow of talk
★ Ask a rhetorical question, which you proceed to answer
★ Thank the person, saying pointedly that you will now continue your presentation
★ Use humour to regain the initiative
★ Conduct an instant poll among the audience
★ Get the audience doing something to your instruction

V

Variety (see also New and Unexpected)

Variety is the soul of pleasure.
APHRA BEHN (1640–89), ENGLISH WRITER AND ADVENTURESS, *THE ROVER*

Presentation audiences soon lose interest or become bored. To counter this tendency, keep adding variety throughout the performance and from one performance to the next.

For example, if you give a regular team briefing, people can find the same approach each week or month extremely tedious. Adding variety to what you do and how you do it will keep them guessing and wanting to know what you'll do next.

Ten ways to add variety

★ Alter the pace of presentation
★ Increase or decrease your loudness and pitch
★ Change your present style, moving to or from more intimacy
★ Experiment with different standing or sitting positions
★ Alter the mix of facts and arguments, stories and example
★ Talk less and involve the audience more
★ Walk around the room, mingling with the audience
★ Move locations
★ Get the audience doing a quiz or solving a problem
★ Use visual and audio aids to break up the presentation

Choose changes that will enhance the impact of your performance, rather than just introducing more elements for the audience to handle.

Venue (see VENUE in main body of text on page 63)

You're important and need showing off. The venue can support or undermine your performance. Whether you're presenting to a handful of people or a ballroom of a thousand, check it out.

When you receive an invitation to speak, ask for information about environment and discuss creative ways it might be changed to enhance your impact. For instance, if you're due to give a boardroom presentation what effect would it have if you added some flowers for once? At a conference, can the backdrop be altered to suit your style and material? How can the lighting be focused where you need it? How flexible is the audio-visual technology?

Master presenters sometimes use set designers to create a powerful backdrop for their performance. Even when you cannot afford this you can certainly still take responsibility for making the most of the facilities.

Think about how to make the place instantly more interesting and inviting for your audience. For example, if you're speaking after a coffee break, why not place your own colourful, eye-catching WELCOME sign at the entrance for when people return? Would it be possible to add some stimulating pictures, quotations or relevant strange objects around the walls?

Verbiage (see main body of text on page 35)

Nothing is more despicable than a professional talker who uses his words as a quack uses his remedies.
FRANÇOIS FÉNELON (1651–1715), FRENCH WRITER AND PRELATE

Vernacular (see Idioms and Interpreters)

Video (see Technology and Video News Release)

People want to hear you, rather than watch a video or film clip. The stronger the screen images the more these may come between you and your audience. Only if the video message is compelling, rather than just entertaining, is it likely to work well as a presenting aid.

Video works best when you incorporate it fully into your performance, rather than using it as an add-on to liven up the proceedings. The technology is useful for

★ Presenting your message in a lively way
★ Giving performance feedback
★ Conveying large amounts of information quickly

Although it's relatively easy to create material, making a high-quality video requires almost as much planning and time as using ordinary film stock.

How will your video be shown? If run on a small television screen, for example, it may have far less impact than you planned, while a giant screen may highlight any amateurish aspects.

Pros	Cons
★ Conveys ideas, feelings and messages well	★ Can be an audience distraction
★ Production costs are falling fast	★ May slow down your pace
★ Easy to replay to make a point	★ May not fit well in a factual presentation
★ Can enliven at just the right time	★ Can be hard to produce to high quality
★ Tends to be underused in presentations	★ Needs integration into a performance
★ Particularly useful for video conferences	★ May fail at the crucial moment

Short video bites are increasingly being incorporated into presentations and can even be held on the computer as part of a multimedia presentation. In a business presentation a video insert longer than around a couple of minutes may begin to detract from your performance and turn the proceedings into a film show instead.

Tips on using videos

★ Check the equipment works
★ Pre-set the right audio level and contrast
★ Dim but don't turn off room lights
★ Keep video clips short – usually not exceeding a couple of minutes
★ Use only if appropriate: if they enhance your message
★ Prepare meticulously, so that clips start and finish to plan
★ Avoid talking while playing the video
★ Be ready to cope with the technology failing – carry a back-up tape
★ Obtain a licence for video clips such as film extracts
★ To make an image stick in people's minds use a freeze-frame
★ Show interest in the tape and watch it with enthusiasm
★ Summarise the main points after showing the tape

Video conferences

Some people love video conferences, taking to them immediately. Others regard them as purgatory, the ultimate presentation nightmare. These hi-tech sessions are growing in popularity, though, as the price for staging them constantly falls. They can be one-way, two-way, or from multiple locations.

Ten ways to survive a video conference

★ Prepare your main points in advance
★ Prior to the event talk to the other people by phone or in person
★ Circulate the agenda in advance, showing how long each item will take and its main purpose – there should be no surprises
★ Avoid taking a prior public stand against something that will be discussed
★ Use plenty of energy – normal gestures and facial expressions can look limp or tired on a monitor – so that people don't need to rely on watching your lips move
★ Introduce yourself the first time you speak

★ Avoid loud colours, striped ties and large jewellery which may distract people

★ Use visual aids and check in advance how these can be incorporated into the conference

★ Be a good listener – as interruptions or side conversations may trigger voice-activated systems and make you the focus of the camera's unwelcome attention

★ Stay alert the whole time as if constantly the focus of attention – you may be when you least expect it. For example, if you doodle, or make pithy comments on your pad about participants, keep these out of range of overhead camcras

Video is also a useful personal tool for practising your presentation. Preferably watch it with a colleague so that you get objective feedback as well as your own observations. It can be worth building a small library of your performances so that you can watch yourself developing and you can track the eradication of any irritating or distracting habits.

Video news release (VNR)

Essentially it's the same as a news release, in video form, though costing much more. Businesses are increasingly using VNRs for important events and presenting your message this way can be extremely effective.

If you expect broadcasters to use the material, even a three-minute VNR can be demanding of resources and technical know-how. There are many angles to consider about being an effective performer for these types of communication and it's best to work with an expert to ensure you stand a chance of having the material used. For example, you almost certainly can't keep mentioning the name of your company because if you do, the networks will see the item as just another piece of PR.

Visualisation (see NERVES in main body of text on pages 71–73, also AFFIRMATIONS)

> *When I dream, I believe I am rehearsing my future.*
> DAVID COPPERFIELD, US MAGICIAN

Master presenters usually create a mental picture of what success would look and feel like. As if running a film through a projector, visualisation lets you 'see' yourself doing something well and this builds confidence.

The more you rehearse the mental image the stronger its

THE ULTIMATE · BUSINESS · PRESENTATION BOOK

power becomes to influence your actual behaviour. Here's how to do it:

Step 1:
Make a quiet period in which to practise, somewhere uncluttered and preferably spacious.

Step 2:
Do some relaxation exercises such as deep breathing and stretching.

Step 3:
Close your eyes, try to empty your mind of busy, day-to-day thoughts, allow your 'inner eye' to 'see' just black space.

Step 4:
Choose a simple mental picture, like the audience congratulating on your performance or you delivering the presentation with passion and confidence.

Step 5:
Develop the picture by filling in details, 'viewing' it from different angles. Make the picture as real and complete as possible.

Step 6:
Keep returning to this mental image regularly throughout the day and last thing at night.

Recall your visualisation even as you give your actual performance. It sits in the back of your mind, a constant reassurance that you are achieving what you want.

Be creative and let your imagination run wild. It doesn't matter how absurd the image you create, or how unrealistic the story it tells. The more outrageous the picture you devise, the more memorable it becomes. The more frequently you 'visit' these mental images the more power they have to affect your confidence.

Give yourself permission to go over the top, developing dramatic and memorable mental pictures of success. For example, have fun imagining

★ The CEO calling you for advice on presentations
★ Winning a world award for the best business presentations
★ Becoming a millionaire from giving brilliant presentations
★ The audience carrying you shoulder-high in triumph
★ An airport bookstall filled with a book of your brilliant speeches

★ Being promoted as a result of your presentations
★ The audience at a sales pitch begging on their knees to be allowed to buy your services

Whenever you feel negative or downhearted about your presentation, call on the visualisation to support and stimulate you.

Visuals (see main body of text on pages 40–45)

Vocabulary (see main body of text on page 35)

I want my vocabulary to have a very large range, but the words must be alive.
JAMES AGEE, *LETTERS OF JAMES AGEE TO FATHER FLYE* (1962)

What reads well on paper can sound cumbersome and formal when spoken aloud. Spend at least some of your rehearsal time listening for whether the words sound stilted or ill-chosen. If unsure, ask colleagues to comment on this aspect of your performance.

While you may be comfortable with certain words your audience may be confused or feel patronised. Your choice of vocabulary should be strongly dictated by what the particular audience needs and this may be influenced by

★ Experience, education, time pressures, expectations

Like jargon, vocabulary can be a double-edged weapon. Keep your choice of words and phrases simple; no one ever failed in a business presentation by using easy to understand words.

Voice (see main body of text on pages 74, 100)

The higher the voice the smaller the intellect.
ERNEST NEWMAN (1868–1959)

Vulgarism (see also Vernacular)

Vulgarity begins when imagination succumbs to the explicit.
DORIS DAY IN A. E. HOTCHNER, *DORIS DAY* (1975)

Coarse words or expressions seldom enhance a presentation. Even if you think you are pandering to your particular audience, some may actually resent your use of such material.

Swear words and crude expressions are best left to stand-up comedians.

Vulnerable (see PASSION in main body of text on pages 77–80)

Better to be wounded, a captive and a slave, than always to walk in armour.
MACRINA WIEDERKEHR, *SEASONS OF YOUR HEART* (1979)

Audiences want to see you as human, with failings just like them. This is particularly so if you are a senior manager talking to subordinates. Some of the most experienced presenters deliberately show their vulnerability, often to great effect.

For example, admitting that 'I made a bit of a mess of that slide' or confessing that 'I'm a bit anxious about talking to such an experienced audience' makes you seem human rather than unprofessional.

It doesn't work if you continuously refer to your failings, or trade on people's sympathy. Yet an occasional sign that you are not perfect adds a touch of humanity that an audience really appreciates.

You also show your vulnerability when you permit your natural emotions to shine through. For instance, if you tell a moving story and are genuinely affected by it, your audience will be too. Even if it brings tears to your eyes, this won't do you harm. You might say, 'That story always brings a lump to my throat.'

Obviously the presentation setting is important, since becoming tearful during a pitch for new business would hardly be helpful.

W

Waffle (see JARGON in main body of text)

One never repents of having spoken too little, but often of having spoken too much.
PHILIPPE DE COMMYNES, FRENCH STATESMAN AND HISTORIAN
(1445–1511), *MÉMOIRES*

Waiters (see INTERRUPTIONS in main body of text on page 101–2)

They also serve who only stand and wait.
MILTON, SONNET 19 (1655)

Walking

People seem to think there is something inherently noble and virtuous in the desire to go for a walk.
MAX BEERBOHM, 1920

Moving around during a business presentation adds interest to your performance. You also energise yourself to inject more into the delivery. Just the act of standing up can give fresh momentum to how you communicate.

When presenting to an audience in a formal theatre-style room, it can make a huge difference if you refuse to stay stuck behind a desk or podium. Get physically closer to the audience, either by going among them, or at least by moving nearer while on the platform.

Endless pacing, however, can irritate if people have to watch you trekking from one place to another without any real purpose. To allow you freedom to rove about check out any logistical problems, including the limitations of fixed-place cameras and microphones on leads.

★ Make your walk slow and deliberate, rather than rapid or shuffling

Wardrobe (see IMAGE in main body of text on pages 88–96)

Any garment that makes you feel bad will make you look bad.
VICTORIA BILLINGS, *THE WOMANSBOOK* (1974)

Warm up (see main body of text on pages 64–6)

Watch (see TIME)

A watch is always too fast or too slow. I cannot be dictated to by a watch.
JANE AUSTEN, *MANSFIELD PARK* (1814)

Keep a watch with a large face nearby when you present, so you can monitor the amount of time left. If you prefer to wear your watch, slip it so the face is on the inside of your wrist so that you discreetly glimpse it, without letting the audience see your actions.

Avoid using a built-in alarm that goes off when you are nearing your time limit.

Water

Often it's your nerves urging you to drink before a presentation. Avoid drinking too much liquid, otherwise you may begin to feel uncomfortable in the middle of the presentation. If your throat needs moisture try sipping hot tea or a little water.

It is always worth checking the drinking water before you start speaking. It needs to be fresh and not excessively iced.

Alternatively, consider keeping some mild fruit juice on hand. It can be distracting to the audience if you keep sipping away, constantly lifting the glass and putting it down again. Your natural saliva will soon return and chewing your tongue slightly will encourage it to appear.

WC (see TOILET)

> *No one is ignorant that our character and turn of mind are intimately connected with the water-closet.*
> VOLTAIRE, SLOW BELLIES (1764)

Wear (see IMAGE in main body of text on pages 88–96)

> *From the cradle to the coffin, underwear comes first.*
> BERTOLT BRECHT, *THE THREEPENNY OPERA* (1928)

Web sites

There are numerous Internet web sites devoted to offering advice, tips, technical information and discussion about presenting and speaking.

General links, articles, and advice pages
http://www2.truman.edu/~rstjohn/publicspeakers/research.html
http://www.kinkos.com/presentations/quiz.html
http://www.computouch.ca/preslnk.htm
http://www.presentations.com/
http://www.presentingsolutions.com/
http://www.busicom.com/
http://www.nsaspeaker.org/
http://www.toastmasters.org/
http://www:maynardleigh.co.uk

A subscription service for business speakers, including tips and an effective quotation data bank with good search facilities, is at http://www.idea-bank.com/. You can try it free for a while.

Clip art
http://www.webplaces.com/html/clipart.htm
http://www.bitbetter.com/index.htm

Quotes
There are hundreds of quotation sites and most can be searched by topic, not just author. Some of the search engines like Yahoo also have a special page devoted to finding you quotations.
http://www.yahoo.com/Reference/Quotations/

Other quotation sites include:
http://www.cc.columbia.edu/acis/bartleby/bartlett/
http://www.cc.columbia.edu/acis/bartleby/bartlett/
http://www.starlingtech.com/quotes/search_a.html
http://www.excite.com/search.gw?search=quotations
http://www.inx.net/catalog/quote.htm
http://www.futurehealth.org/quotatio.html
http://www.mcs.net/~jorn/html/blake.html
http://www.geocities.com/Athens/Aegean/1994/qindex.html
http://www.empowerment-now.com/inspiration/quotations/
http://quotations.sm.to/
http://www.quotations.com/w_qo_res.html
http://www.ashleighbrilliant.com/
http://webpages.ainet.com/gosner/quotationsarc
http://www.fn.net/~degood/quotes.html
http://www.quoteland.com/
http://www.quotationlocation.com/
http://www.quotations.com/w_qo_res.html
http://www.freeality.com/phrases.htm – has Thesaurus, Phrases and Quotations
http://startingpage.com/html/quotations.html – has links to scores of quotation sites

Speech writing

You can have your speech written for you by professionals and e-mailed within days. Two US services that operate across the globe are:

http://speeches.com/open.asp
http://www.speech-writers.com/

PowerPoint tips and tricks
http://www.bitbetter.com/powertips.htm

Welcome

Can you be creative about welcoming people in some way to your presentation? For example, some presenters place a large colourful WELCOME sign outside the place where they are presenting. Another way of achieving the same effect is on arrival to create your own, either on a flip-chart sheet or using locally available computer facilities.

A particularly nice touch when addressing a small audience of under twenty people is to add the first names of those attending to the welcome notice.

Other ideas for a welcome include:

★ Put a give-away on the seats which the audience finds on arrival
★ As people arrive, hand out a welcome note with a visual puzzle to solve, while waiting for you to start
★ Play a video of some attractive scene, or your own 'welcome' video

Why (see PURPOSE in main body of text on pages 4–8)

There is nothing more to say – except why. But since why is difficult to handle, one must take refuge in how.
TONI MORRISON, *THE BLUEST EYE* (1970)

Why are you giving a presentation? For example, do you want to

★ Provide information?
★ Represent your role or company?
★ Entertain?
★ Fill in a free slot?
★ Pitch for new business?
★ Demand action?
★ Seek debate on a report?
★ Be provocative?
★ Defend a situation or past action?

What evidence might confirm you had achieved your wish? This can help you clarify what your central message should be.

Wig (see IMAGE and GROOMING in main body of text on pages 88–96)

Men will confess to treason, murder, arson, false teeth, or a wig. How many of them will own up to a lack of humour?'
FRANK MOORE COLBY, *THE COLBY ESSAYS*

John manages a well-known research company that specialises in the children's market. He often gives business presentations and because he owns the company no one wants to tell him that his wig does him a disservice.

While there is nothing wrong with a toupee, it does indicate that you are trying to hide your baldness. What else might you be trying to hide? Make sure if you wear one that it is meticulously clean and discreet.

Win (see PITCHES in main body of text on page 115, and VISUALISATION)

Whoever said, 'It's not whether you win or lose that counts,' probably lost.
MARTINA NAVRATILOVA IN ROZ WARREN (ED.) *GLIBQUIPS* (1994)

When Nobel Laureate Jonas Salk was asked how he went about inventing the polio vaccine he replied: 'I pictured myself as a virus or a cancer cell and tried to sense what it would be like.'

Winning a pitch can be tough, even if you are one of the well-resourced big players. Throughout the often prolonged preparation period everyone can benefit from keeping a clear mental picture of the presentation winning the business. Some teams re-enforce this image by putting inspiring posters on the wall or other reminders that they intend to triumph.

Winging it (see IMPROVISE)

Jump off cliffs and build your wings on the way down.
RAY BRADBURY, US SCIENCE FICTION WRITER

Wisecrack (see HUMOUR in main body of text on pages 83–86)

Too much improvisation leaves the mind stupidly void.
VICTOR HUGO, *LES MISÉRABLES* (1862)

Wit (see HUMOUR in main body of text on pages 83–86)

Wit is a treacherous dart. It is perhaps the only weapon with which it is possible to stab oneself in one's own back.
GEOFFREY BOCCA

Words (see PASSION in main body of text on pages 77–80, and VOCABULARY)

Research shows that less than 10% of the effectiveness of a presentation is through words. Non-verbal behaviour and symbols have far more importance. An example of this is when talking to foreign audiences. The words may be only partially understood, yet you can still be an outstanding success so long as the non-verbal and symbolic behaviour is powerful.

How you stand, what you wear, your expressions and gestures can totally support the verbal message or undermine it.

This does not mean that words are irrelevant. They certainly count, and even a single wrong word can have a disproportionate effect. But words are always within a wider context – you are that context.

Simple, rather than complex words, down-to-earth phrasing, rather than pompous structures, get an audience quickly on your side and send the message that you value their understanding.

Worry (see Nerves in main body of text on pages 71–73)

> *Without anxiety life would have very little savour.*
> MAY SARTON, *THE HOUSE BY THE SEA: A JOURNAL* (1977)

Write (see Frameworks in main body of text on page 23, and Prepare)

> *It's a nervous work. The state that you need to write is the state that others are paying large sums to get rid of.*
> SHIRLEY HAZZARD, *NEW YORK TIMES* (1980)

Writing is different from presenting verbally. The written word often sounds awkward when spoken. If you are presenting a report, avoid reading directly from it, except when you are wishing to draw attention to a particular passage where the phrasing seems important.

No matter how well you write a report, people will find ways to misinterpret it. That's why you need to present in person.

Y

Yawn (see Audience in main body of text on page 4, 123, and Attention, Sleep)

> *A yawn is a silent shout.*
> GILBERT KEITH CHESTERTON (1874–1936),
> ENGLISH CRITIC, NOVELIST AND POET

They say you're an engineer if you think that when people around you yawn it's because they don't get enough sleep. A yawn is an unmistakable signal to a business presenter that the audience is mentally leaving. Are you going to wait for the rest to follow?

★ Yawning, like laughter, is contagious. It's time to act now!

People often yawn because the room is stuffy, rather than through boredom. Make sure the venue is well aired and if necessary open a few windows, especially after lunch.

Yes (see Persuasion in main body of text on pages 26–39)

One half of the troubles of this life can be traced to saying 'yes'
too quick, and not saying 'no' soon enough.
JOSH BILLINGS (HENRY WHEELER SHAW) (1818–85),
AMERICAN HUMORIST

Yourself (see also PERSONALITY in main body of text on page 89)

You already know more about you than anyone else. Yet
sometimes a professional who does not know you can take a
fresh look and make a big difference to your eventual
performance.

If you consider someone a great presenter it's fine to use this
to inspire you to new heights. But once you are in front of the
audience

★ Be yourself

Suppose you tend to be a rather serious person, then you almost
certainly have room in your presentation to be humorous and the
audience won't conclude you're not a serious person. Likewise,
if you are a humorous person by nature, then you certainly have
scope in your performance to be serious occasionally.

★ Being yourself means letting the audience see you in depth,
not a one-dimensional cut-out

Z

Zest (see ENTHUSIASM)

What hunger is in relation to food, zest is in relation to life.
BERTRAND RUSSELL, *THE CONQUEST OF HAPPINESS* (1930)

Zip (see CLOTHES)

First you forget names, then you forget faces, then you forget to
pull your zipper up, then you forget to pull your zipper down.
LEO ROSENBERG

ZZZ (see AUDIENCE and SLEEP)

Index

This index conforms to BS ISO999. Alphabetisation is word-by-word.

Subheadings relating to entries in the A-Z Section are given in the form in which they appear in that section.

Locators solely to quotations in the A-Z Section are italicised and prefaced by '*q*'

A

E

THE ULTIMATE BUSINESS PRESENTATION BOOK

M